Noble Street

Noble Street

John L. Cooper

Writer's Showcase
San Jose New York Lincoln Shanghai

Noble Street

Writer's Showcase
an imprint of iUniverse.com, Inc.

For information address:
iUniverse.com, Inc.
5220 S 16th, Ste. 200
Lincoln, NE 68512
www.iuniverse.com

ISBN: 0-595-16882-5

Printed in the United States of America

Dedicated to Mrs. Mabel Marie Scriven Cooper

CHAPTER ONE

It was Christmas Eve. My mother had vowed that her children would not go hungry on the holiday. I went with her to Catholic Charities. She wanted me to backup her story that our family was without food. She told me all I had to do was look hungry. That was easy, under the circumstances, because I had been hungry for days.

When the two of us entered the Offices of Catholic Charities, my mother immediately fell to her knees before a group of nuns. She began writhing, her head bowed, and her hands clasped before her with rosary beads between them. She was not praying to God. She was begging, and I was shocked. Why was she doing this?

Being a very young child, initially I did not understand what was going on. Then I began to feel ashamed. First the mortification was aimed at me, but I soon directed my humiliation at my mother. There she was, on her knees, begging for food, and she wasn't even a Catholic. Those beads were just a prop to help support her performance, and quite a performance it was. Tears were flowing down her face as she called out for mercy, and she rocked back and forth, almost collapsing to the floor when she bent forward.

What a sight to see, my mother deprecating herself like that. It made me feel sad, angry, and scared. Nevertheless, she got what she wanted, food from Catholic Charities for her children, but the image of her on her knees, begging for help, is emotionally backbreaking for me even today. My mother was one of the hardest working women in the world when it came to taking care of her children. Why did she have to become a beggar to prove it?

I was born John Cooper in Philadelphia, Pennsylvania on a cold day in March, 1936. I was the sixth child born to Mabel Marie and Allen Albertus Cooper, and five more children were to come to the table in the next five years. My birth occurred at the height of the Great Depression, that period of economic collapse in America when bread lines snaked across the land and sky high unemployment was common to every one of this nation's cities and hamlets. As if to give voice to the nation's agony, a cry of desperation was heard echoing across the land, "Brother can you spare a dime?" It was a bad time for America, but it was the time for me to be born.

I was not a hospital baby. I was born in a dilapidated house near Fourth and Catherine Streets in South Philly, barely a stone's throw from the Liberty Bell. My mother told me that I came into the world screaming at the top of my lungs, which is unusual for a newborn baby. The crying that babies make at the time of their birth is most often caused by the smack on the bottom that they receive from the doctor who delivers them. It is also true that most newborn infants stop crying after a short period of time, once the shock passes. But even without a spanking, I kept right on crying.

Because I did not stop crying, suspicion was growing between my mother and the welfare doctor that I was suffering from some kind of illness or discomfort and preparations were about to be made to remove me to a hospital. Then it dawned upon my mother that maybe her newborn son was hungry. Newborn babies do not normally eat within a matter of minutes after birth, but if food would make me shut my little mouth, then the doctor and my mother were willing to try it.

So, I was given a bottle of milk and allowed to feast myself. Glory be, Little Johnny, having finished the entire bottle, quieted his infant crying and went to sleep like a normal newborn baby should. I had been crying because I was born hungry, and there was a very good reason for that. My mother had not eaten anything for more than a day prior to my birth, and when a baby is resting in his mother's womb, and she goes hungry, so does her unborn child. As I grew up, my mother told me many times that I was a natural born malcontent, but who wouldn't be if he came into the world hungry and possibly suffering from malnutrition?

If I was born to be a malcontent, then my Mom was born to be a mother, and I do believe she was the best mother any child ever had. Being a mother was not just her duty or responsibility; it was her life. My mother's mother had died when she was extremely young, and the memory of that loss was never far from her consciousness. In her heart, she believed that her mother was watching her from the spirit world to see that she would be the best parent she could be. At the same time, my Mom maintained a firm conviction that God wanted her to be a good mother and to have plenty of children, and she did not disappoint the Lord.

My mother gave us love in abundance. She did not want us to grow up without motherly affection as she did. Particularly, her loving showed in her cooking. She was a superb cook. She could make practically any dish you could name, but the secret in her mastery was the taste of her prepared meals. Whether it was hamburgers, pot roast, eggs and rice, gravy and rice, fried sweet potatoes, or peaches and shortening bread, she made the food taste divine and absolutely special. Somehow, she transformed the food into a meal that was one of a kind. Her meals were so delicious that at times when we ate them, we would literally cry for joy. The meals were so individually tasty; we believed we would never eat anything like it again. Then we would be surprised when the next meal would be just as delectable as all the others before it.

I never got to know my father. He was a closed-mouthed man, and even my mother didn't know much about his upbringing or family background. It was as though, in many ways, she had married a perfect stranger and the mask of his identity was never removed. The only thing that Mom definitely knew about him was the fact that he was born somewhere in South Carolina. Both of my parents were transplanted Southern Negroes. They met in Philadelphia and were married there.

My father was a mean-spirited, sorrowful package of a man. I don't think he was born a mean person, filled with hate and rage, but something happened to him in his early life, and it was only through anger and viciousness, directed at his family, did he seemed to be able to relieve himself of the awful psychic pain he must have been feeling. It was that pain, I believed, that made him a stranger to us, and I often wondered how my mother could sleep with a stranger. But, sleep with him she did, and the babies just kept on coming.

Consequently, my parents were faced with raising many children during the worst economic crisis this nation has ever known. As I grew older, I thought a lot about why my mother had so many children when she was poor and the Depression had had its foot on both her and my father's neck. One day when I was a teenager, I asked her why she had had so many children. She was in the kitchen cutting up chicken with a long knife. Her response to the question was to slap me across the face with the broad, flat side of the knife that was away from the sharpened edge. The slap with the knife scared the life out me because I thought she had cut me, and for a moment, as the tears rushed to my eyes, I imagined that my mother had turned into a mad woman, a vicious creature who wanted to kill me, all because of a simple question. But I didn't have anything to worry about. My mother would never hurt one of her children, and besides, I deserved that slap for asking such an impertinent question.

Because there were so many children, no matter how loving and caring my parents might have been, they were in way over their heads with this family thing. For instance, the Depression really hit my father hard. He was an unskilled black man from the rural South. In good times, it was difficult for him to find steady work as a laborer, but during the

Depression, it was all but impossible for him to find work of any kind on an ongoing basis. Add to this the fact that my father was never an emotionally strong man; it is no wonder then that he took to drinking. And by the time I was born, my father was a hopeless alcoholic who had, by and large, stopped looking for steady work.

In any case, whether my father worked or not, there was a household full of children who had to eat. Food and necessities had to be provided for somehow. And so, where did it come from? The household income came from welfare checks and domestic work that my mother would do once or twice a week. She did day work because she needed the money to supplement the welfare checks. The family could not be maintained on welfare money alone. It was just not enough.

She would take trolley cars out to some white neighborhood in one of the better sections of Philadelphia, and there she would scrub floors, do laundry, clean toilets, iron clothes, or do whatever her domestic employment would require. Domestic work was hard work, and she would put in long hours for a measly four or five dollars a day. Then she had to return home to all those children, who were usually waiting at the door for her, hungry and longing for some motherly attention.

Although I was very young at the time, I still have strong memories of those days when Mom was away doing domestic work. It was the time in my life when I felt most neglected. Even though I knew my mother was working, I always felt that when she was away, some other child was getting the love and affection that was rightfully mine. The thought always made me more than a little angry.

I have such a clear memory of those days when my mother was doing domestic work. Invariably, they were days when there was no food in the house and every one of us children at home was extremely hungry. It was a time when we suffered from extended bellies because we drank too much water. We thought that drinking a lot of water would some-how take away our hunger. Having water in our bellies seemed better than having nothing in it.

Moreover, an empty belly has a way of slowing down time, and we would sit at the kitchen table, looking at each other with blank stares, our minds filled with thoughts of the delicious food that Mom would prepare when she arrived home. As the hours went by, there were long periods of time when we would say nothing to each other. But sooner or later, someone would verbalize what we were all feeling, and that would start a chain reaction.

Usually Marion, my oldest sister, would get things started. "I'm hungaree."

Next, I might be the one to chime in. I usually was just waiting for someone to start the ball rolling. "I'm hungry, too," I was likely to mumble. As some of us would begin to speak out about our feelings, the younger children, Donald, whose nickname was Ducky, and Norma, whose nickname was Dotty, Kenny, Jeannie, and Ronnie, would sit around the table without making a sound. They usually fell into a stupor. They had learned long ago that crying did not help. It would accomplish nothing because Mom was not there to feed and comfort them.

However, with the subject out in the open, a chorus of "I'm hungries," might then come from the older children at the table. It was almost as though the admission of it would somehow make us all feel better. But, of course, it made us feel worse now that the cat was out of the bag.

"I'm hungaree," Marion would keep the chorus going. She was like that. She always brought things out in the open. Because of this, she could never keep a secret. Still, she was a person who always told it like it was. She never bit her tongue.

I would usually follow Marion's lead in speaking out during the hungry times, because she was my big sister. If she thought it was better to lay the cards on the table, then I agreed with that. Therefore, I kept the chorus going. "Me too, I'm hungaree."

Then one of my older brothers, Abie, Norman, or Frank might say, "We're all hungaree, but it don't do no good to talk about it."

In thinking back about those hungry days around the table, there is one strange aspect to my recollections of it. I don't recall ever seeing my oldest brother Allen sitting with us. Allen was named after his father, but Junior was nothing like his dad. He was an introvert. He was the brother who most often wasn't there, except maybe when we went swimming or shoe shining He was the phantom sibling, and he did not seem to suffer from the same pangs of hunger, when Mom was away, as the rest of us. Whatever he did to sustain himself, when the larder was empty and our bellies were filled with water, he did not share the secret of it with any of his brothers or sisters.

"I'm hungaree," Marion was likely to stubbornly continue to protest, and I would give her my support.

"Sure you're hungaree," Norman might say. He was the most sympathetic of the older brothers. "But think of it this way," he would continue. "The more hungrier you are, the more you're going to enjoy the dinner Mom's going to cook. Now won't that be nice?" He loved to play games with people's minds.

"But I'm real hungaree," Marion would stay on her protest mark.

"We're all hungaree. So what?" Frank was sure to try to bring reality into the discussion. He was my toughest brother, and the one who was most unlikely to feel sorry for himself. Frank had an aggressive personality, and he was somewhat of a bully. As he grew up, he came to accept the idea that the world was filled with predators. It was a dog eat dog world, and if you wanted to survive in it you had to get the other guy before he got you. That was the kind of general attitude he had about life. "You're hungaree and I'm hungaree, but it don't do no good talking about it. So shut the hell up," he was likely to snarl.

"Maybe the trolley car broke down?" Abie might say. He was always one to think of mishaps and accidents. Abie was the outcast among my brothers. He did not have Norman's intelligence or Frank's strength, and he was forever projecting a surly attitude. He was also quite puny looking, and Norman and Frank tended to shun him or just ignore him. Abie was a boy who never did fit into our family's male-dominated structure. And indeed, my family was top heavy with boys.

My Mom had eight sons, and three daughters in fourteen years. She was also to have one more daughter who would be born when I was twelve years old. But of all her sons, she treated Abie differently than the other boys. She treated Abie somewhat like he was one of the girls. She was very protective of him, and she often said she treated him that way because he had been a premature baby. Abie was always ambivalent about his mother's protectiveness towards him, but at least it was something he got from Mom that none of the other boys received. Speaking very softly, Abie said, "Mom should have been home by now."

"Maybe she should have been home by this time, but she ain't here," Frank shouted. "And that is that."

"Mom is comin'," I would say. I did not want to accept Abie's idea that the trolley car had broken down. "And I'm hungaree like Marion is hungaree."

"We're all hungaree like Marion," Abie would try to keep the group thinking and feeling the same.

"No," Marion was apt to push Abie away emotionally. "My hungaree is not like your hungaree. My hungaree is real, real hungaree."

"I know you're hungaree." Norman would try to be comforting.

"I said we're all hungaree," Frank would say. "Now everybody just keep their hungarees to themselves. I'm tired of talking about it."

That kind of conversation could go on for quite a while, but at some point, Mom would burst through the door, looking tired and exhausted, carrying a shopping bag which was sure to contain the evening's dinner.

She would not even have time to sit down and catch her breath for a few minutes before we would be urging her on to the kitchen stove to begin cooking supper.

We would sit at the table while she hustled to cook the food, banging spoons and forks on our plates, singing a continuous chorus of "I'm hungaree." My father was never there to give Mom a helping hand, but she would carry on like a true, dedicated mother. Somehow, she had strength and stamina to burn. Where she got it from, only God knows.

Sometimes, I'm sure, Mom did become a little annoyed with us when we would bang on our plates with spoons and forks as she was trying to prepare dinner. But I'm certain the feeling came and went very quickly. She could never be angry with her children for any great length of time.

My family did not live very long at that address on Fourth Street where I was born. In fact, we did not live very long at any address during the first few years of my life. We were truly vagabonds. We moved often because the houses we lived in were old and deteriorating, and there was little or no maintenance provided by the landlords.

It was always Mom who took on the burdens of moving and relocating the family. My father never helped her. He refused to be held accountable for the family's living situation. From the way he acted, we were Mom's children and not his kids. From my mother's point of view, my father must have been just like another one of her children. In those early years, when we were moving from house to house, he was always around, but he was never really in the thick our family's struggle for survival.

Not only did we move from house to house in Philadelphia during those early years, but we also moved from city to city. The movement from city to city was often caused by arguments and fighting between my parents. My mother always had a breaking point, and when the fighting with my father became intolerable, she would pick up and leave him, taking the children with her. She had four sisters, two in New York City, one in Trenton, New Jersey, and another in Philadelphia. Mom was quite dependent upon her sisters. She would borrow money from them often, and she would live with them when she was in between houses or when she would leave my father and had no other place to go.

The physical fighting between my parents was emotionally wrenching to me, and I assumed that my brothers and sisters felt the same way about it. I remember vividly one winter's evening when my father came home very drunk, and he attacked Mom. He accused her of becoming pregnant because she wanted to punish him. He then beat her until her face was bloody, and he dragged her to the basement door. He threw her into the cellar, and he kept her down there for a very long time. It devastated me to see my father act so vilely. I saw such behavior many times, and in my child's mind, I would tell myself it wasn't real, even though I cried from the pain I felt from seeing such horror.

Moreover, my father would beat and brutalize my brothers, from the oldest to the youngest and me. When he came home at night, he was always drunk, and he would punch and kick any male member of the family he got his hands on. In a drunken state, he could not stand to look at any of his sons or his wife. But as mean and nasty as he could be, I never saw him hit one of my sisters. Why he refrained from beating his daughters when he would beat his wife, I'll never know.

Whenever my mother would leave my father, the separation would not last for very long. He would soon come after her. He'd say that he would do better, and he would plead for reconciliation. Each time, my mother would give in. Families should be together, parents and children, she believed, and if we were in New York or Trenton, back to Philly we would go to try once again to be one big happy family.

But, the bickering and fighting was sure to erupt again as soon as the family was settled back in Philadelphia, and my father would go right back to his drinking and terrorizing ways. And even when he was sober, to make matters worse, he never talked to any of his children. That is why we knew so little about him. He was a stranger during the day and a monster that invaded our house practically every night.

How he managed to get drunk just about everyday was a mystery to my mother. Except for one very short period, he never had a steady job, nor did he work in any other capacity. But it seemed as though he could get as much to drink as he wanted on any given night.

Both of my parents were short. My mother was about five foot-two, and my father was a little less than that. She had a sturdy build, was big breasted, and she had an attractive figure for a woman of her size. She had an oval, pleasant face, and she had eyes that sparkled when she was happy. Her skin complexion was a mixture of native American and African, which gave it a mellow, brown-reddish look. Her hair was hot-combed straight.

My father was a dark-skinned black man who had a substantial nose and lips and facial skin that was tight and smooth. He was thin, with small shoulders, but he had strong arms and hands and a sinewy, body. Norman was the spitting image of his Daddy.

My father was jealous of my mother's complexion, and because of the lighter hue of her skin, he thought she looked down on him. I also think this feeling would often feed his anger when he was arguing with her. Mom was always after him to get a job and make some money. When they would argue, I would see this consternation come over his face.

"Aw fuck you, woman. Do you think it's easy out there? I ain't no Rockefeller. I'm just a poeass black man."

"I know it's hard, Al, but…"

"But shit. You don't know nothing. All you think about is those kids. You'd do anything for them. You'd get down on your hands and knees to the white man for those children. But I ain't gonna do it. I ain't gonna do it. I kissed enough white asses when I was in the South. That was when the Klu Klux Klan was running around all over the place, but I ain't doing it no more, not for you or those kids. All you gonna do, Mae, is make a lot of ass-kissers out of them, too. Don't you understand, woman? Nobody cares about nigger-kids or any nigger people."

"Al, Al don't use that kind of language around the kids. Don't…"

"Shut up, bitch, and leave me alone or I am going to beat your ass."

After years of being physically abused by my father, Mom went to the family court and got a restraining order against him, but the local police refused to enforce it. There were times when my mother would call the police to stop him from beating her, but when they arrived, they would not arrest him. It didn't matter that my mother was bloodied and battered. The cops would say it was just a family dispute going on. No laws were broken, so it was nothing they could do.

When the cops went away, my father would be furious with my mother for calling the police on him, and I would be very confused. Why didn't the police help? Maybe my father was right. Nobody cared about nigger-kids or any nigger-people.

There is one time that I can remember when my father did get a job. It was a job in a tanning factory where hides were prepared to make leather. The factory was in the neighborhood nearby. My father held the job for every bit of three days, and it gave rise to the happiest days I was ever to know between my mother and father. She was so proud of him, and she scurried about the house trying her hardest to keep the place clean and the children out of his way. Also, it seemed as though he did not touch a drink in those three days, a miracle of miracles. But destiny would not let this situation last for long. After those few days of normal family life, father, mother, and children were feeling a bit out of sorts. Something was bound to break. The calmness of it all was not normal for any of us.

When tanning animal skins, chemicals are used to take the hair off of the hides, smooth them out, and soften them up. I never knew specifically what chemicals were used, but I remember that the smell that came from the factory stunk like formaldehyde. On those days, when my father came home from work, I recall that he smelled like he had spent his work hours wallowing in the waste of an outhouse.

The smell he brought home with him from his job was so bad that we children would leave the kitchen when he came into the room. On that last day of his employment, my father came home and found most of his children sitting around the kitchen table waiting for dinner. Mom was over at the stove preparing a hamburger, rice and gravy meal, a supper that was a favorite of my father's. When he came into the kitchen, smelling like he had been swimming in shit all day, my brothers, sisters and I began to hold our noses and groan.

I don't know what went through my father's mind when he saw us giving him that stinky look, but I would bet it was not a pleasant thought in the least. In fact, he reacted immediately in the negative. "To hell with you little bastards," he shouted, and then right in front of my mother, and all the children in the room, he began stripping off his work clothes. Mom dashed around the table trying to hide our faces, while he undressed right down to his bare, naked ass. He then threw his clothes on the table. Next, he got some water in a basin, took it to the bathroom, and washed up.

As my father bathed himself, I could hear him cursing out loud about the white boss who wanted to treat him like he was a mule. "I ain't no animal," he shouted. "And slavery ended a long time ago. He can take that job and shove it up his ass."

With the stink off of him, he dressed and left the house. All good things must come to an end.

By 1939, the family had come to settle permanently in Philadelphia. It seemed to have been a matter of circumstances that dictated the end to the our vagabond lifestyle. Too many of my brothers and sisters had become of school age and more household stability was needed. We moved into a residence on Noble Street, just off of Third Street. The number was 238, and we were to live there for well over a decade.

Noble Street also became the family's homestead because my mother had made some good friends in the neighborhood, friendships that would last a lifetime. Her friends were also struggling mother-wives, like Mrs. Les who had married so young she never had the experience of being a teenager, or Mrs. Harris, whose husband was so countrified, he found it difficult to us a commode and he preferred using a bucket in the yard because it reminded him of an outhouse. And there was Mrs. Bryant. We actually called her nooky. She had the biggest tokus I have ever seen on a human being. Her behind was so big she had trouble getting into and out of the front door of her house. My mother and all of these women had one major thing in common. They were all married to men who drank too much and worked too little.

The Cooper family's gypsy way of life was also brought to an end by the fact that my mother became a member of a local Quaker Settlement House, The Friends Neighborhood Guild. The Guild was a community center, and the staff there took a great deal of interest in the Cooper family, particularly a social worker named Francis Bosworth, who later became Director of all the Guild programs. He practically adopted the Cooper family as his own. He was genuinely a loving, caring person who believed that all human beings were brothers and sisters, regardless of skin color.

The most meaningful memories of my childhood are all associated with that house on Noble Street. I went back to visit the old neighborhood in the 1970s, just to pay my respects, and I was amazed to find that the old house had been torn down. Even Noble Street itself was gone. The City of Philadelphia had taken over the entire neighborhood and leveled all the old structures that had been there to make way for some government and commercial buildings. It was part of a big renovation program in celebration of the nation's Second Centennial Anniversary. That was the information I was given for the destruction of my old neighborhood, but deep down in my guts I had a different feeling. I honestly felt that the City Fathers destroyed my old neighborhood because of me. They wanted to deny me the proof that I actually did live in a residence that once existed at 238 Noble Street. Without the concrete proof of the house being there, perhaps my memories of growing up in that location were just a figment of my imagination.

But, even if it is only in my imagination now, I will always be connected to Noble Street. Growing up there, I learned so much about the

human condition, the good of it and the bad. And through those har-
rowing years, my mother taught me a great lesson. It is the struggle to
survive that gives life meaning.

We lived in many old houses when I was growing up, but the Noble
Street house was the oldest of them all. It was also located in one of the
oldest sections of Philadelphia, not far from the Delaware River. No
doubt that was near the spot where William Penn first put his foot
ashore in the colony of Pennsylvania centuries ago. Because Noble
Street was situated close to the Delaware River, in the hot months of the
year, the River smells would drift through our neighborhood. The
smells would be of the human waste that poured into the river from the
thousands of toilets in Philadelphia, the rotten odors from the sanitation barges, and the pungent scents from floating dead animals and
floating oil slicks. There were many nights when we went to bed with
funky noses.

The Noble Street House was three stories tall with a pointed roof.
Below the roof, there was a dark and musty attic that had about two feet
of sand in it. The sand was there to absorb the water that might leak
through the roof when it rained. Over the years, I would spend many
long hours playing in that attic, and to be sure I believed that there were
ghosts, or at least one ghost, who lived up there. We all came to call the
ghost Jenson, every member of the family except Dotty. She called the
ghost the Sniffer because she said he was always sniffing her.

The house on Noble Street was an early colonial, row house, with its
pyramid, compact shape that displayed a large window on the ground
floor and two smaller windows on the second floor and one on the third
floor. The house had an English Georgian look that was common to
many of the buildings in the historical sections of Philadelphia. But that
house may have had a unique history of its own. Carved into the wood
boards of the bathroom was the definitive statement "Benjamin
Franklin Slept Here." In later years, that carved statement about
Benjamin Franklin was to come to have more of a risque meaning to

me. I learned that Benny was a man who slept in a lot of different places and with a lot of different women. It is said, in legend and song, the whores of Paris still talk and sing about the wonderful day that Benny came to town. According to the gossip, he was fondly known as the "Philly Dilly." They don't make 'em like that anymore.

There was only one bathroom in the house, but it wasn't really a bathroom. It was located in a shed area in back of the kitchen. There was a commode and bathtub in the little shed room, but there was no hot water or any running water. To take a bath, the water had to be carried in, after first heating it on the stove, and to flush the toilet one had to pour water from a bucket to make the droppings go down. The bathroom was an old outhouse that had once stood separate from the main living quarters. It had been brought into the residence by building a walk-through shed that ran from the house to the privy.

The worst thing about the bathroom that wasn't really a bathroom was the fact that you absolutely could not take a bath in it during the winter months, and even during some of the fall and spring months of the year. It was just too damn cold out there. Once the heated water hit that cold porcelain, the warmth would vanish like a lit match in a windstorm.

We usually took our baths in an old washtub, which would be placed in the kitchen. There was no central heating in the house, and the only source of heat the family was to ever have during the cold months of the year was an old Ben Franklin wood and coal heater. Maybe the great Philly Dilly did sleep in that house after all. In any case, it was nice to have his heater, but the heater was good for heating only one room. And when the girls were taking a bath during the cold months, the boys of the family were sent to the frigid wastelands in other parts of the house.

In the same way, the girls had to leave the warmth of Benny's heater when the boys were taking a bath. However, because she was more protective of the girls, Mom would make the boys wash up much faster than the girls. I was aware of this difference, and I complained about it to my mother often. But my complaining didn't change anything. The girls were still allowed to take more time bathing in the wash tub than the boys.

The house had rickety wooden stairs, a dirt cellar, and no internal electrical wiring. When our family moved into the house, there was a makeshift wire connection that allowed an electrical current to enter the house. There had been an attachment made to a Philadelphia Electric Company pole that stood out in front of the house. The current was allowed to enter the house through a second floor front window by way of a number of exposed, un-insulated, small wire cables.

About two days after we moved into the house, my father came home drunk, and straight away he got into an argument with my mother.

"Al, Al! Look at you! Drunk again. You're always drunk, and I'm sick of it," Mom shouted at him. "Every time the children see you, you're drunk. Drunk! Drunk! Drunk! You're always drunk and stinking of that white lighting. You ain't much of a man. No, you're not a man at all. You're just a drunk."

"Mae, you better leave me alone. I mean you better leave me alone right now before I knock the shit outta you."

"No, I won't leave you alone. I won't leave you alone because I don't understand why you just don't go away for good and leave me and the kids alone."

"They're my kids, too!" my father growled nastily. When he used that tone of voice, he always became physical with her soon after. It was at those times when I wished my mother would back off and stop the argument before he hit her. But Mom could be fearless when she wanted to be, and at those times, when her patience had been stretched too far, she would have put her head in the mouth of a lion if that is what it would take for her to have her say.

"Just because you sleep in the same bed with me, you think that gives you the right to have those children call you Daddy. Well, it takes more than that. You have to give some real time to being a father to your children."

"I said you better leave me alone." He growled through his teeth in a low voice, as he started across the room towards her.

She backed away from him, but she did not stop talking. "Why don't you just get out before I get the police. Maybe they will finally put you out."

"The police. They ain't gonna do nothing. And I told you to stop calling the police on me. But you'd call them anyhow. Why, I'll beat your ass for that." He jumped at her, but my mother was easily able to avoid his drunken lunge.

He tried to catch hold of her a couple of more times, but Mom kept the kitchen table between him and herself. After a few more tries, he backed away from the table and just stood there glaring at her, feeling frustrated and trying to think of some way to get back at her.

Suddenly, his eyes caught sight of the electric bulb overhead in the ceiling socket. It was twilight, growing dark outside, and the lights were on in the house. My father squinted at the light. "So, you like to call the police on me, huh? Well, I'll fix you bitch. You and those kids."

I then saw him stagger forward, towards the upstairs hallway. I was standing with my younger brothers and sisters in the passageway just outside the kitchen at the bottom of the stairs. We had been watching the drama between our parents, scared out of our minds that the two of them would start fighting. We were quite startled when suddenly my father staggered in our direction. We thought he was coming after us. We scattered like scared jack rabbits before he could reach our position, but my father was not interested in us.

He started upstairs to the second floor, swearing and shouting loudly as he went. "My wife thinks it's all right to be calling the police on me, calling the man, the white man." He shouted over his shoulder at her. "You must be crazy, woman. Crazy. You forget that I'm a black man and you're a black woman. And you'd call the white man on me? You're black do you hear? Do you hear? You're black, and I'm gonna fix it so you don't ever forget it."

He had reached the second floor landing now, and he staggered into the front bedroom where he and my mother slept. Mom then left the kitchen and came to the foot of the stairs. She listened intently for his movements upstairs as she tried to make out what he might be doing. We gathered around her, bunching up and straining our ears, listening as she did to the sounds of our father up above.

Then I heard the distinct sound of a window being opened. Was my father going to throw himself out of the window?

Mom took note of the window-opening-sound, and instantly raced up the stairs because the same thought that I had must have been in her mind. My brothers, sisters and I ran after her.

"Al! Al!" My mother screamed, as she reached the second floor landing in a flash. "Get out of that window!"

When I arrived at the second floor landing and looked into my parent's bedroom, there was my father climbing out of the window and pulling himself up to a standing position on the outside window ledge. I thought he was really going to do it. He was going to take a swan dive right down into the middle of Noble Street. All the Cooper children started crying. I especially did not want my father to kill himself. He was a mean, vicious man, but I realized at that critical moment I had some very caring feelings for him.

But then, my mother's movements took up my attention. She rushed to the window and pushed her arms through the raised lower portion of it and caught hold of my father's legs. Apparently, she did not want to see him end his life that way, either. Standing on the windowsill, waving back and forth in a drunken manner, my father kicked my mother's hands away. He was holding on to a thin, electrical wiring pole that ran up the front of the house. It was through that pole the Noble Street house made connection to the Philadelphia Electric Company's current source.

"Get away from me woman." He jumped away from my mother's hands. "You done forgot who you are. You don't know that you're a black woman anymore. You must think you're white. Well, I'm gonna fix it so you remember who you are, and I'm gonna make sure you never forget it."

I was gripped with fear. Was my mean, old nasty Daddy really going to die? I had seen many people die in the movies, but that was fun and entertaining. Watching my father teetering on the windowsill, possibly getting ready to die, was no fun at all. I wished that my father would come in from the window ledge, even if it meant he would start arguing with my mother again.

My mother was trying to grab my father's legs, and at the same time she was pleading with him to come inside. But Allen Albertus paid no attention to her pleading, and he would stomp at her hands as she tried to take a secure hold of him. We little ones boo-hooed and cried, both frightened and fascinated by the sight of our father dangerously hanging outside of the window, twenty feet above the ground.

Then, suddenly, I stopped crying. My father wasn't trying to kill himself. He was tearing out the electrical wiring from that pole on the side of the house. It was just about dark outside now, and as my father tugged at the wires, brilliant sparks sputtered into the air and lit up his face in a very ugly, grotesque manner. It gave him the look of Dr. Frankenstein when he was giving the first blast of energy to his monster. But shortly thereafter, the house went dark.

"Al, Al, what in God's name have you done?"

In the darkened room, I saw a silhouette of my father slipping through the window back into the front bedroom. As he landed on the floor, he pushed Mom away from him.

"What have I done? Can't you see what I've done, or is it that you're blind? I tore those damn wires out. That's what I've done, and now you ain't gonna have no electricity in this house. You see, you done forgot that you're black. Now maybe if you live in the dark, you'll remember that you're black, and maybe you won't ever forget it again."

My father then staggered out of the front bedroom as his children ran in all directions to get out of his path. He went down the stairs, still remarking with disgust, "She thinks she got the right to call the police on me. Call the man! The white man! Well, live in darkness bitch. Live in darkness!"

The family's landlord for the Noble Street house lived just down the street on the corner. Their names were Mr. and Mrs. Schwartz. The Schwartzs ran a neighborhood Mom and Pop candy store, and they had witnessed my father's antics in the second floor window. The following day, Mr. Schwartz said to my mother, "Your husband tore that electrical wiring out. And I'll tell you something, it really angered me. There he was, like a monkey, up there tearing out that wiring. Don't you know that it cost a lot of money to get electricity put in that house. Well, it wasn't your fault, really, and we rented the house to you, but I can tell you this. My wife and I have decided that we will not have that electrical connection repaired as long as you and your family live in that house."

Mr. Schwartz and his wife kept their word. They never did have that electrical connection to the house repaired, and we lived in that house for more than ten years under the light of oil lamps. I never truly understood why they refused to repair the electrical wiring in the Noble Street house. At the same time, I knew my father was wrong in what he had done. But, grown ups were always telling me that two wrongs do not make a right.

Mr. Schwartz was an old man with a large bald head fringed by some grey hair near his ears and on the lower part of the back of his head. Like my father, he was on the small side. He had a fat face, although it was a pleasant face. Mrs. Schwartz was a dried up, wrinkled woman who never smiled. Mr. and Mrs. Schwartz had a daughter whose name was Tillie. Tillie was a middle-aged widow whose hair was beginning to turn gray. Whenever I looked into her face, I had the feeling I was looking into nothing. It was scary. I did not like going into the candy store when Tillie was behind the counter.

The candy store was old looking just like Mr. and Mrs. Schwartz. It was made up of one long counter that had jars and boxes of candy lined up on it. Also, in the rear of the store, to the left of the counter, there was a big ice cooler. All kinds of sodas were kept in that cooler, Coca Cola, Pepsi, and the popular local brand of Franks' soft drinks. There were also boxes of Tastykake pies and cakes on the counter. I thought the Tastykake apple pies were delicious, and it gave me the greatest satisfaction to buy one of the pies for eight cents, take it up to the attic, and eat it slowly without my brothers or sisters nagging me for some.

What made the candy store look so old was the fact that the wooden counter was battered, chipped, and always dusty. The walls of the store were drab and dirty looking. But the strangest thing about the store, was the the back of it. In the area at the end of the counter, away from the street entrance, there was a doorway. This doorway was enclosed with a dark curtain that hung from the top of the door sill to the floor. Beyond that curtain was the Schwartz family's living quarters. Through the years, I went in and out of that store a thousand times, but I never got a clear view of what the Schwartz's living quarters were like behind the dark curtain. It was something I wanted to know, but I never found out.

Tillie had a grown son, George, who was mentally retarded, and he did a strange thing to the children of the neighborhood when they came into the candy store. George enjoyed pretending that he was in fist fights. So, when I, or some other child, would enter the store, he would come running out from behind that dark curtain, almost like a bullet shot out of a gun, and he would rush up to the child, put up his fists, and thump the kid, him or her, gently in the chest. At the same time, he would say, "eee." As I learned, after my first few experiences with George, you were supposed to thump him back in his chest.

George was sort of a burly fellow, with a strong looking body. He was average height, and he had dark, tangled hair that fell down over his forehead. This made him appear as though the upper part of his face was missing. When he came bursting from behind that curtain, it was like being confronted by a man with half a face. It would give me the creeps.

George was always laughing when he made his attack run at a child, and his mother or grandparents would always be nearby. They would usually remind the child that George was only playing, and there was nothing to be afraid of. It was nice of them to say that, but it was still upsetting to have a half-face, grown man come charging at you with a mouth full of "eees".

In spite of George's habits, overall, I thought the Schwartz family were all right. I liked Mr. Schwartz least of all, but one out of four wasn't bad. However, the one thing that impressed me the most about the entire Schwartz family was the fact that they always treated my mother with respect. Mrs. Schwartz marveled at the way my Mom was able to take care of all her children. I think she strongly empathized with my mother. She knew what it was like to struggle with family problems. There was slow-minded George and Tillie's withdrawal from the world, and I'm sure it hurt her to know that her grandson was known as "Crazy George" in the neighborhood. But then, why should her life be any different? Everyone, everywhere, had their problems to deal with.

CHAPTER TWO

Even though the Noble Street house had three floors, with two bedrooms each on the upper floors, the house was still quite small and crowded for the Cooper family. The boys were given the two rooms on the third floor. The girls were given the back room on the second floor, and my mother and father slept in the front bedroom on the second floor.

Living in that old house was like living in the past. When my father ripped away the electrical wiring, we could not have any electrical light in our home, and we could not have any electrical appliances, either. No radio, no electric toaster, fans, irons, washing machine, or refrigerator. That's not to say that my mother would have been able to buy those appliances anyway, but without electricity in the house, she couldn't even dream about them. And whatever the cost was to repair the electrical damage done by my father, she surely did not have the money to pay for it. With one sweep of his hand, my father threw us back into the nineteenth century.

There were dozens of mice and rats living in the cellar and walls of the house on Noble Street. There were thousands of roaches, bedbugs, waterbugs, and millipedes living in every nook and cranny of the place. The house was virtually a reservation for unwanted vermin.

The vermin had lived in that house for generations, and they had pathways that infiltrated the house like a sieve. The cellar was a haven for these pests. With its dirt floor and dampness, the furry creatures and bugs found it a perfect environment for their nests and hideaways. The cellar was dark and uninviting, and it had craggy brick walls that were unplastered and smelled like someone had been urinating on them for years. The cellar reeked with that pee smell, but fortunately, for some strange reason, the odor stayed in the cellar. Even in the hot summer, when the smells from the Delaware River were torturing the family's noses, the pee smell kept itself in the cellar. Norman said that it was probably Jenson who was peeing on the walls in the bottom of the house.

The water and gas pipes in the basement were exposed. They were uninsulated and hung down from the ceiling like elongated trapeze bars, and more often than not, when someone went into the cellar, day or night, big, fat rats could be seen running along the pipes. At night, the rats would raid the kitchen cupboards and make a hell of a racket, trying to get food, very often knocking cans and other items from the shelves. The rats were so aggressive, they would also push pots from the top of the gas range in their efforts to steal the contents within them.

There was no way to rid the house of all the vermin without literally tearing the entire structure down. Right from the start of the family's tenure in the Noble Street residence, we had to learn to live with the multitude of pests.

The third floor of the house belonged to the boys. My three older brothers, Allen, Abie, and Norman, slept in the front bedroom in single, small cot beds. Frank, Ducky, and I slept in one big bed in the rear room. I was never comfortable sleeping with my brothers. There was always a foot or a behind that would get in my way and force me to sleep on the edge of the mattress. How nice it would have been if I could stretch out just one night and not bump into one of them.

However, sleeping in a crowded bed was the least of my worries. What bothered me the most when I went to sleep at day's end were the bedbugs. As far as I was concerned, they were the worst vermin in the house. In the dark of night, when the family was trying to sleep, the chinches would emerge from their hiding places to bite all our bodies and suck our blood. The old wire beds and cotton mattresses were perfect abodes for the chinches to live in, and no matter how many of them I killed, there were always hundreds more waiting in line to get a bite.

The bedbugs were more of a nuisance in the warm weather, but they were capable of being extremely active pests all year around. To make matters worse, they would sometimes get into my nose or ears when I slept. If a chinch got into my nose, usually a good, hard blow would dislodge the little critter, but the smell of a chinch bug could linger in my nostril for days. It was a putrid, revolting ordor.

If a chinch got in my ear, I just had to dig it out.

My mother would spray the beds with insecticide as often as she could, and for a night or two this would help, but then the bedbugs would always return more hungrier than ever. She would use a glass container spray unit, with a long pump handle. After the beds were sprayed, they always smelled like a combination of kerosene oil and street tar. When Mom wasn't home, my brothers, especially Norman and Frank, would often take those spray units, fill them with water, and have spray fights. Sometimes they would let me join into the fun, too.

I thought the bedbugs had a particular dislike for me. They not only bit me and sucked my blood; they seem to have a program to torment me. One night when I was sleeping soundly, just having a nice dream, I felt this nibbling going on between my legs. While I was still dreaming, I reached down and slapped myself hard right where the nibbling was going on. With that slap, I sat up in bed wide awake. Tears slid out of the corners of my eyes as pain filtered up through my groin.

My movements awakened Frank, who slept next to me in bed. On any given night, the chinches bit Frank's body and sucked his blood, too, but they did not seem to annoy him as much as they bothered me. Frank sat up in bed. "Whats-a-matter with you?"

I was in such pain, I could only wave my hand towards my dilly.

It was a night of a full moon, and soft light seeped though the glass of the windowpanes. Frank and I were like shadows, but we could make out each other's movements.

In the dim light of the room, Frank could see where I was gesturing. "What is it? Ya gotta pee or somethin'?"

I shook my head.

"Well." He could tell that I was sniffling. "What you crying about? And why are you waving at your dilly like that?"

Finally, in a very painful voice I managed to say, "A chinch was biting on my nuts, and I..." Then words failed me, and it seemed as though the dark itself was blocking my speech.

"Gawdam." Frank began to laugh so vibrantly, he seemed to draw all the dim light in the room to him, and his cackling voice suddenly seem to standout like a beacon of light. "You mean you punched yaself in the balls?"

I nodded just as I heard Allen call from the next room, "What's all the noise about?"

But I did not answer him.

"Dammit, Johnny," Frank said. "You ought to know better than to do that." He was still laughing. "But it ain't nothin'. Just lie back. You'll feel better soon."

I didn't feel better soon. My balls hurt me all night and for most of the following day. And, many times during that day, I asked the Lord why in the hell did He, the Almighty, put bedbugs on this earth. I concluded that the bedbugs were there to make my life even more miserable than just being poor.

On another occasion, I had gotten to bed late, after spending a very active day playing with my brothers and friends. It had been a day of baseball, hide-and-go-seek, dead blocks, rock climbing, and a walk across the Benjamin Franklin Bridge to Camden, New Jersey. I was exhausted when I finally got to bed that night, and even with the thought of chinches sucking my blood, I fell asleep quickly. Indeed, I fell into a deep sleep.

I had been sleeping for hours when suddenly I sat up in bed and found myself twisting up my nose as though I wanted to sneeze. My right nostril felt stopped up, like I had a bad cold, and there was a familiar, putrid smell in my nose. It was the stink of the dreaded chinch bug. Then I felt a twitching in my right nostril, and I was absolutely sure that a goddamn chinch was in my nose. I held my left nostril closed and blew as hard as I could through the right one, but the little bastard would not come out. I blew through my right nostril again and again, but my actions did not dislodge the chinch.

Then fear struck me like a blast of cold wind. What if the chinch went right down the back of my nose and into my belly? Abie had told me that bedbugs had been known to live inside of a person for a long time. They could live inside the person's stomach and eat up all his food until he died. Abie had said there was nothing that doctors or the hospitals could do about it. Once that bug got into your stomach, you were finished.

I didn't know any better at the time. I believed Abie because he was an older brother. I was only seven, and Abie was twelve. A twelve year old brother was supposed to know the truth of what he was talking about. To me, Abie was almost a grown up.

With this icy fear now gripping me, the only thing that I could think about was my mother. She had to save me from that chinch in my nose.

"Mama!" I bolted out of bed and fled towards the stairs like the devil was after me. "Mommy! Mommy! Mommy!"

It was the middle of the night and the house had been dead quiet. Everyone was asleep, but with my first shout of "Mommy," voices of brothers and sisters could be heard from every corner of the darkness.

"Whats-a matter?" Allen shouted

"Who's makin' that noise?" Frank yelled.

"Is that Johnny?" Marion said.

"Somebody woke me up," Abie said.

"What's all the noise about?" Ducky was heard saying.

"That's Johnny." Dotty said. "Somebody help Johnny."

Then my mother's voice could be heard. "Johnny? Johnny, is that you?"

"I don't see him," Norman said. By that time, he had gotten out of bed.

"Mommy! Mommy! Mommy!"

"Johnny, is that you?"

"Where is that damn fool?" Frank said. He also had now gotten out of bed. My mother and all my brothers and sisters were now out of the bed.

I had jumped out of bed and started down the stairs from the third floor to the second floor with the intention of going to my mother's bedroom. But when I got to the middle of the stairs, I remembered something else that Abie had said. If I got a chinch in my nose, I should not move around because I could make the chinch fall down the back of my nose and into my stomach. But if I stood still, there was a good chance that the bug would come out of my nose on its own accord.

I remembered the second part of what Abie had told me just as I was halfway down the stairs to the second floor, and when it came back to my mind I had stopped dead in my tracks. I was still calling for my "Mommy," even though I was doing it now through clenched teeth. I did not want to open my mouth for fear that I would cause the chinch to tumble out of the back of my nose and into my stomach, and I was not about to move either.

There were no electric lights, so it took sometime for someone to find matches and light a lamp. All the while, there was this shouting and confusion.

"Johnny, is that you?" I heard my mother's voice searching through the darkness, as she came out of her bedroom.

"He's on the stairs," Allen said. "Bring the lamp."

"Johnny's on the stairs, Mom," Marion said as she came out of the girl's room on the second floor.

"Somebody help Johnny." Dotty was still crying.

My mother was out of her room now and coming up the stairs, just about the same time as Allen was coming down the stairs with a lit lamp.

With the light of the kerosene lamp cutting through the darkness, causing eerie figures to dance on the walls, my mother could see me now, crouching in the middle of the staircase, trying for dear life to stay absolutely still.

"Whatta you doin' down there?" Allen said.

"Johnny, are you all right?" Mom said anxiously as she ran up the steps to me.

"Sure he's all right," Frank said as he stood behind Allen on the third floor landing. "You can see that he's all right."

By this time, my mother had reached me. "You all right, Johnny?" She pulled me from the wall to her. First I resisted her, afraid that I would shake the chinch loose in my nose. But then I let her take me in her arms. I was really in need of some comforting.

"Is he all right?" Marion said.

"Somebody help Johnny." Dotty was still singing the same refrain as she stood behind Marion.

"Are ya all right, Johnny?" My mother rubbed my back. "Are ya all right?" She then held me at arm's length. "What was it that bothered you?"

I kept my jaws clamped tight, and I tried to say, "My nose. My nose. In my nose." The words were slurred coming through my clenched teeth.

"What did you say?" my mother said. "Did you say something about your nose?"

"What's he talking about?" Norman said.

"His nose," Abie said.

"What about his nose?" Frank said. "It looks the same as always."

"What about your nose?" My Mom continued to hold me at arms length as she inspected my face. She stared at my nose. "What's ta matter with ya nose?"

Through my clenched teeth I said, "I got a chinch in it, and I don't want it to go down in my belly and eat up all my food."

"What's did you say?" My mother looked perplexed.

Abie began to laugh.

"My gawd, he's so dumb," Frank said.

"Aw shut up," Allen said. "Can't you see that he is really scared."

My mother pulled me closer to her, and she wrapped her arms snugly around me.

At that moment, my father arrived at the bottom of the third floor staircase. "What-ta-hell is all the noise about out here?"

"It's Johnny," Marion said. She was happy to explain the situation because she had understood what I had said from behind my clenched teeth. "He's got a chinch in his nose, and he's afraid its gonna go down into his stomach and eat up all his food."

"Whatta you say, girl? He's got a chinch in his nose? A chinch?"

"That's right, Al. He's got a chinch in his nose, and he's scared."

"He's got a chinch in his nose, and he's scared. Huh! Well, I'm sleepy, and I don't like all this noise out here. Now come here boy."

I did not move.

"I said come here boy. Don't you understand me?" I still didn't move. My father began plodding up the stairs, talking to himself every step of the way. "Being black must knock the sense out of people."

"Now Al, you leave this boy alone." My mother pulled me closer to her.

"I ain't gonna hurt that boy, Mae. He's so dumb, most of his hurtn' is gonna come from himself." My father was now standing on the steps of the stairs right in front of me. "Didn't ya hear me call you boy?" He grabbed hold of my arm and pulled me away from my mother."

"Al, don't you hurt that boy. Don't you…"

"So you got a chinch in ya nose. Well, whatta ya gonna do about it? Ya don't know, huh? Then I'll show you what to do." With that he took hold of my nose with the thumb and pointer finger on his right hand, and he squeezed real hard. I felt and heard the chinch go squash inside my nostril. "Now that chinch is dead," my father said in a very angry voice. "And I want everybody to go back to bed before I start beating some little asses." He went back down the stairs mumbling to himself about how stupid some children could be.

I watched my father disappear below into the dark beyond the glow of the lamplight. Tears swelled up in my eyes. From above, on the third floor landing, I could still hear Abie laughing, and I knew that Abie had told me a lie. I was no longer concerned about the chinch getting into my stomach. It was now plastered all over the insides of my right nostril, and the stink of it rolled down into my mouth and throat, making me feel like I wanted to vomit.

My mother gently picked me up and held me close to her breast. She felt warm, and I felt safe. It was just what I needed to offset the foul smelling stink of the chinch bug in my nose, and I knew I was going to sleep in her bed that night. "The rest of you go to bed, right now," she said. She carried me down to the second floor and into her bedroom.

"Does that stupid boy have ta sleep in here?" my father said as my mother put me in the bed on the far side of the mattress away from him.

"Yeah, Al. Yeah. Now leave the boy alone."

"Aw shit. Being black must cause brain sickness."

My mother had me blow my nose into a handkerchief, but it didn't do much good. The incident was over, but not to be forgotten. The smell of the chinch bug never left me.

With no electricity, there certainly was to be no refrigerator in the house. We had an icebox in the kitchen made of wood, and it had a heavy door at the top that sealed off an inner chamber from the outside air. That was where we put the ice to keep the icebox cold. The icebox was about five feet high, and below the top compartment there was a much bigger door. When opened, it exposed a large inner area filled with metal racks. That was where the food was kept that had to be protected from open air spoilage, like fruits and vegetables. There were strong, metal handles on the doors that made a snapping sound when they were closed. Most of the time, that icebox was empty.

To keep the icebox cold, Mom had to get a cake of ice from the iceman, who came through the neighborhood on a horse-drawn wagon, three or four times a week. He would come driving his wagon down the street shouting "Icesss! Icesss! The iceman is here." Whenever my brothers and I heard that cry, we would rush out of the house as fast as we could. We did not come out to meet the iceman, but rather to pet his horse. I liked horses because they were close companions of the cowboys that I saw in the movies.

There was no need for ice in the wintertime, and I always missed petting that big, beautiful roan horse. I had fantasies of leaping on top of that horse and riding him right out of Philadelphia all the way to the places out West where the Indians lived. I would fight those Indians just like the cowboys did.

The Noble Street neighborhood was laid out in a strange pattern. It was not entirely residential. The area was a mixture of meat plants, tool and dye, knitting factories, and trucking firms. Those commercial establishments surrounded small groups and patches of private homes. There were only a few blocks in the neighborhood that were completely free of commercial buildings.

The neighborhood had probably been totally residential up to the 1850s, but as Philadelphia became an industrial city, these older neighborhoods were the first areas that the factories appeared in. Some of the older homes remained, probably because the rent was so cheap.

The factories in the area were all tall, dark, and rust-colored buildings. They were probably constructed around the turn of the century, and form was dominated by function.

When I was growing up in the Noble Street neighborhood, many of the streets were still cobble-stoned, and they could be quite slippery when wet. Sometimes, horses would have trouble pulling loaded wagons over these wet cobblestones. The iceman's horse had such difficulties on rainy days.

Overall, the neighborhood was drab and dark looking. There was no color to the buildings, and no trees or grass in our locale, except for the grass and weeds that were to be found on a few vacant and storage lots. The closest park, Franklin Square, was about ten blocks away, and it was very small indeed. The environment was quite depressing to look at.

My family lived on the south side of Noble Street, and across the way, a little to the west of our house, there was a tool and dye factory. Behind our house, beyond the fence that surrounded the backyard, there was a large enclosed space where metal and wooden barrels were stored. It was a filthy place that was treated more like a garbage dump than a storage area. The lot belonged to a meat factory that was located a half block East from our house. The barrels were used to transport freshly cut meat, and there were always little bits of it left clinging to the sides of many of the barrels when they were stored in that back lot area. Those bits of meat were a dinner call for the neighborhood vermin.

The rats found that back lot area so irresistible, they would often raid the barrels in broad daylight. When my brothers and I would see the rats jumping in and out of the barrels, we would leap over our back fence and go on a rat hunt. Sometimes we would trap a rat in a barrel, and then we would drop bricks on it until it was crushed to death. Other times, we would catch a rat in a small wooden box and burn it alive or drown it, or get the bow and arrows and use the rat for target practice. That kind of treatment of rats was a common practice among the boys in my neighborhood.

That back lot area was like our own private jungle because it was overgrown with weeds in some spots. Along with the rats, there were grasshoppers, caterpillars, and a few wild alley cats, and at night, fireflies. Norman used to say that going on an adventure in that back lot area was better than going on a safari in Africa because there were no creatures in our jungle that could win over us, certainly not an alley cat, rat, or a grasshopper. We were the kings of our jungle.

Nevertheless, because there were so many commercial buildings in the area, the private homes were relatively small in number. Consequently, the neighborhood was not very populated, but it was, in the words of the civil rights movement, an integrated neighborhood; that is, if you ignored the crazy-quilt, patch-like, residential puzzle arrangement of the community.

Noble Street ran east to west. My family lived between Third and American Streets. The south side of Noble Street was reserved for black families. White families lived on the north side of the street, with one exception. There was an elderly white man named Freddie who lived next door to us.

Freddie was an outcast, a reject among the white families in the neighborhood. He drank a lot, as most of the men in the neighborhood did, but he also hung out in the black bars in the area. Freddie was also very unconventional in his habits. He was some kind of technician or engineer who did work on assignment. He was often walking around the neighborhood during normal work hours, and he was even up and about during the very late hours of the night. But Freddie's worst stigma was the fact that he was more friendly to blacks than he was to whites. The fact that he was living on the south side of Noble Street was an indication of that.

Freddie's behavior might have seemed strange to other people, but to him, he was just trying to live a life of absolution. My Mom told me the story about Freddie's background. He was born into a wealthy New England family, and when he was growing up, he attended the best prep schools in the northeast. When he left high school, he went to Harvard, where he got a degree in physics. Through all those early years, he never had to want for anything, and when he graduated from Harvard, he got a very good job at a commercial research laboratory.

However, Freddie was never happy with the fact that materially he had always had so much and so many poorer people had so little. He finally reached a point when he could not live with the situation any longer. He left his job and the affluent lifestyle he grew up in and moved first to Boston, then Hartford, and finally Philadelphia. He specifically wanted to live in a working class or a poor neighborhood, especially one that had Negro residents.

Most of the time, Freddie tended to stay to himself. He didn't like being around more than a few people at a time, except when he was in the bars drinking. Actually, he didn't seem to care much for people. Nevertheless, there were a few individuals he did show some interest in. But, by and large, he was an oddball, an outsider in the neighborhood, and there were always strange stories floating around about things that went on in his house. He was thought to be a lawless man who frequently had meetings late at night with thieves. It was known that he was not a church going man, so there was the word in the neighborhood that he was in league with the devil, and that evil worshippers met in his house on Halloween and on other satanic holidays of the year.

Freddie was of medium build with a hard looking face that was crowned with white, silver hair. He tended to wear a brooding expression, and he had gloomy eyes. His physical appearance made him seem even more mysterious to the people in the neighborhood, and the fact that he wasn't married didn't help his image either. Stories circulated through the neighborhood that he was some kind of sexual pervert, and little children were warned to stay away from him. However, a woman did live with him.

My family did not pay much attention to the stories that went around the neighborhood about Freddie. He was our next-door neighbor, and the stories we heard never matched up to the man we knew. Freddie took quite a liking to my brother Frank. Freddie seemed to like the arrogance and defiance of authority that was so much a part of his personality. He would even invite Frank into his house, and he often sent Frank off on errands for him. Regardless of the stories, I liked Freddie a lot. I saw him many times help my mother with heavy shopping bags when she was struggling home from the store. I also admired Freddie's independence. He did not care that most of the people in the neighborhood didn't like him.

To the south of Noble Street, for four blocks or so, there were only factories and meatpacking plants. But to the north, on Buttonwood Street, Green Street, and Fairmount Avenue, was the area of the neighborhood where most of the people lived. At the same time, these streets had that same crazy quilt, racial pattern. There would be whole blocks of nothing but white residents, and then there would be whole blocks of only black residents. The streets would alternate like that throughout the area. These separations were barriers between the two ethnic groups. The barriers served as reminders that blacks and whites could live in the same community, but that did not make them genuine neighbors.

Most of the white and black adults who lived on Noble, American, and Buttonwood Streets knew each other on a first name basis. They would even exchange formal greetings to one another across the barriers, but for them, that was usually as far as it went. Neither group would ever think of inviting the other into their homes. Only Freddie challenged that restriction.

There was much more fraternization among the children of the neighborhood, and that was for good reason. All the children in the neighborhood went to the same schools and were classmates. Moreover, just about all the young people went to the Friends Neighborhood Guild community center to play sports and engage in other kinds of classes and craft activities. But when school was over and the Guild closed down for the day, the black and white children would return to their places behind established neighborhood barriers.

I played my part in those odd relationships, but I never felt comfortable about it. I always harbored a wish that some white kids would invite me to their homes. After all, white people were movie stars, presidents like Washington and Lincoln, and schoolteachers. They had to have nice homes. If nothing else, they certainly had electricity, and radios, refrigerators, and all that stuff. But then, maybe those luxuries were not meant for black people. It was probably best that I didn't visit any white homes. It would make me feel more deprived than before.

Just because the adults would say "hello" and "good morning" to one another, and their children went to the same schools and played games together, doesn't mean that there were no raw, racial tensions in the neighborhood. There were, but they were kept in check. It was a poor and working class neighborhood, and both the whites and blacks were more concerned with economic survival than racial differences. At the same time, racial tensions might show themselves when the white and black kids were playing games at the Guild, or in the competition that was so much a part of the activities in school, or when a youngster of one group strayed across geographical boundaries onto the turf of another group.

I had many white classmates in school, and I played with many white kids at the Guild. I never had any trouble with the white kids I knew, but if I happened to stray into an unfamiliar white locale, it could turn out to be a lot of trouble for me.

It was probably the influence of the Quakers at the Guild that helped a great deal to keep the community pot from boiling over. The Quakers were constantly telling us, black and white people, that the color of our skin might be different, but in God's eyes we were all the same. "Praise the Lord. He loves all His Children Equally."

The white and black children of the Noble Street neighborhood could mix and be together at school and in the playground, but that was with a very strict and definite proviso. There was to be no close contact between black boys and white girls, or black girls and white boys, in school or at the Guild. If there were large group activities, like playing games, or putting on shows, black boys and white girls were allowed to get physically close and participate in the programs together, but that was always an awkward situation. There could be no displays of overt pleasure and enjoyment with the company. In most instances, when the two groups participated together, they were expected to act like robots. They were not suppose to show any personal feelings or emotions toward one another.

My oldest brother Allen was a lone wolf. In my family, siblings who were close in age tended to become companions. Frank and Norman hung out together, and when I was not going around with my older brothers, I would hang out with my younger brother Ducky. Even Dotty and Marion would do things together. But Allen refused to buddy-up with Abie. More often than not, Allen did things by himself.

Allen was only thirteen, but he did not seem to have any need for other boys of his age. Moreover, he rarely smiled or laughed. He did not like sports, nor did he like being around large crowds of people. He rarely participated in full family functions, parties, picnics, and those kinds of things. He was truly the phantom brother of the family, and I noticed that he always seemed to be deep in thought and far way from his immediate surroundings.

I liked my brother Allen a lot, even though I did not know him all that well. But more interestingly, white girls tended to like Allen, in the most romantic sense. They were always flirting with him at the Guild. For some reason, he could get away with breaking community mores while others could not. Many times I saw white girls staring at Allen across a room with such intensity and hunger, I could do no less than feel sorry for them. I imagined they thought of him as sexy chocolate thunder. I wished white girls would look at me the way they looked at Allen.

Across the street from our house, two doors up, on the east side of the tool and dye factory, there lived a white girl of Allen's age. The girl's name was Delores. She had the hots for Allen. Delores was a brown-haired perky sort of girl with smooth features. She was a little on the heavy side, but that did not take away from her girlish prettiness. She was quite cute, and there were many days when I saw her sitting across the street, on her front steps staring at Allen with leering eyes. She looked like a lion salivating over raw meat. It was really exciting to see such a young girl filled with so much declarative sexual fire, even though I did not fully understand the stimulating feelings I was getting from looking at her looking at Allen. I was too young then.

One summer's day, I had been playing dead blocks with some friends on American street. It had been a good game, especially because I had been winning, but then I felt the need to pee. Consequently, I had to give up my good position in the game to go to the toilet. When I reached my house, I found the place quiet, and there seemed to be no one at home. But as I was about to leave again, I thought I heard some noise from the third floor. That put me on the alert because it was common in those days to leave your front door unlocked.

I could not hear the sound clearly, but I thought it was the noise of someone sighing, quite loudly. I listened. Yes, it was the sound of someone exhaling. I stood still and quiet at the foot of stairs. Now the house seemed deathly silent. Then, again, I heard the sound.

But, for some reason, rather than calling out, I decided that I would creep silently up the stairs to see what might be going on. My instincts were telling me that something interesting was probably happening. Resting my back against the wall of the staircase, I glided up the steps. The walls of the staircase were cool, and they felt comforting against my hot, perspiring skin. The blood was pounding in my temples, and I did not know why I was feeling so excited. When I reached the second floor landing, I realized that the sound was coming from the third floor.

When I reached the third floor, I first looked into the back bedroom, and I saw that it was empty. However, when I looked into the front bedroom, I saw Allen leaning out of the window, intently watching something. Allen was making that noise, a groaning, grunting, exhaling sound. I watched him for a few minutes, and I noticed that he was moving his hand between his legs. I thought, "Why was he doing that? And what could he be looking at?" Then, it suddenly occurred to me, that maybe he had lost his mind like crazy George. He was doing strange things with his hand just like George. In any case, whatever Allen was doing, I knew it was none of my affair, but I felt I had to know what it was that was causing him to act so peculiarly, even at the risk of getting my block knocked off for nosing into his business.

With a lump in my throat, I crept silently towards Allen. A warm breeze was blowing in the window, and there was a strong perfume smell in the air. I moved forward without the slightest sound giving away my presence. I moved close enough to him until I could see over his shoulder. Allen was so involved with what he was doing, he did not take any notice of me being there. Peering over his shoulder, I followed his eyes through space, to the other side of the street, to a yard area that sat between the tool and dye factory and some residential homes to the right of our Noble Street house.

In the yard area, beyond a six-foot high fence, sitting in a tree swing was Delores. She was swinging back and forth and waving up to Allen, while she laughed and giggled, but that was not the only thing she was doing. In between waves, she would lift up her dress and rub her panties where her nooney was.

When she would rub her nooney, Allen would moan and dig his hand down between his legs. The second time she rubbed her nooney, I suddenly felt hot and excited between my legs, and without noticing it, I gave out with a grunt and moan just like Allen. As I did, he turned around quickly. "What are you doing here?" He pushed me back from the window, but Delores had already caught sight of me. She bounded from the swing and disappeared behind the rear of her house.

"Now see what ya done." Allen bounced his fist off the top of my head, but he did not hit me hard. He was one brother who never beat up on the younger kids.

Allen got up and stood there for a while staring out of the window. There was a look of great disappointment on his face. Sighing, he took one last glance at the empty tree swing across the street, and then he went downstairs. I remained up there on the third floor, and I stared out that window, hoping with all my might that Delores would come back to her swing. I liked the feeling I had gotten when I saw her patting her nooney, but even though I waited for more than an hour, Delores never returned.

It was a few days later, in the evening, around dusk, and I was just starting up the stairs to get a lamp for my mother, when I passed Allen coming down the steps. He was moving swiftly, jumping two and three steps at a bounce. I didn't know why but I had a feeling that something was up with him. Instead of getting my mother the lamp, I went up to the front bedroom on the third floor and carefully peeked out of the window. My hope was that I would get a glimpse of whatever Allen was up to.

As I looked out the window, I did catch sight of Allen, who was galloping up Noble Street, and at the corner he took a quick turn North onto American Street. Could this have anything to do with Delores, I wondered? There was an alleyway that led off of American Street, and it ran behind Delores' house.

At the very moment that I saw Allen sweep around the corner onto American Street, my mother called me. "Johnny, are you bringing me that lamp?"

"Yeah Mom," I called back. "I'm bringing it right now."

After I gave my mother the lamp, I went outside and sat on the front steps. It was my intention to stay right there until Allen returned. Why I did this, I was not sure. I certainly was not going to question him about what he was up to, but I still could not get myself to move from the front steps.

It was about a half an hour later when Allen came sauntering down the street. When he passed me, there was a slight grin on his face. I got up from the stoop and followed him inside. He went straight upstairs to his bedroom, and he was not seen downstairs for the rest of the evening.

The next morning, the entire family was up bright and early; everyone except Allen. He stayed in bed, and he didn't even come to breakfast. Mom asked him if he was sick, and he told her no. He said he just wanted to stay in bed and rest. Since it was summer time, and no school, she let him stay in his room.

I thought there was something strange about Allen staying up in his bedroom. I didn't know what, but I had a feeling. So, as soon as I could, after breakfast, I crept up the stairs again to peek at him. It wasn't easy doing it, either, because I did not want the other members of the family to know what I was up to. Everybody was so nosey. With some dodging and faking moves, I was able to make my way up the two flights of steps without any member of the family asking me what I was doing. Besides, I told myself that I knew they could not see me sneaking around because I had clouded their minds like The Shadow did in the comic books.

When I arrived at the third floor landing, I crouched very low, down near the floor so that my brother, who was lying in the bed, would not be able to see me. I did not think I had the power to cloud Allen's mind because, after all, he was my oldest brother. I also had to be careful sliding on my belly because the old wooden floor was frayed and cracking. I could easily get splinters in my hands, arms, and knees. I once got a big splinter of wood, about an inch long and about a sixteenth of an inch in diameter, stuck in my foot, and it stayed there for weeks before I got it out. I didn't tell my mother about that splinter because I did not appreciate the way she opened up my skin to get a splinter out. She would probe the area where the splinter was with a needle, and her actions were always very painful.

When I reached the doorway to the bedroom, I pushed myself up from the floor so that I could see Allen lying in the bed. The first thing I noticed was that he had his head under the covers. But then, after a while, his head came out from under the covers, and I saw him smell his hand. Immediately thereafter, he put his head back under the covers, and seconds later he uncovered his head again. He did this two or three different times, and each time his head appeared he would smell his hand and smile while saying, "Ha, Delicious Delores."

"What could that mean?" I wondered. But when I saw the outline of Allen's hand go down under the covers to a place between his legs, I began to put two and two together. When I realized that his behavior had something to do with Delores and that nooney business, I got my butt out of there as quick as I could, without making any noise, of course. In hurrying the way I did, I was not being as careful as I should, and as a consequence I got a couple of splinters in my hand. But I got both of them out later without much trouble.

After peeking at my brother, I was feeling odd for the rest of the morning. Just thinking about Allen thinking about Delores' nooney made me feel hot and bothered. It was a nice, wholesome feeling, but it scared me because I did not understand what was happening to my body.

Allen finally came downstairs for lunch, and the entire family, except my father, was sitting around the dining table waiting to eat fried sweet potatoes and pork sausages. That was the day the bi-weekly welfare check arrived. Check day was always a good eating day, and there was no better cooking smell in the world than the smell of frying sweet potatoes and pork sausages. Everyone at the table was in the best of moods, anticipating the delectable meal they would soon be eating.

Mom began dishing out the food, and when Allen got his plate, he started to eat, holding the fork in his left hand. The fork wobbled in his fingers, and he could hardly pick up the food from the plate and get it to his mouth. Allen was right handed. All the Cooper boys were right handed. When I was very young, right up to the time I was four or five, I preferred to use my left hand as my primary hand, and if it was not for my brothers Abie, Norman, and Frank, I would have grown up left handed. But my brothers declared that there would be no left handed boys in the family. To break me out of the habit of using my left hand, whenever I was caught using it to eat with or throw a ball, one of my older brothers would place my left hand on the floor or ground and stomp on it. They would crunch my knuckles under their heels, and the stomping was very painful. It is a wonder that they never broke my hand, but in any event the stomping was enough. It convinced me that I should be right handed like all of my brothers.

But there we all were, sitting at the lunch table, and Allen was trying to eat with his left hand. His right hand he kept below the table. He had it hidden in his pant's pocket.

"Why you eatin' with your left hand?" Norman said.

"Yeah," Abie said. "Why ya eatin' with ya left hand?"

"Aw, shut up." Allen looked menacing at them.

"Is something wrong with your hand?" Dotty said. "Somebody help Allen. His hand is hurt."

"I thought you kids were hungry," Mom said. "Now what is all this talk about Allen hurting his hand?" She came over to the table from the stove and she stood near Allen.

"There ain't nothing wrong with my hand," he grumbled, looking very annoyed.

"Then why are you hiding it under the table?"

"Yeah," Frank said. "Why you hidin' your hand?"

"I ain't hidin' nothing."

"Allen," Mom spoke in a serious voice. "Let me see your hand. Right now. Let me see it."

Allen was an obedient son, and he usually did exactly what Mom told him to do, but this time he hesitated.

No one was eating. All eyes were on Allen. The entire family was just sitting around the table staring at him, waiting for the mystery of his missing hand to be cleared up.

Finally, Allen pulled his hand from his pocket and put it on the table.

"He's got a glove on," Marion said with great surprise.

"Why you got that glove on ya hand?" Frank said.

"Cause I wanna."

"Is it hurt?" Dotty said.

"It ain't hurt."

"Then why you hidin' it?" Mom stared hard at Allen.

"There's somethin' on it," Marion said. She wanted to be the one to solve the mystery of the missing hand. She did not want Norman to figure it out first. "Yeah, there must be somethin' on it," she said again, and this time more emphatically. "That's why he's hidin' it."

"That's right," Frank said. "There's somethin' on it, and he don't want us to see it." Frank was challenging Allen, and nothing Frank loved more than challenging the oldest of the big brothers.

"Now, Allen." Mom put her hands on her hips, which meant she was really anxious and serious to resolve the mystery. "What in the devil are you wearin' a glove for in the middle of the summer time?"

"It's a disease or somethin'," Dotty said in a sorrowful tone.

"No, no," I finally said. "It ain't no disease." I had heard enough of all this speculation, and enough was enough.

"Then what is it?" Frank said.

"Well…" I looked at Allen, and it appeared to me as though he was giving me the okay to speak out. I looked around the table, and all eyes were on me. I swallowed hard and said, "Well," I stammered a bit. "It's Dee-lishous Delauris. He's got Dee-lishous Dee-lauris on his hand."

"What?" My mother glared at Allen.

Allen Junior slid right out of his chair and landed underneath the table. Never before, and never since, have I ever seen him so embarrassed and wiped out.

"Dee-lishous what?" Frank began to roar with laughter. He seemed to know immediately what I was talking about, while the rest of the family stared at each other completely stupefied.

After a long moment, my mother began to wrinkle her nose as a look of comprehension came over her face. She turned away from the table and faced the stove to keep her children from seeing how much she wanted to laugh. While Mom had her back turned, Allen crawled out from under the table and made a fast exit from the house. He was outdoors for the rest of the day, and he was one very hungry boy when he finally did return home.

Conversations about Allen's hand and Delicious Delores filled the house with discussions throughout the afternoon and evening, but by the following day, the family had grown tired of the subject. For a time, I was right in the middle of all the talk because, except for Frank and my mother, the other family members wanted me to explain this business about Delicious Delores. I buttoned up my lips. I wasn't about to tell them what I saw Allen doing in bed, and what I saw him doing when he was watching Delores from the third floor window. I certainly was not going to say anything about that girl patting her nooney.

I never found out how Allen squared himself with Mom. I never mentioned the name Delicious Delores to him or her ever again. The reference was just allowed to fade away as a family topic, but I thought about it a lot. And I know that Norman and Frank talked about it. After a day or so, Allen acted as if nothing had happened, and he wasn't even angry with me. That was one of the nice things about Allen. He didn't hold a grudge.

CHAPTER THREE

My brothers and I were born adventurers. We loved to go tramping off to other areas of the city when the weather was nice in the spring, summer, and fall. As a consequence, we came to know the city very well. One of the things that caught our attention early on was the way the different streets were paved. All the major thoroughfares were smoothed over with a tar face—streets like Market, Spring Garden, Girard Avenue, and Broad. But the back streets, like Noble Street that ran through the poorer neighborhoods, were mostly cobblestone.

When we weren't walking, we would take the trolley cars or the subway-El system. When the subway came out of the ground, it traveled on elevated tracks high above the street, and that is when it became the El, the elevated train.

I also became very familiar with the most historical section of the city—the area that Ben Franklin lived in during colonial times, which was located around Market Street, Front Street, and Delaware Avenue. Noble Street was just a few blocks from that old section where the historical sites of the Liberty Bell, Elfreth's Alley, and the Betsy Ross House still remained. The Nation's history was at our doorstep. Even Independence Hall was only eight blocks from Noble Street.

The most important area of Philadelphia sat on a narrow strip of land between two rivers, the Delaware to the East and the Schuylkill to the West. The heart of the city, both literally and figuratively, was at the junction of Broad and Market Streets. City Hall sat right in the middle of this junction, and the most important local government and commercial buildings were also found in that downtown section.

Because the main area of the city was situated between the two rivers, I often thought of the city proper as being an island. If you went to the top of City Hall, you could see the two rivers clearly on both sides of the City. It was quite an impressive sight, and it made me feel small. I was always happy to return to ground level afterwards. The view from the top of City Hall also showed me how big the city really was, and I saw that it had many different neighborhoods.

I learned more about the city when my brothers and I traveled around, from place to place. The city was not laid out uniformly. It swerved and twisted between the two rivers, and it sloped downward from north to south. North was uptown and south was downtown. The further north you went, the better the neighborhoods became, and the more up-to-date and modern the houses were. The streets were cleaner, and the neighborhoods became increasingly communities of all white residents. Noble Street was decidedly downtown.

Because much of the land of the City sat twisted between two rivers, I also thought of Philadelphia as being a crooked city, and that made me think of myself as being a character in one of the childhood stories that my teacher used to read to me in kindergarten class. It started like this: "There was a crooked man, who lived in a crooked house." To be sure, to be crooked to me meant to be poor, frequently hungry, and living in a house that was infested with vermin. Why didn't the teacher tell me about the quality of life of the crooked man in the story? There should have been more details. Nevertheless, it didn't matter how crooked the city was, it didn't stop us from traveling from one end of it to the other.

There were times when my brothers and I, usually Norman and Frank, would go downtown to Market Street, to where the big department stores were. I would do things with them that I would never do on my own. We would go into the department stores and look at all the beautiful clothes, toys, and home appliances up close. It was a much better experience than staring at the items in the department store windows. That was one of the reasons why I liked traveling with my brothers. They were so bold, and being with them made me feel bold, too.

When we were not going down to center city, we would often take the trolley car and go out to Fairmount Park. The park ran for miles on both sides of the Schuylkill River, beginning around Twenty-third or Twenty-fourth Street. It was filled with wide fields of grass and trees, and there were many ponds and creeks to explore. Deep in the park, there were even some thick forests. But what fascinated us the most when we went on a trip to Fairmount Park was the caves in some of its small mountains. They were so dark and scary.

Also, we truly enjoyed playing in the waterways of the park. We loved swimming in the ponds, and we got a great deal of pleasure from hunting for crayfish in the creeks. Moreover, the water was clear and clean enough to drink, and there were times when we would do just that. But most often, the waterways were used to play in. There were occasions when we would build a raft and go sailing on one of the ponds. We would imagine that we were whale hunters out on the high seas, or we would imagine we were floating down a crocodile-infested African river.

Fairmount Park was the biggest park in the City, but there were other parks, like Pennypack Creek Park, which were fun to visit. Pennypack was located in the northeast section of Philadelphia, and it was much further from Noble Street than Fairmount Park. Even though it was a greater distance from our home, we enjoyed going to Pennypack Creek Park because it was one of the most secluded parks in the entire city.

Traveling to the parks was great fun for us. We would often ride in those old wooden trolleys, with their clanging bells and those long iron connections that stretched up from the top of the trolley to an electric wire overhead. There was a roller on the connecting rod, which bounced along the electric wire, and periodically, it would shower sparks in the air. That was exciting, and it made riding in the trolley car an adventure. The seats of the trolley were a yellowish brown, made of lacquered wood, with cushions stuffed with horsehair. When riding on a trolley car, my brothers and I would bounce around a lot. The vehicle always gave us a rough ride. The trolley had a herky-jerky motion because it had a different mechanical system than a bus or subway car. The trolley motor did not hum. It moaned and groaned as though it were straining, and the sound of the trolley made me think of it as being a beast of burden instead of a machine.

To get to many of the parks, we had to travel through communities where no black people lived. I usually felt very uncomfortable going through those white neighborhoods. It made me feel like I was an alien in a foreign land and often my skin would itch, and I wanted to run home, jump into the washtub, and take a bath.

Moreover, white communities tended to surround the parks where we liked to go, but we did not let that stop us from going to them, either. One hot, humid August day, my brothers and I decided we wanted to go swimming. One of the best places we knew of to take a swim was in Pennypack Creek Park, and on that day, even Allen wanted to go along. Usually, it was Norman, Frank, and I who made those trips to the Park, but Allen enjoyed swimming so much, he would often give up his lone wolf status to join us.

Some areas of Pennypack Creek Park were so dense, it was like being out in the country, and I was attracted to Pennypack paticularly because of that quality. But I also liked going there because we would have to travel by the Subway-El all the way to the northern end of the line, and then we would have to take a trolley for a very long distance before reaching our destination. It gave me the chance to hear the hum of the El motor, and afterwards the moaning and groaning of the trolley car motor, all in one trip.

We left Noble Street late in the morning, traveling first by the Frankford El, which ran above Front Street through East Philadelphia.

The El wound itself through clusters of red brick, dark industrial build-ings that once constituted the main commercial area of the city, but in the l940s, industrial progress was already leaving that area behind.

The El passed through Kensington before it reached Frankford, and the further north we went, more and more residential housing began to appear.

At the end of the El line, we left the train and went down from the elevated tracks to the street level. There we caught a trolley that went up Frankford Avenue. The trolley would take us right to the gateway of Pennypack Creek Park. The Frankford trolley traveled through alien territory, but even with that itchy feeling I usually got when I was in white neighborhoods, I still thought it looked like a nice place to live. The houses looked so new. I would have liked it if my family and I lived along Frankford Avenue.

Reaching the park, we charged into the area and made our way to our favorite swimming hole. The smell of the park was wonderful. It had the grassy, flowery smell of the country. The environment was filled with color, green, white, and red foliage, and there was also the odor of lilacs and mulberries in the air.

The swimming hole was off the beaten track of the park. It was a backwater stream area that was somewhat hidden by a canopy of large trees. The area probably wasn't exposed to the average park visitor, and we enjoyed swimming there because of the secluded nature of the spot and because the water was always clean and cold. On hot days, when the humidity was high and our bodies felt clammy and sticky, the first plunge into that cold water would cool us right off.

When we reached our swimming spot, near a big rock that jutted out into the stream, the four of us rushed to see who would be the first one in the water. We began tearing off our clothes, and Frank got tangled in his pants. Consequently, he fell behind the rest of us. But Frank was not to be outdone. He dearly loved to be first in everything we did. He real-ized that if he took the time to put on his bathing suit, he would have been the last one in the water. So he didn't put on his bathing suit. He plunged bare ass into the water, shouting as he did, "I'm first. I'm first."

"No fair. No fair," Allen said. "You didn't put on your bathin' suit."

Allen knew that Frank was competing with him. Frank did not care when the rest of us got into the water. He just wanted to be ahead of Allen. He lived for the test of wills, strength, and power between him and Allen. He would even engineer situations that would bring on confrontations between him and Allen Junior.

There was a great deal of competition among all the brothers. To be in good standing as one of the Cooper boys, you had to have a healthy ego, and each brother had his own particular way of nurturing his ego. Allen was an elitist and that is partly why he stayed very much to himself. Abie may have been a scrawny outcast, but he was the best looking one of the Cooper boys. He had sharp features, a clear unblemished face, and very black, curly hair. He used every opportunity he got to let his brothers know that he was the best looking boy in the family.

Norman was a strange fellow by any account. He was intelligent like Allen, but this intelligence was never exhibited in school. He would rather use his intelligence "getting over" on somebody—being slick and devious. He also had a tremendous facility for using the language. He was a born speaker, and he could entertain the family with jokes and stories for hours when he was in the mood. He certainly knew how to deliver a punch line. None of the other boys had such talent.

Frank was the most aggressive boy in the family. He was robust and strong, although, like all of the Cooper brothers, he was not very tall. He made up for it, however, by being built like a fireplug. Frank was fearless, and he would do almost anything to prove that he was the strongest and bravest of the brothers. On more than one occasion, he almost got himself killed when he did something reckless, like rolling under a freight car of a moving train.

I was the youngest of the big brothers, but I really was not very big at all. I was just a little kid who followed his bigger brothers around.

Nevertheless, I was a person in my own right. I was affable and what some people would call a charmer. I looked like my mother. I had her native-American, high cheek bones, spread-oval face, and brown-reddish complexion. But more importantly, I had an ability to attract people, people who wanted to be kind to me, people who wanted to give me emotional, and sometimes, material support. They saw in me something different that they did not see in my brothers, and I liked that idea.

When I first starting going to the Guild, social workers there took a liking to me right away. They would tell me I had such cute manners. Some of them would often take me to the candy store on Green Street and buy me ice cream cones, sodas, and sometimes even a taskykake apple pie. I was very happy about the attention they gave me, but I was glad my brothers never heard those Quakers say I had "cute manners."

My second grade teacher was a nice woman, too. Her name was Miss Levin, and she had gray hair and brown liver marks on her hands. She used to say love was something that was good for everybody, and we could never get enough of it. I don't know if she was right about that, but she did do some good things. The winter I spent in her class, she brought socks and gloves to school and gave them to me. Once when it was snowing real hard, she gave me a muffler. I don't know why, but people just did things for me.

My younger brothers, Ducky, Kenny, and Ronnie and my sisters, Marion, Dotty, and Jeannie never went on any of these trips to the parks with the older boys. In fact, I had very little to do with my sisters, except on holidays, picnics, and things like that. I never played games with them because that would be too sissified.

Ducky and I were close, and he was of a different sort than all of the other Cooper boys. He was one of the nicest individuals I have ever known, and unlike my older brothers, he seemed to be a fellow without any ego. He was an easy going guy who had nothing to prove to anyone, and he tended to have good feelings for everyone. He was generous and helpful at all times, and when he and I would play games, he didn't care about winning.

The game Ducky loved to play the most was checkers. He had a natural, intuitive knack for it. He was able to see three and four moves ahead. He was so good, he won the Guild's checker championship. He was emperor of the board in our house. I couldn't beat him at checkers if he played blindfolded. However, when he and I faced off, I always won half the games we played. He just wanted the two of us to enjoy playing together.

Because of his unselfish, generous nature, next to my mother, Ducky was the most loved person in the family. But he wasn't on the Pennypack Creek trip, and the older boys were flashing their egos as usual. Frank was treading water, looking smug and successful. "You didn't say anything about havin' to have your bathing suit on," he shouted back to Allen. "Leave yours off if you wanna."

"Yeah," Norman said. He threw his bathing suit aside and dove into the water.

I was the last one in, and since my brothers were all bare assed, I left my bathing suit off, too.

The water was great. It was just right, nice and cool, and the swim was certainly worth the long trip up from Noble Street. For about thirty minutes, we frolicked and swam around in the water of the creek having a wonderful time.

About twenty-five feet from the shore, there was a high sand bar where we could stand up on to rest while still being in the water. In between the sand bar and the shore, there was a dip in the bottom of the creek that went down about six feet. It was a perfect location for intermediate swimmers like us. Taking advantage of the location, we swam back and forth between the shore and the sand bar.

We were having so much fun we didn't notice the two men in gray uniforms who suddenly appeared next to our clothes laying on the ground near the water's edge. They were Park Guards, tall individuals, carrying nightsticks and guns.

"Hey you kids," the one on the left shouted, "What are you doing there?"

The Park Guard doing the talking was the taller of the two, and he had a swarthy complexion. What caught my attention the most about the man was the unusual character of his face. It appeared to be bloated or swollen, and the contours of it were very uneven. I could not be sure, of course, but I believed this was his normal face and the puffiness and distorted shape of it was not due to illness or accident.

My brothers and I stopped splashing about in the water and just dog paddled to keep ourselves from sinking.

"I said what are you doing there?" the swarthy Guard shouted at us again.

Frank finally spoke up. "We're having a swim."

"You're having a swim," the second Guard said. "Well you just get ya little asses out of there. Right now!"

The second Guard was more muscular than the first, and he had freckles and red hair. I could tell that when he was not scowling, he probably had a very pleasant face, a more boyish face than his partner.

With trepidation, I followed my brothers to the bank of the creek, and I pulled myself out of the water. We stood in a line, and I took the last place on the right.

"All right, all right. Stand up, and keep your head up," the puffy faced guard ordered.

We tried to stand straight, but it was difficult because we were naked and feeling embarrassed about it. At the same time, as we were feeling our nakedness, we were trying to hide our private parts with our hands.

The puffy faced Guard looked at Frank, Norman, then me, and lastly he stared Allen straight in the eye. He flinched a nasty smile. "Don't you know that it is against the law to go swimming in this Creek naked?" I saw him wink at his partner. "Do you know what that's called?"

None of us answered.

"I said: do ya know what that's called?"

"No," Allen said.

"Well, I'll tell ya what it's called." The puffy face Guard walked right up to Allen. "Its called indecent exposure. It means you were showing your black asses in public. And don't you know…" He bent way down to look Allen directly in the face. "No one wants to see yo-oh sunnyside black asses. I bet yo mammy don't even like ta see yo sunnyside black asses. So, what do you do, you bring those midnight asses up here to show it to the world." He stood up and stepped back from Allen.

"Say, Harve," the red headed Guard said, as he came over to his partner. "Do ya see that?" He gestured towards Frank. "Do ya see that?"

"See what, Jake?"

"The cock on that one over there." He pulled out his nightstick and pointed directly at Frank. He started to chuckle, "its as big as mine."

"Come off it, Jake. That boy can't be more than nine or ten years old."

"No, no Harve. I'm not kidding. Take a look."

Both men stepped over to Frank. Jake took his nightstick and hit Frank gently on the knuckles.

"Move your hand, boy."

Frank hesitantly withdrew his hand.

Harve stared for a second or two. "Well, I'll be goddamn. He's hung like a horse. They say some of those black bastards have joints like animals. This one sure has."

"And Harve." The cheeks of the red headed Guard became flushed. "Look at it. It ain't circumcised. None of them are circumcised." He glared in turn at each one of our penises that could be seen in our hands as we tried to cover them.

"Yeah, I see," Harve stepped back a little further so that he could get a better view of us. And then a mean, twisted look came over his face. "And do you little fuckers know that that is unsanitary, and its against the law, too."

When I first got out of the water, I had been nice and cool, and I had not been particularly afraid of the Park Guards who were confronting us. I had seen Park Guards many times before, and as long as we weren't doing anything wrong, they would usually leave us be and let us play in the park. But these two Guards were different, and they were not leaving us alone. They were making me scared.

The coolness I had enjoyed in the water was now all gone. Instead, I was feeling unusually hot and sweaty, and I felt like a fool using my hands to hide my private parts. Moreover, I was having a difficult time trying to do it. My balls kept plopping out of my cupped hands, and I feared that one of those Park Guards would hit my balls with his night-stick; the same way Jake had hit Frank on the knuckles. And those Guards had guns. "God," I shivered through my sweat. They might shoot my balls off.

I was scared, and my brothers looked scared too, even Frank, who was the toughest of us all. When he got scared, that meant there was something for me to really be scared about, and when Jake rapped Frank on the knuckles, it made me wince. Tears came to my eyes.

But instead of crying, my body began to throb with anxiety and anticipation. Maybe we had broken the law by swimming naked in the creek, but I knew there was more to it than that. It was that black, white stuff that was making these Guards act mean and nasty, that same kind of stuff that cut the Noble Street neighborhood into its crazy quilt pattern. Harve had made it very clear. He was angry at our black asses, and it didn't matter that our black asses had not done anything to him.

I wondered if the Park Guards would really put us in jail for indecent exposure. Mom would have a fit if she had to come way up to Frankford to get us, if she could get us at all. Maybe we would be kept in jail for a long time.

"Well, Jake do you think we ought to arrest these little fuckers?"

Jake put his hand to his mouth and played with his bottom lip for a second or two. "I'm not so sure, Harve. It would probably cost too much money to feed these little African monkeys."

"Then what should we do?"

"We could just teach them a lesson, like beating their asses or somethin'."

I looked over at Allen, and I saw him swallow hard, as he shifted his weight around from his left to his right foot. The grass rustled loudly under his feet, and I guess he was trying to think of something that would keep those Guards from beating us. His movements were probably an indicator that he was worried about me. Mom told him that the oldest brother was always responsibility for looking after the younger ones, and that was particularly true whenever we were away from home.

As Allen was shifting his weight, I stole a glimpse at Norman and Frank. They were throwing side-glances at each other. Obviously, they were trying to communicate without speaking, and their eyes told me what was going on in their minds. They were trying to let each other know what they thought was the best course of action under the circumstances. There was also a great deal of fear in Norman's eyes. He didn't like guns, and he was practically staring down the barrel of two of them.

I could also see in Frank's eyes that he was getting mad. He was scared, too, but the look he gave Norman said that he was not taking an ass whopping without a fight. He also transmitted that same message to Allen. Allen didn't seem crazy about the idea, but what other choice did he have if those Guards came down on us?

That was the silent message Frank was sending to Norman and Allen, but I did not want to fight the Park Guards. The Guards had nightsticks and guns, and they were big grown men. The thought of fighting them had me just about in tears. I did not want an ass whopping, and as I tried to contain my tears, all I could think was, "Where is my mother when I need her most?"

The two Guards stepped back from us and huddled together to decide what to do. They whispered and talked in very low tones. The four of us looked at each other. We did not want to speak, but Allen made it clear, by nodding his head, that we should all get the hell out of there. Norman gestured the obvious with his head. We didn't have any clothes on. Frank then grit his teeth. I just looked at Allen, pleadingly.

Before we could make any kind of move, the Guards came back over to us. Harve stood directly in front of us while Jake collected our clothes from the bank of the creek. When Jake had gathered up all our clothes, he came over to Harve.

"Now we gonna teach you little fuckers a lesson, especially you," Harve came up to Frank. "You ain't got no right to have a joint like that." He pulled out his nightstick. "Didn't any body ever tell you that you ain't no horse." He rapped Frank hard on the knuckles, which made Frank pull his hands away from his penis. "Only horses are supposed to carry around that kind of baggage." He tapped his nightstick against Frank's dick, but fortunately he did not hit Frank's joint very hard. Nevertheless, Frank acted as though he had been smashed in the penis by a bulldozer. He literally screamed and jumped in the air, almost toppling backwards into the water.

At that moment Jake threw all our clothes into the creek, and they began to float down stream.

"Now you little fuckers go and get those clothes and get your black asses out of this Park and keep them out."

The two Guards then walked away from us, and Allen, Norman, and I circled around Frank as he squeezed his penis to take away the pain. Then in an instant, we all remembered that our clothes were floating away down stream. We had avoided an ass-beating, but now we had no clothes to cover our asses.

Frank's pain was suddenly all gone, and the four of us turned to the creek to locate our clothes. They were about forty yards ahead of us being gently carried along by the current.

"Let's go," Allen said. "We have to get those clothes."

We started down the shore, running like deer being chased by a pack of wolves, We were naked and looked like freshly plucked chickens, but we did not let that stop us. And so we ran like racing cars, hardly feeling our jingles that were jangling against our thighs. We were catching up to our clothes, but suddenly they disappeared from sight around a bend in the creek.

"Faster," Allen shouted, as he gulped deep mouths full of air to keep his wind up. "There's a waterfall down there, and if they go over that, we could lose our clothes forever."

We began running faster, and my bare feet plopped and padded on the dirt and grass along the creek's bank. I was also stepping on little rocks and pebbles and my feet hurt, but I dare not stop. Moreover, I was having trouble keeping up with my brothers. I couldn't run as fast as they could, and I was falling behind.

Suddenly, the riverbank began to swerve, and then it curved around a bend. There, right in our path was a family of four out on a picnic. They were sitting on a blanket, with food spread out around them, down near the water's edge.

As the thundering hoof beats of my brothers and I bore down on the picnic party, we found ourselves hemmed in on both sides. On our left, there was a row of trees, and to the right there was the flowing stream of the creek. The family was sandwiched between the trees and the creek, right in front of us. We would have to go through them, or over them, or else go into the water of the creek in order to continue to chase our clothes.

There was a man, a woman, a boy, and a girl lounging on the blanket. It was the ideal American family. The woman looked as though she had a suntan, and she had dark hair that was tied in a bun in the back of her head. Just as we came thundering upon them, the woman was preparing a plate of food, and the boy and girl were sprawled out on the blanket reading comic books. The man was lying on the blanket with his eyes closed.

Hearing the sound of rushing feet, the woman looked up just as three dark flashes went over her head, and she heard the sound of a big splash in the water nearby. At first, she did not know what to make of it. Then, she began shaking her head as if in doubt of what she had just seen. The man never opened his eyes, and the boy and girl kept right on reading their comic books.

To avoid running into the picnicking family, first Allen, then Frank, and then Norman dove right over the woman and plunged down under the water. I had been running on the side of the pathway furthest from the creek. It was impossible for me to dive over the man, the woman, and the two youngsters and be able to land in the water the way my brothers had done. There was too much distance between the shoreline and me. I chose the next best option.

I put on a strong burst of speed, and when I neared the blanket, I closed my eyes and leapt into the air like a gazelle. I had to go right over the head of the man, but since my eyes and his eyes were closed, neither one of us saw the other.

I did not open my eyes until my feet had touched the ground on the other side of the picnic blanket. I had made it, hurdled completely over the man and the blanket, without breaking speed. In just a few seconds, the picnicking family was behind me, and as I ran from them I heard their voices.

"Morris," the woman said very loudly. "Did you see that? A naked kid just flew over your head, and before that three other naked kids dove over my head into the water."

I heard the woman's voice clearly, and I imagined Morris opening his eyes and giving out with a ho-hum look and saying nothing.

"I said Morris, did you see that? Did you see that!"

"No dear, I didn't see anything," I was sure he finally said.

"Then you must be blind."

The woman was loudly chastising the man, and the sound of her voice made me slow down. With my bare ass still flapping in the wind, I glanced over my shoulder at the family behind me. What I saw was the woman on her knees staring intently after me, the man still lying on the blanket, seemingly gazing up at the sky, and the boy and girl were now on their feet looking in my direction.

I swung my head back to the front of me, and as I did I heard the boy, who was probably about thirteen and the girl a few years younger, shouting, "I see a hiney! It's black and shiny!"

Upon hearing the boy's shouting, I turned up the speed and started running faster. At that point, the shoreline along the creek turned again and the family disappeared from sight, and I slowed down to a walk as I looked out over the water of the creek. I was tired and out of breath, and I was looking for my brothers. In the middle of the creek, I saw Allen, Frank, and Norman swimming just a little ahead of me. Apparently, they had stayed under the water as long as they could before they came up to the surface near the turn in the shoreline. They, too, were now out of sight of the picnickers.

Our clothes got caught on some waterweeds near the shoreline, thanks to the way Jake had rolled them up together, and Allen was soon upon them. He brought the clothes over to the creek bank, and my three brothers got out of the water. We began putting on our water-soaked clothes, happy to have our pants to cover us, and as we were dressing we heard loud laughter nearby.

Up on a small ridge that overlooked the creek, just behind us, we saw the two Park Guards again. They were laughing like hell.

"You black bastards can really run," Harve shouted down at us. "And the way y'all flew over those people having a picnic back there was the greatest. I didn't know niggers could fly." With that comment, Harve broke into another fit of loud, roaring laughter.

Trying not to be distracted by the laughter of the Guards, we finished putting on our clothes. They were wet and clammy, but I felt much better having them on.

"We don't have our shoes," Frank said.

In our haste to chase down our clothes, we had forgotten about our shoes. Jake had not thrown them into the creek with our clothes, but he had left them lying on the bank where we had dropped them.

"We gotta go back and get them," Allen said.

"Yeah, Mom will kill us if we don't get them," Norman said.

We bunched together and started back up the shoreline from where we had come.

"Hey you boogies. Where the hell do you think you're going?" Jake shouted.

"We're goin' ta get our shoes," Frank shouted.

"Like hell ya are," Harve said. "We told you to get out of the Park and that is what we meant. Now beat it before we come down there and kick your little asses."

The two Guards made a gesture like they were going to come after us, and we spun on our heels and were on the run again. We didn't stop running this time until we were on the main path that led out of the Park. "Motherfuckers," Frank growled in a low tone, as we all slowed down to a walk.

"My feet hurt," I said. "It's cause of all these little rocks and twigs I been stepping on." My feet were actually becoming bloody from cuts and bruises.

"I know how your feet feel, " Frank said. "My feet feel the same way."

With the knowledge that Frank's feet were hurting, my feet seemed to start hurting twice as much. Of all the brothers, Frank would resist giving into pain the most. It was part of his personality of being the tough guy. If Frank admitted that his feet were hurting, then I knew all our feet were taking a beating.

We did not meet up with many people as we gingerly walked down the path to the entrance to the park. There were never many people in Pennypack Creek Park during the week. The area was too isolated.

"Oh, my feet are really hurting," I stopped and leaned against a tree.

"Don't talk about it," Norman said. "I think I have a hole in the bottom of one of my feet."

"Let's just get out of here," Allen said.

"And my wet clothes make me feel funny," I said.

"All right, all right," Allen said. "We still gotta get outa here, and you'll just have to wear those wet clothes."

After what seemed like forever, and with our feet aching from the battering they had taken, we finally reached the street outside the park.

We made our way to the trolley car stop, and soon a trolley came along. I had been hoping that a trolley would arrive quickly because I wanted to sit down and rest my feet. I was also happy to see the trolley because I wanted to get home to my mother, even though she was going to be very angry with us. We had lost our shoes. But I was anxious for her to tell me about the nature of my black ass and why those guards were so interested in it.

The trolley stopped, opened its front doors, and we started to get aboard.

"Hey you kids." The motorman of the trolley stopped us. "You can't get on here like that. Why you ain't even got any shoes on. Off! Get off!"

"But wait a minute," Frank said.

"No, I'm not waiting a second. Get off!"

The motorman started to close the doors, and we had to jump out of the way or get mashed by them. Once we were on the street again, the motorman took off. I watched those passengers on the trolley car stare out their windows at us and shake their heads. "Just look at that. Those little Negro boys were trying to get on the trolley all soaking wet and with no shoes on. Those people will do anything." That is what I imagined the passengers were saying, but it was not true. I would not do anything. I would never spit on anybody, even if it was a bad white person.

"Damn," Frank said angrily. "I'm gonna get on that next streetcar whether the motorman likes it or not. They can't keep us off the trolleys."

"You're right," Norman said. "We gonna get on whether they like it or not."

"No," Allen said shaking his head. "We're not gonna get on any trolley. Our carfare is gone." Allen usually held the money when the four of us would go on park trips. The money was normally safer with one person. "It must have gotten lost when that Guard threw our clothes in the creek."

"Whatta you mean?" Frank said. "You mean we have to walk home from all the way up here?"

"Yeah," Allen said trying to be as emphatic as possible. He wanted the reality of the situation to sink into all our minds.

"Aw no," Norman stamped his foot on the ground, giving him a moment of unanticipated pain. "Goddamnit." He did a little dance to subdue the stabbing needle sensations that were coursing through his foot.

"I can't do it," I said. "My feet are already hurtin' too much."

I was ready to cry again. It had been a long ride on the El and then on the trolley to Pennpack Creek Park, and the idea of having to walk all the way back to Noble Street seemed impossible to me. "Allen, I can't do it. I can't do it." I was now fighting back the tears.

"You have to." Allen stared sternly into my face. "We gotta do it. We can't stay up here in this white neighborhood. We probably gonna get beat up if we do, and if night comes, and we're up here, we're gonna get put in jail. The cops know we don't live 'round here."

What he said made a lot of sense, but my feet were still hurting.

"Shit," Frank said. "If we gotta do it, then let's do it."

And that started the Cooper brothers' long walk in the sun. We were many miles away from home, bare-foot, wet to the bone, and without carfare. But the worst thing about our circumstances, no matter how we sized up the situation, was the ugly fact that we were in hostile territory.

With a collective sigh, we turned southward and started towards Noble Street, padding quietly along the pavement, while the soles of our feet burned from the heated concrete on that hot August afternoon. We walked down Frankford Avenue, trying our best not to look at the white people who passed by us. Frankford Avenue was a wide thoroughfare with trolley cars and many other vehicles going in both directions. The houses along the street were big and beautiful, with porches, hedges, grassy-green lawns, and flowerbeds. They all looked so clean and modern.

As we trudged down the Avenue, some of the people in those good-looking houses were sitting on their porches, trying to catch a cool afternoon breeze. The porch sitters stared down at us, gesturing with their hands and commenting softly about the strange little black boys who were trampling through their streets.

I remembered how downtrodden and dejected I felt. It was as though the poverty I lived in was apparent to the people on those porches. I felt they were looking right inside of me. Damn, I thought. Why couldn't those people be nice? I would have loved a cold drink of lemonade or a soda.

Some distance from Pennypack Creek Park, Frankford Avenue became something on the order of a shopping mall, a place where there were many stores and shops bunched together in a commercial corridor. Local people went there to buy food, clothing, household goods, and just about anything else they needed. It was a busy area where mothers gathered in the afternoon to talk and gossip with friends as they did their shopping. Their young children, of course, would be with them.

When we came upon this area, which stretched for blocks and was crowded, my heart jumped into my mouth. Frankford Avenue was a public street, but I did not want to walk amongst a crowd of white people looking the way I did. It would surely be like walking into a lion's den, and even if the lions did not bite me, I was sure to feel like I had been bitten all the same.

I felt the heat and anxiety rising up in me again. I looked over at Allen, hoping that he would turn off of Frankford Avenue and go beyond this shopping area on another street, but that was not realistic. The streets off of that main drag were even more residential than Frankford Avenue. My brothers and I would be even more scrutinized on the side streets than we would be on this major thoroughfare. Our presence there would be readily taken as a black invasion. In white neighborhoods, streets were like castle moats, and if a black person, crossed over one of those moats uninvited, he was sure to be seen as storming the palace gates.

Seeing all those white people crowded on the pavements of Frankford Avenue, I was willing to take the chance of traveling on a more residential street, but Allen kept his course and led us into that valley of the lions. The sidewalk was crowded with shoppers, mostly women and small children, and as we moved among them, the people fell back away from us, up against the storefronts. They did not say anything at first. They just stared at us, and I felt sick from their scru- tinizing, piercing eyes. My stomach was rolling like I had eaten some- thing rotten, and I wanted those people to take their eyes off of me. But those white people just kept staring and staring, and my insides kept right on churning.

I moved closer to my brothers in the hope that they would give me protection from those piercing eyes, but it didn't work. My wet clothes began to feel like lead weights pushing me down into the pavement, and I welcomed the feeling. If I were down under the ground, I would be out of view of those piercing eyes, and none of those white people would be able to say anything about my black ass.

I was following close behind Allen, and I think he was concentrating on the distance in front of him, beyond the crowded area where all the shoppers had gathered. He was trying hard, most likely, not to let those staring eyes distract him. We had a long way to go, and he was responsible for seeing that all of us got home safely.

Norman was sizing up the crowd as best he could out of the corner of his eye. He was sure to have been thinking about what he would do if those white people attacked us. Looking at Frank, I saw that he was flexing the fingers on both his hands. No doubt, he was thinking about how those Park Guards had pushed him around, and he had had enough of that crap. If these people wanted to get nasty, then he was going to get nasty, too.

"Where did they come from?" a voice spoke from crowd.

"There's no Negro people who live around here, is there?" someone said.

"Mommy, who are they?" a child said.

"Oh, it's nobody dear. Just some strange kids passing by."

I heard these questions and comments, but I did not look at the individuals who were speaking them. I just looked straight ahead and kept on moving.

"They are just passing through, aren't they?" an uncertain voice said.

"No shoes. They don't have on any shoes, and their clothes are all wet."

"Niggers."

"What did you say?"

"I said niggers."

"Oh Maggie, they're just kids."

"They're niggers all the same, and I don't like them walking around here like that. Look at them—no shoes, and they're all wet. They'll scare our kids. I'm gonna tell Harry when he comes home, and he's gonna be damn angry."

At the word nigger, Frank balled up his fist and stopped walking. He turn to look into a crowd of fifteen or twenty women and children, and he was trying to determine who had made that nigger crack. I didn't know what Frank would have done if he discovered which person had made the remark. He wasn't going to punch one of those white ladies.

I recoiled when I heard the word nigger. When white people used it on me, it was worse than cursing my black ass. The word nigger made me feel helpless and bad all over, like someone had beaten me into submission. I felt like I wanted to pee, and then a desperate feeling, of wanting to hide, came over me. But there was no place to go. I looked to my brothers to give me guidance, but what could they do? Nothing. I knew the best course of action for me was to just keep on walking, as fast as I could, because I suddenly felt separated and alone in the lion's den.

The concrete pavement was hot, and the soles of my feet were stinging. I had to skip along to lessen the pain and to keep up with my brothers.

"Look at that one. He's dancing while he walks."

"You know what they say about them. Those people are born with rhythm. It just naturally pours out of them. You remember how Bo Jangles Robinson always danced when he walked?"

"But wasn't it just shameful to see him dancing with Shirely Temple."

"Shameful?"

"Yes, shameful."

"Hey Mom, don't they look like monkeys?"

"Yeah, like little monks."

"I'm gonna throw them some peanuts. Monkeys like peanuts, don't they?"

Suddenly a shower of salted peanuts came down upon our heads, and we all tried to defend ourselves with our hands by waving and swatting at them as they cascaded down upon us. Immediately, some of the people standing against the storefronts began to laugh.

Frank stopped walking. He was furious. He turned to face the crowd of women, and his eyes searched the group as he tried to ascertain who had thrown the peanuts.

At that moment, a man came charging out of one of the nearby stores, He pushed right through the crowd of women and children and went right up to Allen, stopping him, and all of us right in our tracks. He was a big man in weight and height, and he had on a white apron that was splashed and tattered with blood. The sight of the blood on the man's apron made me feel sick on the inside, and I began to cry openly because I believed that something dreadful was about to happen to us.

The man shouted at us, "You...You black kids, get the hell out of here. Go on. Get the hell away. You don't belong around here, so move on."

"Yeah," someone said. "Get your niggerselves out of here."

At that moment, I noticed that more men were arriving, and they were surrounding my brothers and me. We were now in a worse situation then when the two Park Guards had confronted us.

I looked down at the ground. Whatever was going to happen, and I did not think it was going to be something pleasant, I did not want to see it coming. I kept my eyes on the ground, wondering all the while what was going through my brothers' minds. I knew that even though they were all youngsters, they would fight if they had to. Out of fear, if nothing else, they would fight grown men. Not that they had much chance of winning. We were outnumbered by too many white people. It was an impossible situation, but they would lock egos and make a last stand if that is the way it had to be.

I was still crying, when I suddenly heard Norman shriek like someone had stabbed him with a hatpin or a knife. It was a hideous, chilling sound that made me shake, and my heart fell right out of my chest into my stomach. Norman had been standing away from me to my left, and he was not in my immediate view. The first thing that I thought of was that someone had attacked Norman, but when I snapped my head around to see what had happened to him, I was surprised to see that there was no white person near him. Norman was swaying back forth as though he were drunk or dizzy or something. Then he began to twitch and hump his shoulders, and at the same time he leaned way back and his eyes rolled to the top of his head.

"Norman," Allen said, "are you…"

Allen never finished the question. At that very instant, white foamy spit began to ease out of Norman's mouth. Allen was taken back by the sight of it.

"Hey," shouted the big man with the bloody apron. "One of these little nigs has got something wrong with him. He's foaming at the mouth."

"Oh my God!" a woman shouted. "Get these kids out of here. It's a rabid nigger."

The shouts of "rabid nigger" became a chorus as the whites around us, both men and women, scuffled to get themselves and their children out of harm's way. Even the big bad man with the bloody apron was cautiously backtracking. But he kept his eyes glued on Norman all the while.

But then, I heard Norman say out of the corner of his mouth, in a sort of whisper, "Come on, let's go. Follow me." With that, he staggered forward at a half run, leaning and swaying from side to side, like he was ready to collapse any minute. He looked like James Cagney playing a drunk in one of his movies.

The people in front of him fell back rapidly. Mothers were shouting and screaming as they grabbed their children and dashed for cover in one of the nearest stores. "Rabid nigger! Rabid nigger!"

Frank, Allen, and I followed behind Norman trying to make his every move, a swing to the left, a stoop to the right, a stagger step forward.

"They're all sick and diseased," shouted the big man. Get out of their way. "Get out of their way!"

A path had now been made for us, straight down the center of the pavement, and behind Norman we juked, swayed, and played our way right out of the shopping area. The people just fell back to the nearest storefront or they took refuge inside a store to let us pass unimpeded.

Even though our feet were hurting us, we bounced along the pavement in a sick, staggering gate until we were a block away from the shopping area. Then Norman broke into a full scale, top speed run, and we all did the same. The houses and people just whizzed by. I never knew I could run so fast and so long on bruised and battered feet. We did not stop running for another five or six blocks, not until the shopping area was far behind us. Then we all stopped and stood there on the sidewalk, huffing and puffing trying to catch our breath.

After a while Norman shook his head violently, and then he began to spit out a white foamy saliva. "Whew," he said. "That stuff taste awful."

"I thought you were sick," Allen said, sounding relieved.

"Naw, I ain't sick. I just crushed some aspirins in my mouth to make those white people think I was sick. I figured I could scare them off if they thought I had some real bad sickness. I slipped some aspirins in my mouth when that big man came running out of that store. They were in this tin box in my pants, and its a good thing that they didn't get wet when that guard threw our clothes in the creek."

"You slicky," Frank said. He started to smile. "There ain't nothing wrong with you."

"Naw. Big Coffee taught me how to do that. When people think you're sick with a bad disease, they'll leave you alone in a hurry."

Big Coffee was a walking buddy of Norman's, and I thought that the trick he pulled off was just the kind of stunt Big Coffee would know about. Big Coffee was about six-foot four, very dark, and one of the nicest friends Norman had. If he had a real fault, it was the fact that he liked to play jokes on people. On this occasion, I was happy that Big Coffee had taught Norman the aspirin trick. There was no telling what might have happened if we had not gotten out of that situation when we did.

Allen started to laugh, and then Frank did the same.

"Did you see how they got out of our way when that stuff started coming outta Norman's mouth?" Frank laughed louder.

"You're a damn clown," Allen said.

I joined into the laughter. "Yeah. I thought you were really sick."

"That's what I wanna you to think." Norman stuck his tongue out of his mouth and wagged it from side to side.

At that moment a group of white adults walked by, and they noticed Norman's antics. They stared disapprovingly at him, and we were suddenly reminded that we were still in alien territory, far from home.

"Hey y'all, we ain't home yet. We still got a long way to go, and looking at these white people makes me feel like running," Allen said.

"I feel like running too." Frank bared his teeth.

"Me too," I said, as the words just jumped out of me. I was surprised at what I said because I knew I would have to struggle to keep up with my big brothers.

"Then let's go," Norman said. "Let's go."

With our bare feet padding on the pavement, we did a lot of running on our way home that afternoon, and when we arrived at our doorstep the sun was going down behind the Inquirer Newspaper Building on Broad Street. That building was a landmark for us whenever we returned to Noble Street from a long trip away from home.

Mom gave us all hell for being so late and losing our shoes, but when she heard the full story we had to tell, she laughed and then she cried. It would be difficult for her to replace the shoes right away, but she was just damn happy that her boys were home.

Chapter Four

The first school I went to was Paxson Elementary School. It was a public school located at Sixth and Buttonwood Streets, a short three and a half blocks from my Noble Street house. The school was a huge, four-story, stucco building. My first day at Paxson as a kindergarten student was filled with apprehension. My mother brought me to school, and as we walked the distance from my home, she talked to me every step of the way. She kept telling me how much fun I was going to have in kindergarten, and the new things I would learn, and the new friends I would come to know. She tried to be very convincing, but she couldn't relieve my anxiety. No matter what she said, I knew she was going to leave me alone at school, and I would be separated from her and my siblings for the first time in my life. The thought was terrifying.

When we reached the school, my mother located the classroom on the ground floor. She took me into the room and introduced me to the teacher, a young white woman. The teacher told me to go and play with some of the other children, but I ignored her suggestion. I did not move from my mother's side. My mother stood there with me for five or ten minutes before she kissed me and said, "I'll see you later." She then left the classroom. As she disappeared through the door, there was a moment of supreme dread. I had been abandoned. But before I could cry, a girl came over to me and asked me if I wanted to play building blocks with her. She was really cute and I let her take me by the hand

and lead me to the blocks. We sat down on a soft rug and began playing with the blocks, and as we did, my anxieties and dread soon dissipated.

But I did much more that first day of kindergarten than just play blocks with a cute girl. The teacher put all of her first time students through a full program of activities. There were the games, like ring-around-a-rosy and patty cake, patty cake baker's man. She read fairy tales to us. There were morning and afternoon breaks for cookies and milk, with lunch being sandwiched in between, and there was also morning and afternoon naps. The whole day was planned and regulated, and even though I was very young, the teacher's control over all my school activities bothered me. That attitude was to be a problem for me throughout much of my stay at Paxson Elementary School. In fact, I got into a number of contentious situations with teachers because of it.

On that first day in kindergarten class, it was that cute black girl who made my introduction to public school palatable. She was what we called in those days a "high yellow," which is to say she had a very light complexion. The girl's name was Juanita Price. It was a lovely name, and it suited her just perfectly. I said she was cute, but that was not the half of it. She was pretty, and I could even say beautiful. And little, young me was mesmerized by her and infatuated with her from the first moment I saw her.

Jaunita and I would go all the way through elementary school together as classmates, and my infatuation with her never waned. We became good friends as we grew older, but never boyfriend and girl-friend. Nevertheless, that did not stop me from fantasizing about her until the day we separated upon graduating from Paxson. More importantly, it was my feelings for Jaunita, that began that first day in kindergarten that gave me the desire to go to school at the outset. If Juanita had not been there to invite me to play with her, I am sure I would have run out of school after my mother. But after spending a day in Juanita's company, school suddenly had a more inviting and exciting quality.

I did not like the way that the teachers programmed the school day minute-by-minute and hour-by-hour. To be around my older brothers, I had to be more of a free spirit, but there was to be none of that spontaneity of action in school. Nevertheless, because of Juanita and some other friendships I made at Paxson, I managed to get through the first three grades of elementary school without any extreme behavioral problems.

I was not a "goody-two-shoes," or the teacher's pet. I did my share of spitball-throwing, firing paper bullets at other students with rubber bands, mocking and baiting other pupils, and I even talked at times when the teacher's back was turned. But I never did anything really bad.

Thinking back about my elementary school days, I now realize that when young children accept their parental abandonment, and become students, they do not do so because they want to learn how to read or write. First they do so because they have no choice. But second, they probably do so because they want to learn more about other children like themselves. It is a way to get an outside measurement of who you are by comparing yourself with your peers. Certainly, that was the nature of my relations with Juanita. She was a light-skinned black person, and I was on the dark side as a black person. I thought her prettiness had much to do with her skin complexion, and it made me feel good being with this high yellow. Well, in my mind, she was closer to being white.

I enjoyed the company of my peers in those first years at Paxson, and so I went to classes regularly. But I did not open myself up to what the teachers were trying to teach me. I did just enough to keep them off my back. I came to school to be with Juanita and my other friends, and I did not give a damn about reading, writing, and arithmetic.

However, when I reached the fourth grade at Paxson, the Philadelphia Board of Education began a new policy, which stated that students of my class standing had to be reading at grade level. If a student was reading below grade level, he would be removed from his regular class and placed in a special section for underachievers. Each homeroom teacher was instructed to evaluate her students and determine if they were reading up to par.

My homeroom teacher for that year was Mrs. Loreli Newsome, a tall, bossy woman who was more suited to being a sergeant in the Army than a teacher of young students. Moreover, she was a full-bosomed woman with raven colored hair that reminded me of the evil witch lady in Sleeping Beauty. The most distressing thing about her was how intolerant she was toward her students when it came to behavior she deemed "improper." She was so strict with our class that I honestly believed she did not like children, yet she was an elementary school teacher.

I don't believe that Mrs. Newsome's attitude had anything to do with color. She was white, as all my teachers would be throughout my school career. But, specifically, more than half of my class was white, and the overall percentage of the school was approximately the same between blacks and whites. Mrs. Newsome's disdain for students was equally expressed for pupils of all ethnic groups. She was just a mean woman who enjoyed pushing around individuals who were smaller than she was.

If you did not do what Mrs. Newsome wanted immediately, then to her, you were being insubordinate. She used to say, "You students are all knuckleheads," an unflattering term she often threw in our faces when she was annoyed with us. "Your heads are more suited for a carpenter's workbench than a classroom," she would bark. How I used to wish that she would ask me what I thought her head was more suited for. I would have gladly told her that her head was more suited to being at the bottom of the sea with the rest of the whale shit.

My classmates and I called Mrs. Newsome "Gruesome Newsome," and there was a common consensus among us that she would have made a wonderful wife for Frankenstein. I disliked the woman so much it was difficult for me to look directly at her when she was talking to the class, not to mention when she was specifically speaking to me.

At the start of the school year, Gruesome Newsome told us that during the first few weeks of class, each student would have an individual reading session with her. She said the reason for it was to find out how well we were reading. She did not mention what the consequences might be if a student was found to be reading at a lower grade level. Indeed, she presented it as though it was not a serious matter.

During the coming weeks of the term, Gruesome would take a couple students aside in the morning and afternoon, and she would have them do some extended reading for her out of a book that was not from our regular reading materials. She would take the student to be evaluated to a corner in the back of the room, away from the rest of the class. She and the student would sit together, and using her finger she would point out the lines from the book she wanted read, and she wanted the student to read at random from any page she chose. The reading session would last about thirty to forty-five minutes.

A number of students went through that exercise with Gruesome before my name came up, and I dreaded every waiting moment. When the day came and I approached the back of the room where she was waiting, the bottom of my stomach fell out. I would have to sit close to her. Nevertheless, we sat down together, and I tried to read for her.

I could not do it. I could not read with any consistency with that woman so near to me. She was so close; I could feel the heat from her body. How was I supposed to concentrate on what she wanted me to read? The only thing that I could keep my mind on was how close she was to me, and secondly, how much I didn't like it. The heat from her body made me feel as though I was being cooked in a frying pan.

I read poorly for Grusesome. In fact, I hardly read at all. I just mumbled unintelligible sounds as I tried to fend off the heat coming from her body. She pressured me to read for about twenty minutes, with no success, and then she gave up. Now, Gruesome had to know that I could read some, or else I would never have gotten to the third grade with the rest of my peers, but in spite of that fact, she never asked me to read for her again. Apparently, she had reached certain conclusions about my reading skills and that settled the matter for her.

As I was to learn later, Gruesome not only found me to be reading below grade level, which was technically correct, but she also judged me to be slightly retarded. The school authorities informed my mother of their conclusion, and she was told that it was best if I was removed from the normal fourth grade class. My mother did not tell me about any of this. She went to Mr. Bosworth, the Director of Guild programs, for help. She could not accept the idea that I was mentally retarded. She wanted him to help her convince school authorities that they were wrong about me, but as it turned out his help wasn't needed. I took matters into my own hands.

A couple of weeks had passed since my reading evaluation with Ol' Gruesome, and I had all but forgotten about it. I arrived in school one morning at about eight-thirty, hung up my jacket in the cloak room, and then walked to my desk. As I was about to sit down, Gruesome called me.

"John Cooper," she said loudly. "Come up here."

At that moment, the classroom was about half-filled with students who were talking among themselves. It was the normal activity that always went on at the start of a school day. But when my name was sounded, the conversations stopped and every little pair of eyes in the room turned on me.

I was wondering what I had done. I said nothing, and I went up to Gruesome's desk. I wasn't really apprehensive, just confused. After all, I had just walked into the classroom, and I had not committed any type of improper behavior. Moreover, it was unusual for her to talk to a student at her desk before she called the roll.

As I came up to her, she looked at me over the top of her glasses. "John," she said. "I want you to collect all your things from your desk, pencils, notebooks, everything, and then go to Room 108."

Suddenly, I was apprehensive. Room 108 was on the first floor close to the principal's office. It was the room where all the student flotsam and jetsam were sent when some administrative action was being taken against them. Chronically late and chronically absent students were sent there. Disruptive students were sent there, and sickly and retarded students were sent there. The room was the schools holding tank, and any student who went there gained a notorious reputation. Notorious students had a way of falling behind the pupils in the regular grades, and many of them disappeared from Paxson Elementary School altogether.

I straightened my back and tried to give Gruesome a serious look. "Did you say room 108? Why do I have to go to room 108? I haven't done anything wrong."

Gruesome looked passed me to the classroom filling up with students, and she wrinkled her nose a bit. "Now be quiet, John. Just do as I told you. Get your things, and I'll have one of the other students walk you downstairs."

I searched Gruesome's face trying to get some clue as to the reason for this call for my banishment, but her powdered, lipstick splashed face revealed nothing.

"Why? Why do I have to go? I haven't done anything. For real, I haven't."

"John." She leaned back in her chair and put on her sternest face. "Get your things and do as I told you."

"Why do I have to go?" I tried to make my voice sound woeful and pleading. "Why?"

She did not answer me, and I could see that her eyes were focusing on the students behind me again. If there was ever an example of improper behavior, I was presently exhibiting it, and I was doing it right in front of the entire class. Gruesome surely did not like that.

Suddenly I knew that I needed support. My pleading words had bounced off of Gruesome's hard face like stones bouncing off of concrete. If I could get no response from her, then maybe my classmates would help me. With that thought in mind, I turned around to look at them. The room was now full. All my classmates were in attendance that day, and I suddenly felt bolstered by their presence.

In a hurried glance, my eyes swept across the faces of my peers, students that I had gone to school with for years. I knew the individuals behind many of those faces very well. Some of the others I hardly knew at all, but that didn't matter, because I needed their help that morning. I stared at them, and they stared back at me. I could see in their faces that they wanted to know what was going on with me and Gruesome.

"John, get your things like I told you. Get them this minute!"

Her voice came over my shoulder like a strong gust of wind, and I had to stiffen to keep myself upright. I continued to stare at my classmates with sorrowful, begging eyes.

"Do as I told you, John. Do…"

I turned around to face her. "Why are you sending me down there? Why? Why? I want to know why?"

"Now control yourself, young man. Control yourself." She stood up behind her desk.

"I wanna know. I wanna know," I shouted as tears filled my eyes, and I could not help but feel that this banishment had something to do with the fact that I was poor and that I lived in a vermin infested house.

"You're making a scene, John. You're making a scene. Now stop it. We're doing this for your own good." When she said that, she seem to grow taller and I seem to grow smaller. Could Juanita see me at all?

"What is for my own good? What is? What is?" I pressed her verbally and backed it up by moving closer to her desk.

"Well," she said in a lower, calmer voice, as she sat down again. "I was going to come downstairs later and talk to you about it. You're being put in a special class because you need more help with your reading than I can give you."

"You mean you're taking me out of this class because of my reading?"

"Now keep your voice down, John. What I'm telling you is for your information and not the entire class. Also, your mother has been told about this change in class for you."

Now it was beginning to make some sense. "Are you saying that I can't read?"

"I said you need help with your reading."

"But you think I can't read good enough. Ain't that right? That's why you're putting me outta this class." I didn't wait for her to reply. I spun around and faced the class again. I hurriedly looked at as many of them as I could, and I said in the most hurtful voice I could conjure up. "She says I can't read good enough, but I can. I can." I was appealing directly to them for help.

Then I heard Gruesome's chair scratch the floor in a screechy sound as she suddenly stood up again. "John!" Her voice was loud and stamped with anger. "John Cooper! Enough of this, now. The decision has been made. Now get your things like I told you."

I swung around again to face her, and without even thinking what I was saying, words just begin to pop out of my mouth. "No! No! I won't go. I won't go because I can read good enough."

"John, John." Gruesome tried to talk to me, but I cut her off.

"I can read good enough." I turned to face my classmates again. They were sitting at their desks, staring at me and Grusesome, looking bemused, confused, and interested. I saw a spark of encouragement coming from their faces. "I can read good enough and I will show you."

"John, stop this," Gruesome said. "Stop this right now."

I ignored her because something had snapped in me, and I was not consciously in control of my behavior. Moreover, she had me backed in a corner, and my brothers told me whenever you're in a position like that you have to come out fighting. I could not let her separate me from my friends. I needed them, and they needed me. I started school with these kids, and I wanted to stay with them.

Spinning on my heels, I swiftly circled around Gruesome. Behind her desk was an open bookcase. That was where she kept her books. It was from her collection of books that she read the class fictional stories and historical essays.

"John." Gruesome reached for me, but she missed, as I swept by her. "Stop this immediately and do as you've been told."

But I wasn't paying any attention to her, and when I reached her bookcase, I grabbed a book from it just as she tried to take hold of my arm. But I quickly backed away from her. "I can read!" I shouted as I put the desk between her and me again. "I can read good enough. I can."

"Give me that book, young man," she said through clenched teeth. "Give it to me this instant."

"No!" I said, and I stepped back further from her. "I can read good enough to stay in this class. I can. I can. Please let me read, and I'll show you."

Gruesome clenched her teeth tighter and shook her head.

I turned away from her and looked desperately into the faces of my classmates. I felt a strong need to connect with them, and I was hoping that they felt the same way. For a split second, I was in limbo, but I quickly shook off the feeling. I could not afford to entertain it. What surprised me most about that moment was the fact that Gruesome did not pounce on me from behind and take the book away from me. She could have easily done so, but I think at that point she, too, was getting caught up in the drama of the situation.

I stared hard at my classmates, the white ones and the black ones, and to my relief there were sympathetic looks on their faces. There was compassion and understanding in their eyes. I could see it, and why shouldn't there be? Like me, most of them thought that Mrs. Newsome was a gruesome sergeant-type.

And then it began. "Lettim read," a voice spoke softly from the back of the room. I looked in that direction, but I couldn't make out who had spoken.

"Yeah, let him read." Another voice came from the second row of seats, and I knew who had said it. It was Mushface Morgan, a black kid who had a face that looked like a squashed tomato. It was unusual for him to speak out in class.

"Let Johnny read," came a girl's voice from the middle of the class on the left side of the room. I thought it was the black girl, Jellybean Susie, who had said it. Just hearing her voice made me feel better about the situation. Jellybean was always laughing and full of humor. She could find something funny in any kind of event or happening, and when she laughed, everyone around her tended to laugh with her. "Go on, Jellybean," I thought. "Get Ol' Gruesome to laugh about sending me to Room 108." Maybe she would then change her mind.

Otis McAlily raised his hand like he was going to ask a question, but instead he said, "Mrs. Newsome, I think you should let Johnny read." I was not surprised to hear him speak. Otis was one of my walking buddies, and I liked him a lot. Teachers liked him, too, because he was always so well mannered and formal. That morning was probably the first time he had ever done anything in class that Gruesome might call "improper behavior."

Right behind Otis, Shelton Pelzer and Henry Washington spoke.

"Let him read."

"Yeah, go on and let him read."

Shelton and Henry were also my walking buddies. If Otis was willing to throw caution to the wind, then they were willing to go along with the program. Moreover, Shelton never liked being overshadowed by Otis, in particular when it came to the friendship between the three of us. Henry, on the other hand, had a compliant personality. He was the tallest of my closest friends, but he was also the darkest. He was quite ashamed of his complexion. Because of it, he lived with the fear of rejection, and consequently, he tended to go along with whatever Otis, Shelton, and I decided to do. But that morning, I was happy he had that follow-the-leader attitude.

As I tightly clutched the book in my hand that I had taken from Gruesome's bookcase, voices of support were popping up all over the classroom. "Let Johnny read!"

Looking over my shoulder, I could see that Gruesome was puzzled by what was going on, and it would seem that she did not know how to handle it. What she needed was a clue. At just that moment, a girl in the first row raised her hand to get Gruesome's attention, and she was a very special girl. The thing that made her special was not the way she looked. She was a high yellow, but she was not as pretty as Juanita. She was bright and funny, but not like Jellybean Susie. She was special because of her name.

The name of the girl who raised her hand was Yula Mae Christmas. That was not a nickname. She was baptized Yula Mae Christmas. To say her name always made me think of Christmas and the good times that went with it, the singing, the presents, the good food that Mom cooked, and the spirit of joy that made the holiday special. By virtue of her name, she was a young lady of good tidings.

Gruesome acknowledged the girl's hand with a nod and Yula Mae spoke. "Mrs. Newsome, let Johnny read and everything will be all right."

"Speak for me, Sister Christmas," I said under my breath, not knowing just how fortuitous it was for her to speak out at that moment.

I turned and looked at Gruesome. She had her head cocked to one side, and she was staring at Yula Mae. She opened her mouth to speak but another voice from the chorus stopped her.

"Let Johnny read." It was Mary Cunningham, who had spoken as she stood up next to her seat. Mary was a ruddy-faced little white girl, and even though we started school together in kindergarten, I didn't know her very well. She had high buttocks and long skinny legs, and when you put the two together it made her look like a chicken. But chicken or not, I was happy for her support that morning.

Gruesome put a weary eye on Mary Cunningham, and then she glanced back at Yula Mae. "All right," she said, as she looked at me. "Let

Johnny read." She plopped down in her desk chair, removed her glasses, and stared intently at me.

Mary Cunningham sat down, and she and the other students fixed their gaze on me. They were waiting for me to read, but Gruesome was waiting for me to fall flat on my non-reading face.

When I went to Gruesome's bookcase, I had grabbed the first book my hand fell upon. I had no idea what book it was, but now as I looked down at it in my hand I realized that it was a familiar item. It was a small book with a brightly-colored cover. The colors were red, green, and white. In the middle of all this color, there was an image of a fat round man, clothed in a red velvet suit, stepping from a sleigh that was being drawn by a bunch of reindeer. That was the book that told the holiday story "Twas The Night Before Christmas."

When I recognized the book, a tingling warmness circled through me, and my apprehension disappeared. I knew that story, or more accurately I knew that poem. I had heard Clement Moore's poem of a visit from Old St. Nick many times. My previous teachers had read it during the holiday season, and renditions of it had been offered at the Guild on a number of occasions at Christmas parties. But, the main reason why I knew the poem so well was because of my sister Dotty. She loved the poem, and every year on Christmas Eve, she would drive the family crazy with her stand up, dramatic, repetitious presentations of the poem. She got a tremendous kick out of reciting the poem as though it were a mystery story, rather than a holiday fable about lovable Santa Claus. I went to bed on many a Christmas Eve night with the sound of Dotty's voice in my head reciting Clement Moore's poem.

"We are waiting for you to read, John Cooper. Now, read."

I swallowed hard and opened the book. I stood up straight and faced the class. Gruesome was directly behind me. I held the book up to my face, and I began to speak:

Twas the night before Christmas

And all through the house

Not a creature was stirring

Not even a mouse.

The words flowed easily from my mouth, and I tried to imitate the dramatic way Dotty performed the poem. In particular, I tried to pronounce the words exactly the way she said them, and I tried to put the feeling of excitement and mystery in the story of Old St. Nick as she did.

I was looking at the book and turning the pages, but I was not reading the words in the book. I was reciting from memory. Nevertheless, I was doing a good job, and I determined this by occasionally taking a quick peep over the top of the book at my classmates. They were sitting quietly and listening attentively to me. They were probably thinking about Christmas that was coming in the next few months and the gifts they were going to receive at that time. But, whatever was on their minds, I could tell that I had their full attention, something that Gruesome also had to be aware of.

As I articulated the poem, I found myself being caught up in the recitation. I was enjoying the sudden rapport with my classmates. It was a new experience for me, and as the poem drew to its conclusion, I felt a little sad that it was coming to an end.

And a Merry Christmas to all

And to all a good night.

As I finished the poem, I closed the book as though I had read through to the last page, and there was a dead silence in the room. And then Mary Cunningham started clapping, and the rest of the class soon followed. They were giving me a loud round of applause, and I felt compelled to smile.

I turned half about to look at Gruesome. She had not clapped, and she looked dead-eyed at me. I don't know what was actually going through her mind, but she must have been thinking about how I had pulled off a fast one on her. Was I reading or reciting from memory?

Then, from the back of the classroom, I heard a student ask, "Is it Christmas time? I didn't know that Christmas was here."

Gruesome did not answer the person, but she stood up at her desk. The students had rendered a verdict, and now the anarchy was behind them. She took a long look at the class before she looked at me. "John Cooper, go and sit down at your desk. It is time for me to take the roll."

I had won. I knew I would stay in my class now, with my friends.

I walked to Gruesome's desk and handed her the book. She took it with a hint of a begrudging smile on her face, and she had to be thinking, "You little bastard. You pulled that one off."

I went back to my seat, and my reading was never an issue in Gruesome's class again. The reason for it was not only because of my coup that morning, but also because soon thereafter I made a strong effort to better my reading skills as quickly as I could. I began reading much more in school, out of school, at the Guild, and at the Public Library. And when I was home, I would get my older brothers to help me read. I even began reading the daily newspapers whenever I could get them. To be sure, I read voraciously for a time, and I soon became an excellent reader.

If I had gone to Room 108, I would not have been there very long. I would have been sent on to the O-B class. I don't know what "O-B" actually stood for, but I assumed it meant something like off-balance on the dumb side, or class for obsolete brains, or overly-black. I stress the last description because without a doubt the overwhelming majority of students who ended up in the O-B class were black. Moreover, if a black student went to the O-B class and his learning skills did not pick up, he was sure to be shipped out to either the Madison School or Boone School. Both schools were known as the dumb-dumb schools, institutions where "uneducable" kids were sent, students that the public educational system had given up on. They were schools for throwaway students.

My confrontation with Mrs. Newsome could have had a much more negative impact on my life than she let on or that I knew, and unbelievably, I did not learn my lesson from the experience. I was to put myself in educational jeopardy again.

George Washington and Abraham Lincoln are two of America's most celebrated Presidents. Washington is said to be the father of our country, and Lincoln is described as the Great Emancipator. Both Presidents were born in February. I learned about these American icons early on in elementary school, and every year, on their birthdays, my school would have special programs to acknowledge their importance in this nation's history.

I did not mind so much hearing about George Washington on his birthday because I liked the history of the colonial period. But I did mind hearing stories about Lincoln because invariably they were linked to the Civil War and all that business about him freeing the enslaved people. During my grade school days, we were taught that the Civil War was fought to free the Africans in bondage, and that was the sole reason for the war. Of course, that was not the case. There were many other issues involved.

I suppose I was not really upset with Lincoln, but I did not like hearing about black people being enslaved. It made me feel uncomfortable. If hearing about the Great Emancipator was not bad enough, my classmates and I were required to sing songs about enslavement and the happy life whites and blacks had in the old pre-Civil War South. Stephen Foster, who wasn't even a Southerner, composed most of these songs. Nevertheless, he wrote songs like "My Old Kentucky Home," "The Old Folks At Home," and "Massa's in The Cold, Cold Ground." These songs romanticized the Antebellum South. If you believed Stephen Foster, the South was not a bad place for the enslaved people, but even as a young boy, I wasn't buying that malarkey.

The worst of Stephen Foster's songs had to be "Old Black Joe." It was a song about an old enslaved man who was nearing the end of his life, and his greatest regret is the fact that he can no longer serve his master. He was happy being an enslaved person, if you can believe that nonsense. Maybe Foster believed all that make-believe about the old South, but imagine teaching black children to sing its praises in school. It happened, at Paxson

Elementary School back in the 1940s. The singing of "Old Black Joe" was a classroom staple. We sang that goddam song every single time we had our music hour.

The teacher I associate with the singing of "Old Black Joe" was Mrs. Riley. She was a shapely woman, on the young side, with the longest, sexiest legs in the whole school. She did not seem to be a very bright woman because whenever she was asked why we were reading a certain book, or studying a certain period of history, she would only reply, "That is what the schedule calls for." She ran our class by schedules and lesson plans. I presume she ran her private life the same way.

With as much passion as a young boy could have, I hated "Old Black Joe," and I had the impression that the other black kids in the class felt the same way about it, and I wandered why Mrs. Riley always made us sing that song. To say that it embarrassed me to sing it before my white classmates and white teacher, severely understates the case. Whenever the class was about to sing it, I wanted to run away and hide. Just think of it. There was a pathetic, old enslaved man whose greatest feeling for life was that of hanging his head low in acknowledgement of his coming demise and out of respect for his Massa. He was the picture of a worn out, decrepit old fellow who had given up on life because the enslaved life he had known had given up on him. The idea of that enslaved person deprecating himself because he had grown old was excruciatingly humiliating.

Every time the class sang "Old Black Joe," I would always sense the eyes of my white classmates staring at me, and my stomach would always start churning. The white kids knew that I was putting myself down every time I sang that song. How could Mrs. Riley be so insensitive? How could she not realize the negative impact of such a song on her black students? Or was it that she didn't care? In any case, whenever I sang that song, it had the tendency to ruin my entire school day.

I was an impulsive young boy, and when I became upset, it was difficult for me not to show it. There came a day when I was fed up with "Old Black

Joe." We were going to have a singing hour that day, and I knew Mrs. Riley was going to tell the class to sing that infamous song. But, I had made up my mind that I would never sing that song again, never.

When we had singing hour, every student was expected to sing unless he or she had a cold or some other kind of ailment. Mrs. Riley said singing was good for our lungs and that was why she wanted us to do it, but I believed she wanted everyone to sing because the schedule called for it.

Nevertheless, on that morning when she told the class to turn to page 125 in The New Blue Book of Favorite Songs, I closed my book and sat it on the desk in front of me. The other students had followed her instructions. They had their books opened to page 125, but Mrs. Riley noticed that my book was closed.

"John," she said as she came down the aisle between the rows of desks. "Open your song book to page 125."

I did not move, and I stared straight in front of me.

"Did you hear me John?" She was now standing right over me. "I said open your songbook to page 125."

In a low voice, I said, "No."

"What is that?" She was taken back.

"I said no."

"No?" She raised her voice, and every student in class was clued into the situation. Johnny will not open his songbook.

Some of my classmates giggled. Others gasped at my refusal. Still others looked sheepishly away from the scene at my desk. They did whatever they thought would indicate to Mrs. Riley that they were not in agreement with me.

"Yeah." I looked up into her face. "I'm not gonna sing it. I'm never gonna sing that song again, never."

Mrs. Riley stood there for a moment wrinkling her brow as if she were trying to understand what was going on in my mind. "Now, why have you decided to never sing that song again?"

I turned to the side in my seat so that I could face her more directly, and I gave her a hard, studied look. It was quite easy for me to buck Mrs. Riley's authority because I never felt intimidated by her. She had those sexy legs, and that always made me think of her as just a pretty woman rather than my teacher.

"That song is 'Old Black Joe', and I ain't never gonna sing it again."

Mrs. Riley crossed her arms and sighed. "John, why don't you want to sing that song? You have sung it before."

"Yeah, but I'm not gonna sing it now."

"Why?"

"Cause I ain't."

She uncoupled her arms, and then she coupled them again. "We're suppose to sing this song," she said, shaking her head in dismay. "We're supposed to."

"Not me. Not anymore." I shook my head.

She tightened her arms around her body. She was now becoming annoyed. "Stop this nonsense right now," she said. "Stop it and open your song book."

"No," I said with such force it surprised even me.

At this point, my refusal to sing that song was no longer the issue between Mrs. Riley and me. The situation had developed into a contest of wills. Could she make me open my book and sing "Old Black Joe," or would I make her back down? I kept my eyes focused on her face, and I did not look around the room to see how my classmates were responding. I suspected that they were still emotionally distancing themselves from me.

Mrs. Riley was decidedly angry, and she ordered me to open my song book, but again I refused. She then told me to stand up, which was a routine tactic that a teacher used when she found herself in a confrontation situation with a student during class time. When the student stood up, it made him stand out, and he was separated from his peers who were sitting down. It was a way of isolating the misbehaving pupil and make him feel alone, and one on one with the teacher.

Once she got me on my feet, Mrs. Riley demanded to know specifically why I did not want to sing "Old Black Joe," and she pressed me hard for an answer. My thoughts became jumbled under her pressure. I knew I wasn't going to sing that song, but I did not know if I could tell her the reason. How could I explain the negative feeling the song gave me. I began to hem and haw and lose confidence in the stand I had taken. I then looked away from her and glanced around the room. My classmates were all staring at me, and she was staring at me. It made me feel like the guy in the middle with no place to go.

I started getting nervous because I knew I had ruined her schedule for the morning, and she did not like being off schedule. The singing hour was just that, an hour, and she was using up the time questioning me. I was also worried because I realized that if I did not give her a satisfactory answer, she would likely send me to the principal's office for disrupting the class schedule. If I went to the principal's office, there was always the chance that I might end up in Room 108.

"All right, John." She lowered her arms. "You won't open your song-book, and you won't tell me why you're not going to sing 'Old Black Joe.' Therefore you leave me no choice, but…"

"I…I…" My words cut her off. "I don't want to sing…sing that song because it makes me feel bad. Mrs. Riley, I don't walk around with my head bent over like I've done something wrong, and I don't feel like that person in the song. I feel ashamed and like nobody when I sing it."

As I was speaking, I saw the right corner of Mrs. Riley's mouth twitch nervously, and finally I heard my walking buddies say, "We don't like that song either." Better late than never. When I finished speaking, Mrs. Riley suddenly looked as though someone had just punched her right between the eyes, and within an instant, her angry mood had changed. She then asked me to sit down, and she returned to the front of the room. As she sat down at her desk, she told the class to turn to another song in the book.

I sat down as she told me to do, but I felt uneasy. Why didn't she send me to the principal, Mr. Ross? Disruptive students were usually sent down to his office with dispatch. I thought maybe she was going to send me later. Me and my big mouth. I really did not want to go to Mr. Ross's office. As a principal, he was an extremely strict disciplinarian who did not care for students who talked back to their teachers or who did not follow instructions. Next to Mr. Ross, Grusesome Newsome was a piker. There was even the word around school that he had a strap in his office that he used to beat students with as a form of punishment. I had my doubts about the strap idea, but I didn't want to be the student in my class who found out if it was true.

In refusing to sing "Old Black Joe," I had inadvertently raised the question of racial insensitivity, if not racial prejudice. Certainly, at my young age, I was not specifically aware of having done so, but I had apparently put the thought in Mrs. Riley's mind. That was probably why she did not send me to the principal's office. She ended our class confrontation, but the entire affair was not over.

When the morning session of school came to a close at noon, Mrs. Riley asked me to remain after class for a few minutes. She told me ahead of time that she did not want to punish me, but rather she just wanted to talk. After the classroom had been cleared of the other students, she asked me to sit down at a chair next to her desk. She then proceeded to tell me that she never wanted me to feel bad in singing "Old Black Joe." She stressed the idea that Stephen Foster's songs were all nice American songs about a special period in our history, and that is why students were asked to sing them. She tried very hard to convince me that there was nothing malicious about her, or the school's music policy, and that I should not take the substance of the song personally.

But, after hearing her out, I was totally unconvinced. How could I not take the song personally? She had to know that. The enslavement period of the South was hardly a time that served to enhance the self-image of black people in America. It was a time that black people could not look back upon with pride. And, as my mother told me, black people in the South were still being beaten and lynched by white supremacists as we sang "Old Black Joe" in Paxson Elementary School. Was I to understand that she did not know anything about the KKK? Mrs. Riley could not have been that naive.

That incident with Mrs. Riley occurred way back in the middle forties. I was just a grade school kid. My actions had nothing to do with protest in the civil rights sense. I was just acting out of emotions, against something that individually irked me. Many years would pass before I would begin to grasp the concept of institutional racism, but at the same time, I knew it was wrong for my teacher to force me to sing a song that made me feel bad. Perhaps after I stood up to Mrs. Riley, she realized that, too.

Besides my walking buddies, some of my other black classmates told me afterwards they were glad that I had spoken up because they did not like singing "Old Black Joe" either. And to my surprise, Mrs. Riley stopped asking us to sing that song and some of Stephen Foster's other songs that tended to put a benevolent, loving, happy glow on enslavement and the Antebellum South. Also, a few weeks after Mrs. Riley and I had our confrontation, the class found itself on a field trip. Mrs. Riley took the class to Freedom House.

Freedom House was located downtown near City Hall, and it was an establishment that had come into being to aid in the war effort. Freedom House consisted of three floors of an old colonial house that had been refurbished as a small historical museum, which paid tribute to America's multiracial and multiethnic population. The theme of the museum was that of "Americans Pulling Together" in the times of crisis for the good of the nation.

Freedom House was mostly photographs and artwork about Americans working together, praying together, and fighting together to keep the nation strong and free from totalitarianism and fascism. Along with the photographs and pictures, there were appropriate, inspirational commentaries that appealed to the patriotic nature of visitors. The highlight of the visit to Freedom House was a short film that starred Frank Sinatra.

The film began with a fight between a group of white boys who were beating up another white kid who they did not like because he was Italian. The fight occurred in the alleyway behind a recording studio where Sinatra was cutting a record. He was taking a break from the recording session when he came outside and found the kids brawling. He broke up the fight and then delivered a sermon to them about the non-importance of a person's ethnic background. "No matter what country our forefathers came from, we are all Americans now." He made a special case for cooperation that was needed among American fighting men during times of war. Sinatra ended his sermon by singing "The House I live In," which I think was the title of the movie. The movie ended with the bad boys seeing the error of their ways, and making friends with the Italian kid.

The Sinatra movie really wrinkled my brow because I saw right through the charade of it. The concern in the movie was not with the boy who had gotten beat up, but rather with the notion that Americans should cooperate for the good of the nation. The movie was saying that the welfare of the nation was more important than the welfare of the individual, minority individuals in particular. But even worse than that, there was another message that came at me from the movie. To speak of the welfare of the nation was to also speak of the welfare of whites and their dominance and control of all the good things in society.

Being a black boy in America, initially, I identified with the Italian boy who got beat up, but I could not agree with Frank Sinatra that ethnicity did not matter. If it did not matter, why did my teacher make us sing "Old Black Joe?" Mrs. Riley, perhaps out of her own naiveté, Paxson School and the Philadelphia Board of Education, as a matter of policy, and probably white people in general, wanted me to bend my head low as an American. Know your place boy. Know your place.

In one fashion or another, teachers were always trying to put me in my place, but from the time I was very young, I was doing a lot adventuresome things with my brothers. They taught me how to be a free spirit. In school, I found myself in a controlled environment, and I was frequently unable to reconcile these two different patterns of behavior. That was one of the reasons why I would occasionally get into trouble with my school mentors.

CHAPTER FIVE

Officially, the great Depression may have ended around 1940 or '41, but for my family, and for most of my friends' families, the Depression continued until the early 1950s. Of course, the hardest times for us were the early years on Noble Street when my brothers, sisters, and I were very young, and the support of the family was squarely and solely on my mother's shoulders. But, as we boys grew older, we tried to help Mom meet the family's needs by obtaining money and food in a number of different ways.

To begin with, as each one of us older boys reached the age of responsibility, which was five years old, we became the recipient of a shoeshine box. It was our time to enter the world of work. Allen, Abie, Norman, Frank, and I all became bootblack entrepreneurs a week or so after our fifth birthday. "Shoeshine, mister? I'll do a good job, and it's only ten cents." We became business children, scuffling to make a profit, and it wasn't all that easy.

Shoeshining was primarily a warm weather, weekend business. In fact, the best times for shoeshining were Friday evening and Saturday morning and afternoon. It was during those times that the men of the Noble Street community, and probably working class men all over Philadelphia, liked to dress up and go to the neighborhood bars to have some drinks with their friends. They were often natty and meticulous dressers, and they loved dearly to have their shoes spit-polished and sparkling. I found this a strange attitude. What was the importance of having shined shoes inside of a dark bar? The shoes would probably not even be noticed, but then that was not my concern. As a bootblack, it was my job to shine the shoes and not think about where they went after I finished with them.

I would never forget the first shoeshine box I ever had. My brothers made it for me, and it was a big mother. It had dark lacquered wood, and a footrest that was twice the size needed. It looked like a tank, and, unfortunately, it felt like one when I carried it. But I was one happy, proud little boy when that shoeshine box was given to me. Now I had the chance to make some real money and help my mother. Having a shoeshine box meant that my mother now considered me to be one of the big boys, but it also meant that I would have to become a business rival of adults.

Individually, my brothers and I never made much money shining shoes. There was a lot of competition out there on the streets. It seemed as though every poor mother's son over five years old was out hustling with a shoeshine box on the weekend. However, my brothers and I worked as a collective, and we pooled our money together at the end of a workday.

Friday evenings were always a short work day, just a few hours, and we didn't make much money because we could not start shoeshining until early evening when the men had returned from work and were making their way to the bars. Also, my mother did not like her sons staying out late at night. But on Saturday, if we stayed out on the street all day, that is from about nine in the morning to five o'clock in the afternoon, we could make about three dollars on an average day. That doesn't sound like much, but since there was four or five of us working, three dollars apiece could amount to twelve or fifteen dollars total. That was quite a bit of money.

We always split our earnings right down the middle with Mom. It was her idea. Even if we wanted to give her more, she would not take it.

She would always say, "You earned it. So, you have a right to get some enjoyment out of it." For Mom, an extra seven or eight dollars a week was a windfall. She used to boast that she could feed the entire family for a week on five dollars.

Of course, the shoeshining money meant a lot to each one of us boys, too. With a dollar and a half of our own, we could go to the movies three or four times in one week, and we could have potato chips and pretzels or Goobers candies to eat at the movies. A ticket to the movies was only ten to fifteen cents, and pretzels and candies were only a nickel a bag or a box.

Having that shoeshine income also gave us carfare money to go on our trips around the city and to the parks. It gave us money to buy small play items from the five and ten cent store on Second Street. We always needed marbles and balls to play with during the warm weather months of the year. As working brothers, we would also give the younger kids, like Ducky, Marion, and Dotty, money that they could spend on frivolous things.

However, shoeshining had its limitations. Business was good only during the warm months when there was a lot of foot traffic on the pavements. It was not a good business in the Wintertime, and there was little or no business when the weather was damp or rainy. And there were other problems with shoeshining, like carrying that heavy shoeshine box, staying out on the street all day, and having strange kids make fun of me because I was a bootblack.

Nevertheless, I liked the idea of shoeshining, but I detested the fact that most of the money had to come from shining white people's shoes. White patrons could be so condescending, saying, "Now do a good job, boy," and they would look down on me like I was dirt. They made me feel so small, so insignificant, and like a beggar. Invariably, they would behave in a fashion that would give me the impression that they were doing me a favor by letting me shine their shoes. To whites, this was not a business transaction between them and me;

that is, pay for services rendered, but white customers tended to act like they were giving me a handout.

Actually, condescension was not the worst indignity I had to put up with. Frequently, the white customers would make a deal with me before they would allow me to shine their shoes.

"Shine Mister? I'll do a good job."

"Shine, huh?"

"Yeah, I'll do a good job, a real good job."

"Well, I'll tell ya what. I'll let you shine my shoes if you will let me rub the top of your head."

"Rub my head?"

"Yeah. Just a little bit."

"If I let you rub my head, then you will let me shine your shoes?"

"Yeah and I'll give you something extra, too. I heard it was real good luck to rub a black boy's head. I need a lot of luck right now. Things ain't going too good in my life at the moment."

With a grimace, I would usually agree, and then I would get down on my knees. "Put your foot up."

"Yeah, sure, but let me rub your head first. I want that luck to start right now."

"Can't you wait 'til after I shine your shoes?"

"No. I want that luck to start right away."

"Okay."

"Come over here then and let me touch those nappy beebees. Ha-hah. Yeah, I can feel that luck jumping through my fingers like sparks. Goddamn you people are something."

"Can I shine your shoes now?"

"Oh yeah, sure you can, but you coons are something else. If I could put that luck of yours in a bottle, I'd make a million bucks."

It was the servicemen who wanted to rub my head the most. It was the time of the Second World War, and there were always plenty of soldiers, sailors, and marines walking the streets of Philadelphia, especially in Center City along Market and Broad Streets. Many of these service-men would be on leave before going overseas to fight the Axis enemies, and they would reach out to anything or anybody if they thought it would give them a better chance of surviving the deadly battles that lay ahead. Even though I did not like that head rubbing, in my own way, I was still doing my part for the war effort. I thought that by letting the servicemen rub my head, I probably made a number of them feel spiritually stronger and better prepared to go into battle.

The absolute worst part of the shoeshine business was the squabbling and the fighting it often set off between competing bootblacks. On the face of it, the business was simple enough. The shoeshiner asked some person if he wanted a shine, on a one to one, individual basis. The person being asked could say yes or no. Now all of that is quite true, but there were locations, the corners of certain intersections, where a bootblack could station himself, that were much better than others for intercepting foot traffic. One's location could be the difference in making one dollar or three on a day's outing, and it was getting these good locations that gave rise to the squabbling and fighting between the bootblacks.

Usually, the person who arrived at a good location first, on any given day, was allowed to stay there until he left the corner, but there were always mean individuals and strongarmers who would try to throw their weight around and take a good location from someone who got there first. Fistfights and the breaking of a competitor's shoeshine box were not all that uncommon. My brothers and I did not fight each other for locations because we worked together. We would go to an intersection and spread ourselves out on all four corners. The intersection we went to most often was at Fourth and Market Streets. If there were four of us on a given outing, the four corners would take care of our location set-ups. Also, being on joining corners allowed us to watch over each other during the day just in case some trouble came up.

More often than not, on a Saturday, there would be five Cooper Brothers out on the street shoeshining. In that case, four of us would station ourselves at Fourth and Market Streets, and Abie would usually take a location a block away, say at Fifth and Market Streets. Abie liked to work alone, while the rest of us liked to work close to each other. Being on the four corners of an intersection meant that we could intercept the foot traffic from all directions.

Of the four shoeshine locations at Fourth and Market Streets, one location was better than all the rest. Invariably, the person who was stationed on the northwest corner tended to get much more business than individuals on the other three.

The Fourth and Market Streets intersection was our favorite location, but it was also the favorite location of another bootblack known to us as "Snotnose." Snotnose was a black man who looked like he was in his thirties, but we never knew just how old he really was. It was Snotnose who had first clued my brothers in on the fact that the intersection was a good one for getting shoeshine customers. One Saturday morning, when my brothers had just started out for a day of shoeshining, they had come upon Snotnose, who was stationed on the northwest corner of Fourth and Market Streets, doing a landmark business. He had so many customers; the people were waiting in line to get their shoes shined.

Snotnose was a man who could really shine up some shoes. He knew how to give a sparkling spit-shine, something I didn't learn how to do until I joined the Army many years later. But it was not the fact that Snotnose could give a customer a beautiful shoeshine that made him so popular. He drew customers to him because he was a clown and an entertainer who catered to the stereotypical beliefs that many white people had about black people.

Snotnose was a musician, and a good one. He was a guitar player. The way he got customers was to play some gutbucket, down-home blues piece, sitting next to his shoeshine box, while he rolled his eyes around in his head like Mantan Moreland of the old Charlie Chan movies. He would even get up and do a slow, shuffling dance that would suggest that he was dim-witted. And, he loved to show his teeth like Louie Armstrong and say "cha-cha-cha!" He also kept a shaven, baldhead, even though he always wore a hat. But while he performed, he would be constantly taking his hat off to let his customers know that he had just the right kind of head for luck rubbing.

Snotnose had a system all worked out. First he would play his guitar, and then he would dance and sing a medley of tunes. As he did so, a crowd would usually gather about him to watch him perform. When the crowd became fairly large, Snotnose would stop singing and dancing. He would apologize to the people, saying that he enjoyed entertaining them, but he couldn't use all his time singing and dancing because he had to shine shoes to make some money. He would never take any donations because he said that being a bootblack was his job. If people wanted to give him money, they had to get their shoes shined first. After he had shined all the shoes of the people who wanted it, he would then start his routine over again.

Snotnose would call every white man "Boss," and even his shine box was painted red, white, and blue. The reason was obvious with the war on. He was showing white people that he was patriotic, and he supported America in its efforts to defeat fascism around the world. I once asked Allen how much money he thought Snotnose made in a day. Allen said he was sure that Snotnose must have made as much as twenty dollars a day. It was hard to imagine, one person making as much as twenty dollars in one day from just shining shoes.

My brothers called the clowning bootblack Snotnose because he was periodically blowing his nose, especially when he had a crowd around him. Maybe he had some kind of sinus problem or blowing his nose was part of his act. Whatever the reason, he had a Snotnose.

For many weeks, Snotnose would be on the good corner every Saturday when we arrived at our favorite intersection to shine shoes.

Then he stopped showing up, and he stayed away for a month. During that time, one of my brothers would take the northwest corner, but eventually, Snotnose came back. He was there for a few Saturdays, but then he was gone again. It was a strange pattern.

One Saturday morning, we arrived at Fourth and Market Streets, and Snotnose was not there. We divided up the corners among ourselves. To my surprise, I was given the northwest corner. It pleased me very much that I would have the best corner for the day. As I settled down at the location, I smiled at the fact that it was a bright sunny day, and there were lots of people walking the streets. By eleven o'clock, I had already made a dollar and a quarter, and if business kept up I might have a four or five dollar day.

However, about eleven-thirty Snotnose showed up. That had never happened before. Usually, if he was not on the corner when we arrived, he did not show up at all that day. But there he was, sauntering down Fourth Street with his guitar flung over his back, his right hand carrying his shoeshine box, and in his left hand he carried a small stool. He did not get on his knees to shine shoes like we did. He sat on a stool.

I saw him coming a long way off. It wasn't difficult recognizing him with that red, white, and blue shine box, and I welcomed the sight of Snotnose. I did not mind the idea that he and I might share the same corner. I knew that he would draw a crowd and that could mean more business for me. Usually, there was only one bootblack to a corner, but business had been so good that morning I was quite willing to be magnanimous. Plus, I wanted to see Snotnose do his routine up close.

Snotnose came up to the corner and stopped a short distance from me. He stood there for a long moment before he walked over to where I was standing on the Market Street side of the corner. He looked at my shoeshine box and he wrinkled his nose. He did not say anything. Then he took the time to put his shoeshine box down, place his stool in front of it, and take his guitar off of his back. He leaned his guitar against the wall along side of his shine box, and then he stood up and faced me. He wrinkled his nose again, as he pushed his cap to the back of his baldhead.

I started to smile, and I was just about to say, "Good morning, Mr. Snotnose," but he spoke first. "All right, you little bugger, get the hell out of here. This is my corner whenever I'm on the street. Get your box and go."

Snotnose's words surprised me and I winced, but I knew the street rules. I had gotten to this corner first, and I had the right to stay here. I knew that Snotnose did not own that corner, and it was wrong for him to try to make me leave. And then there was the matter of the money in my pocket. As Snotnose glared at me, I felt the coins pressing against my leg. It could be a big money day if I stayed on that corner, a four dollar day. I would be able to give my mother two whole dollars, and I would still have two for myself. "Oh no, Snotnose," I thought, "I know the rules."

"I said get ta hell outta here, ya little bugger. This is my corner."

Looking up into the Snotnose's face, I swallowed hard. "I got here first."

"Ta hell with that. This is my corner."

Allen was on the northeast corner directly across the street from me, and he had seen Snotnose's arrival. He quickly noted that the Nose was hassling me.

"Frank, Norman." Allen shouted across the street. "Snotnose is bothering Johnny. Norman, go get Abie."

Being the youngest of our shoeshining group, my brothers were very quick to come to my aid whenever I was in trouble. The distress call went out, and Norman took off up the block to get Abie. At the same time, with shoeshine boxes in hand, Allen and Frank came running across the street to where I was confronting the Nose. When Allen and Frank reached the spot where I was standing, they plopped down their shoeshine boxes, and they took positions on both sides of me.

Snotnose was somewhat surprised when Allen and Frank stepped up next to me, and he fell back against the wall. "Now what ta hell is this?" he snarled.

"He's our brother." Allen's voice was strong and certain. "And you'd betta leave him alone." Allen had put on his toughest-looking face, and he tightened his lips to try and impress Snotnose.

"Hah, so he is yo brother. So what? I don't give a shit. Ya brother is on my corner, and he's got ta go."

"Nahhhh," Frank said trying to look as fierce as he could in the face of this grown man. "Johnny got here first, and he can stay."

Snotnose must have been five-nine or ten, and he probably weighed about a hundred and sixty pounds. But next to the three of us he looked like a giant. His baldhead has already been spoken of, but he also had a round dark face, which was held together, it seemed, by big heavy lips and pearly-white teeth. Even though his complexion was on the shady side, there was a reddish tint to his skin color. He was dressed in coveralls and he wore brogans. He looked very much like a country boy who had been suddenly plopped down right in the middle of the city.

Using his hands, Snotnose pushed himself away from the side of the building he had been leaning on, and he sneered. "I don't give a damn if he did get here first. I'm here now." At just that moment, Norman and Abie arrived. Snotnose gave them a ugly look. "And whose ta hell are they? No, don't tell me. I know. That's ya brothers, too."

"Yeah," Abie said. He looked as menacing as he could, stepping in line next to Allen. Norman fell in line along side of Frank. "Yeah," Abie said again. "We're brothers."

Snotnose was standing in front of me, and I was flanked by my brothers, two on each side of me. They were going to protect me from any advances from the left or right. The Nose would have to go through them to get to me.

Snotnose put his hands on his hips. Then, using his right hand, he pushed his cap further back on his head. "Look at dat. Five little buggers ready to fight me. Well, bless my soul." He grinned and chuckled.

I stared hard at Snotnose. He had a funny expression on his face. Was he thinking that we were just kids. Allen was the oldest, but he had not yet reached puberty. I was the youngest, not even half Allen's age. We were just kids, but we were Snotnose's adversaries.

Standing in the middle of my brothers, I thought of myself as a link in a chain, and with two of them on each side of me, I felt like I was the strongest link.

Allen shifted his feet around and spoke to Snotnose. "Johnny got here first, and you can't make him leave. Besides, this ain't your corner. This corner belongs to the city."

"Oh horseshit," Snotnose said as he stopped chuckling, and he took one step closer to me. "Take this little kid and get da hell outta here. I ain't got no time to be foolin' around. I gotta make some money."

I suddenly thought of myself being inundated with horseshit, and the idea of it made me shudder. But at the same time, I felt I could face up to the onslaught of Snotnose's horseshit. With my brothers next to me, I felt strong, and, how could I forget that this could be a four dollar day? "I ain't goin', Snotnose," I growled, I looked about at my four brothers. "I ain't goin'."

"What ya say?" Snotnose's eyes glared like fire. "What ya say?"

I stared back at him, and I wondered if the Nose was talking to me.

"What did ya say?"

"He said he ain't goin'," Norman spat the words at Snotnose, and he stared right in the man's eyes.

Snotnose stared back at Norman, and for the first time he looked uncertain about the outcome of the encounter. He took his eyes off of us momentarily, and he stared at the people passing by.

What a situation: five kids confronting a grown man on a busy street in downtown Philadelphia. It was a hostile situation, but people walked by without seemingly taking notice. Some of the passersby even stepped around us because we were in the middle of the pavement walkway, but no one seemed interested in our confrontation with the Nose.

Snotnose glared at us. "What ya say, and I don't mean that stuff 'bout that little bugger not going. What'd you call me?" He took another step forward towards me as he spoke.

"Now you stay away from him." Allen moved closer to me.

My other brothers also moved closer to me.

Allen made a fist with his right hand. He probably thought that the fight was about to begin.

Snotnose kept his distance, but asked his question again. "What he call me? Whatta he say?" He pointed a wavering finger at me.

"He called ya Snotnose," Frank said boldly. "Snotnose."

"Snotnose. Snotnose? Why'd he call me that? Why?" He seemed genuinely hurt and surprised by the name.

"You wanna know why he called ya that? Well, it's 'cause you're always blowing ya nose in front of people," Norman said.

"Yeah," Abie said,. "And 'cause you act like a fool in front of a lot of white people."

Suddenly, I had this feeling that Snotnose was on the defensive. He wasn't the aggressor anymore. He had been pushed back on his emotional heels, and the expression on Frank's face said that he smelled blood. Consequently, he went for the jugular.

"You're a Tom, Snotnose, an Uncle Tom, always grinning and showing your teeth to white people. And nobody like you gonna push my brother off this corner."

Now there were visible signs of pain on Snotnose's face. He took a couple of steps backwards until he pressed against the front of the building behind him again. He seemed to want to retreat further, but there was no more room for him to go. He then made a motion like he was going to pick up his guitar, but he stopped himself before he touched the instrument. He straightened up and stared at our faces.

"Why you say I'm a Tom?" His voice was soft now and totally without anger. "Why?"

"Ya know why." Frank moved closer to Snotnose. "Ya know. Ya act like a nigger, like the way white people talk about us."

"Yeah." Norman nodded. "You act like that."

"But wait a minute, you damn little buggers. Ya don't know nothin'. I have ta make some money. I have ta. That's why I come down here."

"Well, we gotta make some money too." Allen grit his teeth. "We ain't out here shining shoes for nothing."

"Yeah, yeah," Snotnose wiped the back of his hand across his nose. "Ya gotta make money too, but you kids listen. This ain't no game. I really have to make some money. Ya wanna know why? Cause I'm a preacher. Yeah, I'm a preacher. I work for the Lord. I got my own church over in Camden, cross the bridge."

"Oh get outta here," said Frank. I never heard of any preacher who talks like you, and if ya a preacher, why ya shinin' shoes?"

"Maybe I don't talk like a preacher should all the time, and I don't act like a preacher all the time cause it took a while for me to become a preacher. But I'm a preacher, and I got my own church. But there ain't no money in preachin'." He was stooping down now so as to look directly in the faces of all of us. "I come all daway from Camden to make some money so I can keep my church goin'. I do what I have ta for da Lord. For da Lord." He pushed himself up to a standing position, and he nodded. "I do what I have ta for da Lord."

Frank shook his head. Norman shook his head, too. Allen and Abie also shook their heads. I did not understand what Snotnose was trying to get at.

"You don't act like no preacher," Norman said.

"Ya sure don't," Abie said.

"I'm a preacher. A preacher," Snotnose said.

"Well," Frank said putting his hands on his hips. "If ya are a preacher, I wonder what the Lord would say if he knew you been Uncle Tomin' for Him. I wonder what He'd say ta that?"

"Yeah, I wonder," Norman said.

Snotnose looked down at us with a desperate, searching look on his face. He looked as though someone had just put a needle through his ballon, and he was trying to think of a quick way of keeping the air from flowing out.

"Ya don't understand. Ya don't understand. I do it for da Lord, for da Lord." He looked at our faces, searching our eyes, looking for a sign that would tell him that we understood his situation.

"Even if you do work for the Lord, my brother ain't leavin' this corner," Allen said smartly.

I don't think Snotnose even heard what Allen said. He was already collecting his things, picking up his guitar, his shoeshine box, and stool. All the while he kept saying, "For da Lord. I do it for da Lord."

Without looking at the Cooper boys again and with his guitar on his back, shoeshine box and stool in hand, Snotnose shuffled back up Fourth Street. We held our ground until he had turned the corner at Arch Street, a block away. When Snotnose disappeared from sight, then we cheered. The Uncle Tom had been turned away, beaten back.

Snotnose never appeared again at that Fourth Street intersection during the times my brothers and I did our shoeshining there. We heard from other bootblacks that he was seen at a new location on Fifteenth and Market Streets. Frank even said he saw Snotnose once during the middle of the week at that new location, but I never saw him again.

The incident with Snotnose left quite an impression on me. To begin with, it was the main topic of discussion among the boys in our neighborhood for weeks. My brothers bragged to their friends that they had made a grown man back down in a dispute with them. That was pretty amazing, I had to admit. I couldn't imagine confronting my father like that.

It gave me a good feeling in knowing that my brothers and I had stood together and had come out on top in the contest with Snotnose, but I could not understand why I felt so good about it. The encounter with Snotnose also left me confused. It was a long time after that before I learned what an Uncle Tom was.

CHAPTER SIX

There were many ways in which my brothers and I tried to help with the family income. There was shoeshining during the weekend, but through the week, we did other things to get money, and it wasn't always legal.

One thing we did was go trashing. We would get up early in the morning, about dawn, and we would visit the neighborhoods nearby that had trash collection that day. People would put their trash and throwaway items out in front of their houses, and the sanitation workers would come by and collect it. We would arrive in the neighborhoods before the sanitation workers got there, and we would rummage through the refuse on the sidewalks, looking for anything we might be able to sell to the local junk dealer. We would be looking for metals, like copper and iron, or a bunch of old newspapers, or broken household appliances, or cardboard. We never made much money trashing, but every little bit helped.

Invariably, the locations with the most rewarding trash were white neighborhoods, and nothing was more embarrassing than to have some early morning stroller catch us in the act of rummaging through the rubbish receptacles on the sidewalk. That was an annoying price to pay for the privilege of trashing, but I enjoyed doing it with my brothers. There was something very mysterious and exciting about getting up at dawn. The streets were so quiet and empty of people. It made me feel as though I was lost on a desert or a desolate island somewhere. It was like traveling without actually leaving Philadelphia.

There was another thing that I liked about trashing. Usually, when we left our house, the light would be just beginning to break up the darkness of the night before. And, as we moved through the silent streets, the sun would begin to rise above the horizon, and sunlight would splash against the facades of the red brick buildings. The structures would then seem to sparkle, glow, and come alive, and the usually drab looking buildings, the factories, the private homes, would become inviting castles of sunlight. It was the only time during the day when the Noble Street neighborhood seemed bright with color.

We were happy to find anything we could sell to the junk dealer, but we were particularly happy when we found a large quantity of cardboard. The junk dealer paid as much as ten to fifteen cents a pound for it. For many other people on Noble Street, cardboard was a much sought after item, and trashing was only one way to get it. We also got cardboard from a local meat factory. Meat was delivered to the factory in long cardboard cartons, as well as in barrels. The workers would discard the empty cardboard cartons once the meat had been removed.

The cartons would be tossed out of a third story window of the meat factory. They would be thrown into a small street behind our house, next to the back lot area where empty barrels were stored. We never knew exactly when the meat workers would throw the cardboard cartons out of their upstairs window. It was the sound of the cartons hitting the ground that would alert us. When they hit the ground, they sounded like small bombs going off, and everyone in the vicinity who heard that noise knew the meaning of that sound.

So, when the cardboard cartons started falling, individuals, young and old, would dash from their houses to get them. It was an opportunity to make some quick money, and the first person to get to the cardboard had the rights to all of it. It was a sight to see, mothers with babies, old men, and children rushing down this narrow back street to get the prized cardboard. It was quite a rat race, and everyone involved took the matter very seriously.

There were many times when my brothers and I would arrive at the spot below the meat factory window where the cartons were landing in the street at the same time as other cardboard seekers. That meant that everyone had equal claim to the carboard, and what followed was a wild scramble to get it. For the cardboard that was already on the ground, we would get what we could and set it aside. As more cardboard came knifing down from above, we would leap into the air to try and catch the cartons before they hit the ground. All the cardboard we would get, we would put in a pile. One of the brothers would watch over it while the others would try to get more cartons as they came falling down.

Some of these cartons were large, and they came hurdling down through the air. They could really give a person a jolt if they hit him on the head when he was jumping to try and catch them. Once I saw a kid get laid out, knocked cold, when he jumped high in the air to catch a big box that hit him right on the noggin. He wasn't injured seriously, but as he lay there unconscious for a short while, I for one thought he was dead. That made me feel sad. No one should get themselves killed for a few pennies worth of cardboard. At the same time, and very often, getting that cardboard could make the difference in whether someone would eat supper that night or go hungry.

There were a number of meat packing plants in the Noble Street neighborhood. Another way we made money was by stealing wooden barrels from one meat company and selling them to another. The employees of the meat companies were willing to buy them from us with no questions asked. The people in one company must have known that we were taking the barrels from another establishment, but that did not seem to matter. We never stole barrels from the lot near our house. That was too close to home.

As a general rule, during the work day, the employees of these meat companies would leave barrels sitting on the sidewalks, or in a backyard, with no one watching over them, and when my brothers and I were out on a barrel hunt, and came upon such a lax situation, we would swoop down on the barrels and make off with as many of them as we could handle. The way to move a barrel rapidly was to tilt it over on its bottom rim, and taking hold of the top rim, you roll it like a slanted hoop along ground. With a little practice, we could run while rolling a barrel along side of us. In fact, my brothers became so good at it, they could roll two barrels in that fashion—one with each hand. Eventually, even I learned how to roll two barrels at the same time; not as fast as my brothers, but still this was quite an accomplishment considering that the barrels were as tall as I was when I first became involved in these escapades.

We probably stole more than a couple of hundred barrels during the time we lived on Noble Street, and not once was one of us caught by any of the plant workers or the police. That also goes to prove that those workers must have known someone was stealing the barrels. If nothing else, they could count, and they did see us hanging around the meat companies on many occasions, even if they did not actually catch us in the act of stealing. In later years, I came to believe that those meat company workers actually let us steal those barrels most of the time. That was the only thing that made any sense as to how we could get away with it for so long.

However, there were some close calls, like the time when Norman, Frank, and I had stolen barrels from a meat plant near Third and Callowhill Street. At the intersection where those two streets met, there was a hill that slanted down Third Street from Callowhill to Willow Street. Whenever we snatched barrels from that particular meat establishment, there was always a quick getaway because we could roll the barrels down the hill very fast. However, on that occasion, I had gotten a late start. Norman and Frank got away with their barrels easily enough, but a worker came into the backyard of the meat plant before I could sneak away with two barrels. To keep from being discovered, I had to hide behind a row of barrels until the worker went back into the plant. By the time I had my two barrels rolling, Norman and Frank were long gone.

But, when I was half way down the hill on Third Street, I saw the front of a police car suddenly slide into view from the east on Willow Street. I could see the two police officers clearly, sitting in the front seat of the cruiser engaged in a conversation. Because they were so deeply engrossed in what they were talking about, they did not notice me moving with my barrels on the pavement to their left.

I thought the police were going to get me for sure, and immediately that dumb, scared feeling grabbed me. My stomach gurgled as I imagined myself behind bars, dressed in striped prison attire, and shackled with a ball and chain on my right leg. I did not want to go to jail, and to my surprise, I reacted quickly to the situation.

Without even thinking about it, I let go of the barrel I was rolling in my left hand, and it continued to roll and spin on its tilted rim for a time before it crashed broadside to the pavement. The barrel then rolled off the pavement out into Third Street and continued rolling down the hill.

Without watching what was happening with the barrel that rolled into the street, I stopped rolling the second barrel and leapt headlong into it to get out of the police officers' view. But I dove into the barrel with such force, it spun over on its side and began to roll down the hill on the pavement. The barrel with me in it was now rolling straight towards the police car at the bottom of the hill. The police were surely going to get me now, I was thinking, as I saw the sky through the top of the barrel go whirling by. It was like being on a tiny merry-go-round.

Inside of the barrel, I was spinning around and around, waiting for the collision I thought was coming, but it never happened. Before my barrel reached the bottom of the hill, I heard car tires screech, and the next thing I knew, my barrel bounced off the sidewalk and spun around the corner onto Willow Street. It came to a stop against the south curb.

With the barrel at rest, and even though my head was spinning, I could see the police car chasing the other barrel further down Third Street. I guessed the officers wanted to get that barrel out of the street before it caused an accident.

I then popped out of the barrel I was in, and I lifted it up and moved down Willow Street with it. I soon had it sold, and I found my brothers nearby waiting for me. They wanted to know what happened to my second barrel. When I told them I last saw it being chased by two police officers down Third Street, they thought I was just making it up. And they really thought I was lying when I told them I had dove headlong into one of the barrels, and it had rolled down the hill to Willow Street.

Whether my brothers believed me or not, there was no dispute about the fact that twenty-cents a barrel was a good haul for about ten to fifteen minutes worth of work, and Mom could always manage a meal for the family with a dollar. And most of the time that is why we stole those barrels—to get money to give to Mom. If we had any guilty feelings about stealing, they were overcome by the knowledge that we were providing food for the family.

Even with all our efforts to help Mom keep food on the table, they were only stopgap measures. It was a tough situation to beat because poverty engulfed our lifestyle, and there was no letting up. There were just too many days when the cupboard was bare for the efforts of my brothers and me to make a sustaining difference. The welfare checks were frequently being delayed, and Mom could not always get domestic work.

It was a given that the family was always short of food, not to mention clothing and all the other necessities of life. What saved us from going without food, most of the time, was the fact that Mom could depend upon credit from a local merchant, Mr. Katz, who ran a small food market. Mr. Katz was a nice, fat old man with thick eyebrows. His face reminded me of a marshmallow, and that is why I liked him. He always had a good word to say about everyone. That was good for business, but I felt he was sincere. I could not remember a time when an ill word came from his mouth, and he seemed to genuinely like all the children in the neighborhood.

Mom had a slightly different view of Mr. Katz. He gave credit to most of the neighborhood's poor families, and she thought that was very good. But, she would occasionally remark that he overcharged his credit customers for his merchandise, but she really didn't complain about it. It was just an observation she made. She knew that without that credit, she would not have been able to feed her family on any kind of regular basis. Since the welfare checks were never enough to cover the two weeks they were allotted for, she, and the other poor families in the neighborhood, accepted Katz's overcharging as a tradeoff. They paid a little more to get what they needed, with the understanding that they had little choice in the matter.

But, even with Katz's help, periodically, circumstances would arise that would cause our family's larder to be completely empty, sometimes for days on end. There were times when the welfare check was overdue for more than a week, and Mom's credit at Katz's store had reached its limit for the month. There would be no domestic work, and Mom may have overextended herself with her sisters. Moreover, bad weather may have kept the Cooper boys off the streets. We were not able to go shoeshining, trashing, and barrel stealing, and there was no cardboard to collect from the meat company. On these occasions, it would seem as though all sources of income had dried up at the same time, but the family still had to eat.

It was a dreadful sight watching your younger brothers and sisters moan and groan about the emptiness in their stomachs while they looked to a desperate mother to make things right. And it was a different situation than before. We were older boys now, and we could not, or would not, sit around the kitchen table braying about being "hungry" as we did when we were younger. Besides, Mom was home, but there was still no food to eat.

It was strange for us to be sitting in the Noble Street house, with our larder empty, yet we were surrounded by food. There were meat plants all around us, and not far away, a few cobblestone streets from the Delaware River waterfront, there were the wharves, which were made up of blocks and blocks of shed-type buildings where fruits and vegetable produce were stored after they were taken off of boats and trucks. The greengrocers of the city would come to the wharves to buy the produce wholesale that they would then sell in their stores. When a strong wind was blowing east to west, we could smell the fruit and the vegetables from the wharves in our kitchen, and when the meat companies were curing and preparing meats, we could smell the hot dogs, the bolognas, pork sausages, and hams.

With all those food-smells circling around us, it was certain that, at some point, my brothers and I would take up the challenge. When those dire circumstances of an empty pantry presented themselves, and Mom was out of options, it was time for my brothers and I to go into action. We would then plan and execute a caper. We would assume the role of professional thieves and make a raid on one of the places where we could get food for the family.

The closest meat company was Yankee Maid, an establishment that we were very familiar with. We had cased the joint many times, and we knew the behavior of the workers there very well. Consequently, we knew the best times to make a hit, and we knew the best location in the plant to do it.

The meat plant was in a five-story, red brick building. The meat curing and packing was done on the upper four floors of the plant. The first, or ground floor, was where the finished meat products were stored in big refrigerated rooms until they were shipped out. At the front of the building, there was a loading dock where trucks came to pick up the meat that would be delivered to retail stores for sale. After studying the situation, my brothers decided that the best chance for stealing meat was at the loading dock.

At the loading dock, the workers would stack and hang the meats, the bolognas, the hot dogs, on racks that were then positioned on large moving carts. The carts were used to roll the meat in and out of the refrigerators and smoke rooms and right up to the back of the trucks.

The best time to steal meat was just after trucks arrived to pick up deliveries. The drivers often spent time talking to the meat plant workers before they proceeded to load up their trucks, and the talking was usually done off the loading platform away from any complete view of the meat racks hanging on the carts. It was actually quite easy to steal meat off of the platform during the five or ten minutes that drivers would take to chat with the plant workers.

We would sneak up to the loading dock and hide down under the parked trucks, near the back wheels. The platform would be above our heads, and we would be totally hidden from view. This gave us cover until we made our move, but any one of us could have been easily killed, as one of our friends was, if we got caught under a truck when it drove off. Nevertheless, we would wait until we heard the voices of the drivers and workers receding, leaving the docking area, before we would come out from under the truck and take a look up over the end of the platform. If the coast was clear, one of us would jump up onto the platform and take a rack of hot dogs or bolognas and hand them down to the others. One rack of meats was usually enough for a good haul because it could contain as many as four dozen hot dogs or as many as fifteen bolognas. We would divide the booty among ourselves under the truck before the driver would return, and then we would take off running as fast as we could.

Planning a raid on the meat plant was done with a certain calmness and coolness befitting professional thieves. We were aware of the risks, but Norman and Frank would not allow their apprehension to overwhelm them. It was usually Norman, Frank, and I who made the raids on the meat plant, with Ducky coming along on a few occasions.

If my two older brothers were frightened when they were stealing meat, they never showed it. On the other hand, I found the raids scary as hell. I always compared what my brothers and I did to what I saw in Hollywood motion pictures, the stories about bank robbers, stagecoach holdups, or diamond heists. It looked like fun in the movies, outsmarting "the coppers," but it was not quite that way when I was hiding down under those trucks or stealing the meat from the platform. It was also irritating to smell the motor oil and gasoline fumes when I was lying under those trucks. The smell was so strong it would stink up my nose and remind me of the stench of the bedbug.

I was most afraid when I had to get up on the platform to steal the meat. I would be so scared my entire body would be shaking, and the sweat would roll down my face like rainwater. I always had this great fear that one of the plant workers would catch me on the platform, and then the police would be brought in and I would be sent off to the chain gang. No more peaches and shortening bread to eat. That thought alone would make me feel so very sad. But somehow, I would get myself through it. After all, my younger brothers and sisters were depending upon me.

It was quite dangerous to hide under those trucks, but there were other hazards we encountered on these meat plant forays. There was an occasion when Ducky came along on a raid, which was unusual. He probably went more out of curiosity than anything else. He did not have an aggressive personality, nor was he one to engage in bravado. Therefore, it was most unusual for him to want to be involved in any kind of stealing escapade.

Since it was Ducky's first time on a raid, Frank allowed him to go up onto the platform to take the meat off of the racks. Ducky had just approached and circled behind a meat cart that was loaded with hot dogs, and he was about to remove some frankfurters when a worker came back onto the platform. Ducky did the wise thing by dropping down to the floor and sliding under the meat cart that held about a hundred racks of hot dogs. The worker had not seen him sliding under the cart. He came over to that same cart where Ducky lay hidden, and he rolled the cart off of the platform and into a freezer.

The worker's back was turned to where Norman, Frank, and I were peering over the edge of the platform. We saw the worker begin moving the cart, and we thought that Ducky would be discovered. The worker would push the cart away, and there little Ducky would be lying on the floor of the platform. But when the cart moved, there was no Ducky lying on the floor. Apparently, he had grabbed a hold of the bottom of the cart, and he was wheeled away with the rest of the frankfurters into the freezer. The worker closed the freezer door with the cart and Ducky inside, and he then left the platform.

Norman, Frank, and I began to look at each other, twitchy, nervous, and scared. Norman said he had heard that the workers at the meat plant kept the temperature in the freezer down to thirty-degrees below zero. This was not true, but we didn't know that.

"Godd," I said. "Ducky's gonna turn into an icicle in there."

"We gotta get him out," Norman said.

"Jeesus, Mom is gonna kill us," Frank said. "I'm gonna go up there and get him out of that freezer."

But as Frank started up onto the platform, the worker returned, and he had to slip back below the platform quickly once again and hide under the truck with Norman and me. Three or four different times, Frank tried to get to the freezer, but there was always someone about. Ducky had now been in the freezer for about a half an hour.

I started to sniffle. "Ducky is dead, dead, frozen like a popsicle." Even though I said that, I could not really believe my little brother was dead. And then to relieve myself of the sadness I was beginning to feel, I asked, "He ain't really dead, is he Frank? Is he?"

Frank didn't answer the question. "We're gonna get him outta there."

"Yeah, we're goin' to get him," Norman said.

But I didn't believe them because I felt certain that Ducky was already nothing but freezing ice, and I could only shake my head. "All this for a hot dog. Ducky is dead for a hot dog."

"He ain't dead," Frank said emphatically. "He ain't dead."

We were still hiding under the truck, waiting for the opportunity to release Ducky from the freezer. But then we heard footsteps on the platform, and they were coming towards our location. We had to move further back under the truck. As the movement on the platform grew closer to us, we all grew silent.

But I could not keep myself from whispering, "All this for a hot dog. I ain't never gonna eat another hot dog. Never."

Then suddenly, there was the sound of someone jumping from the platform and landing next to the truck where we were hiding. We were about to be discovered, or so Norman, Frank, and I thought, but Ducky came crawling under the truck wrapped in strings of hot dogs from his neck to his waist.

"Dammit." Frank grabbed some of the hot dogs. "Why'd you scare us like that? We thought you might be frozen stiff by now."

"Naw." Ducky laughed. "I wasn't even all that cold. When that man rolled me in that freezer room, I just wrapped myself up with the hot dogs to keep warm, and after a while, I opened the door and came out."

"You weren't even cold, huh?" Norman slapped him gently upside the head. "And we out here were so worried about you." Norman was relieved that Ducky was safe.

"Aw, lets just knock it off and get the hell outta here," Frank said.

With Ducky wrapped in hot dogs, we raced home with dinner for ourselves and the rest of the family. Mom would never ask us how we got the hot dogs or other meats we stole. She just closed her eyes to the reality of it and fed her children. Stealing food may have been morally and criminally wrong, but it was our human necessity.

Stealing the meat was one thing. Getting it home was another. The best route for us from the meat plant's loading platform to our house was by a couple of very small back streets and an alleyway. When we took that route, we would be hardly seen by anyone. But stray dogs that frequently visited the meat plant looking for scraps of food often inhabited those back streets and that alleyway. Many times we had to fight off those dogs while we clasped our stolen meats close to our breast, and a dog or two bit more than one of us, at different times. There could be as many as ten or twelve dogs sniffing around the meat plant on any given day. Nevertheless, there was only one time that I could remember when we lost some of our stolen booty to the dogs.

We would usually run at top speed right through the mingling, hungry group of stray animals, kicking and shouting as we did in order to scare them off before they realized that we were carrying such tasty morsels. But, on one mad dash, with our arms loaded down with stolen goods, Norman lost his balance, and he fell sprawling among the hungry dogs. Two bolognas bounced out of his arms as he hit the alley floor. The dogs scattered as Norman landed amidst them, but as he scuffled to recover the bolognas, the dogs perked up their noses as they realized that a meal had just dropped in on them.

As Norman was still scuffling on his knees, the dogs quickly turned on him, and only his quick thinking saved him from a mauling. He threw one of the bolognas at the dogs, picked up the other one and dashed off after us. We all laughed about it later, but in truth Norman could have been chewed up badly by those eight or so dogs if he tried to hang on to both bolognas. He did the right thing by giving the dogs one of them.

Frequently, when hunger would squeeze our stomachs, it would not be images of hot dogs and bolognas that would dance through our heads, but images of sugarplums. Hunger would give us a particular appetite for Mom's sweatmeats, like her apple pie, sweet potato pie, or the best food of all for beating back hunger, peaches and shortening bread.

That's not to say that when we were hungry, we never thought of Mom's tasty fried chicken, or her delicious pork chops, or her most delectable brown gravy in a pot roast, but when our stomachs were most pinched with hunger, invariably, our thoughts of food would turn to peaches and shortening bread. Peaches and shortening bread satisfied not only physical hunger, but it also quieted the spirit of hunger. Other kinds of food would fill the emptiness of the belly, but peaches and shortening bread could fill the belly and the emptiness of the heart and soul that often accompanied hunger. It was a dream food.

Why that was the case, I'm not sure. Peaches and shortening bread was the simplest and cheapest of foods. It was a combination of cut up, skinned peaches that were boiled in their own juices, with water and sugar added, and baking dough cooked in a frying pan. The peaches and the bread were prepared separately, and then they are eaten together. Take a bite of the shortening bread and then eat a spoonful of peaches with it. You could eat the peaches hot or cold. Now, I couldn't think of a simpler, non-wholesome, lack of protein meal, but to the Cooper children, it was absolutely the wonders of wonders to eat when we were really hungry.

When hunger was in our bellies and thoughts of peaches and shortening bread in our heads, Norman, Frank, and I knew what had to be done. It was time to make a commando raid on the wharves. Usually, at the height of a peaches and shortening bread hysteria, when the young children like Ducky, Dotty, and even Marion had fallen into a repetitious chorus of "I smell peaches 'n' shortnin' bread," we would give Mom that certain look and we would leave the house. She would always shake her head with disapproval as we slipped away. She did not want us to do bad things, but there was hunger in 238 Noble Street and something had to be done about that. She once told me that whenever Norman, Frank, and I would go out to steal food, she would pray to her dear mother beyond the grave to protect her children on their errand of mercy, and she hoped that God would forgive her for looking the other way when her sons were stealing.

Making a raid on the wharves posed a different kind of problem for us than when we would hit the meat plant. Stealing from the meat plant required a clandestine operation and stealth. Stealing from the wharves required much bolder tactics. It required a more open, two-prong attack, with a definite diversionary component. We would have to fool our adversaries in order to pull off the raid.

There were sheds on the wharves, and there were always large quantities of fruits and vegetables stacked in boxes and baskets on the sidewalks outside of these shed buildings so that buyers could have easy access to them. The focus of our raids was always on the fruits outside, primarily the peaches. The wharves were a busy place twenty-four hours a day. The streets around them were always crowded with sellers and buyers. To pull off a caper, one had to be slick, shrewd, cunning, and quick.

The routine for stealing from the meat plant was very much the same each time, but a raid on the wharves had to be planned out according to the situation and circumstances we found when we arrived at the storage market. For instance, the peaches on the outside of the sheds were constantly being moved from one location to another. We had to deal with the peaches where we found them.

The peaches to be stolen were usually in large, wooden lattice baskets that held as many as six dozen peaches in them, and these baskets would be lined up on the curbside. On any given day, when peaches were in season, there might well be hundreds of these baskets sitting out in the open on the pavement. One could easily approach the basket of peaches, but the question was how to get away with one of them and not get caught. That was not an easy matter, since there were great numbers of people traversing through the area. A plan had to be devised. Diversionary tactics were needed, and coordination was required between the person causing the diversion and the others who would be snatching the basket of peaches.

The specifics of a plan would have to take into account what elements like the types of vehicles, trucks, horse and wagons, and the density of the crowd that was present on the wharves that day. These elements would be the determining factor in deciding what type of diversionary tactics we would use. It was quite common to see a number of horses and wagons on the wharves. Merchants used them to haul away the produce they bought.

Horses were very good for creating a diversion, but at times, there would be no horses and wagons on the wharves where the peaches were. Frequently, we focused on a truck as a source for creating a diversion. There were always plenty of trucks in the streets around the wharves. But, there were times when we could not get close to a truck, and as a last resort, we would then use the buyers and sellers themselves for our diversionary tactic.

The best plan always included a horse. Horses are really very temperamental animals. If we disturbed their concentration when they were at rest, they would raise holy hell. The most effective way, we discovered, to break a horse's concentration, was jamming a needle into its ass. A horse might buck and rear up with such force it would sometimes break free of its harness. One horse reacted so violently when Norman drove a hatpin into its rump, the animal overturned the wagon it was harnessed in. The wagon was empty, but it was still one terrific sight to see it crashing down on its side. The falling vehicle gave off the sound of an explosion. I thought it was thrilling, especially when the horse fell over, too. The animal lay there on the ground kicking its four legs in the air in stiff, awkward motions while it screeched, the sound of which tingled in my ears. The sight of it all was better than the action in the Westerns of the serial pictures at the Saturday matinee movies, and when you're able to create that kind of diversion, you can walk off with a barrel load of peaches.

When we used a truck to create a disturbance, one of us might put a piece of cardboard, or a safety pin, or a wad of chewing gum in the horn of the vehicle. That would cause the horn to blast off loudly and continuously. A noise like that always stopped people in their tracks and gathered a crowd. However, the horn noise had to occur close to the shed area where the peaches would be swiped from. Still, the truck could not be right in front of the peach shed.

If the blowing horn trick was not used, Norman or Frank might set some pages of a newspaper on fire and throw it into the back of a truck to make people think the truck was burning. The sheds were made almost entirely of wood, and just the mere mention of fire struck panic into the heart of the wharf workers. All normal activities on the wharves would stop if someone shouted "fire" and smoke could be seen.

I did not care very much for the use of fire as a diversion because it frightened me. I knew how fire could easily get out of control. Once, I took a match, lit it up, and tried to burn the chinches out of the bedsprings of the bed in my room, but instead I set the mattress on fire. I was amazed at how quickly the mattress became engulfed in flames. It flared up like fireworks on the Fourth of July, and if I had not acted quickly, the room would have become ablaze in just a few minutes.

The only liquid available nearby was the pee bucket, which was about half full. I snatched the bucket, and I dashed the pee on the burning mattress. There was a loud sizzle sound as the pee splashed on the flames and smothered the fire. I remember shuddering at the thought of the Noble Street house going up in flames, and I was thankful that the pee bucket had not been emptied, as it should have been the last couple of mornings. And the stink from that sizzling pee was so acrid and pungent that I actually gagged. For a time, I could not breathe.

Because of my bad experience with fire, I was never at my best when it was used as a diversionary tactic on the wharves. When all else failed, the people themselves had to be used to create a disturbance. That could be done rather easily once we realized that men particularly did not like to be blamed, belittled, or embarrassed in public, especially when that public was largely made up of other men. And to be sure, working class men did not like their masculinity being questioned. If we could play upon any of these themes among the orchestra of men in the market, some guy was sure to get hot under the collar.

During the daylight hours, seven days a week, the streets around the wharves were always extremely busy. The horses and wagons, the trucks, and even pushcarts would be coming and going on the cobblestone streets, which caused the moving vehicles to bounce and squeak when they traveled. Buyers and sellers flooded the sidewalks.

As raiders, we would drift in among the merchants and wholesalers as business deals were being negotiated. The buyers and sellers were usually too involved in their transactions to notice the black kids mingling among them. The minds of the buyers and sellers would be on fruits and vegetables, but our minds would be solely on peaches. We would wander about the wharves until we found a location where a group of baskets, loaded with peaches, sat near the curb.

While two of us would lounge inconspicuously near the peach baskets, the third member of the raiding party, usually Norman, would pick out an unsuspecting man nearby, and he would slyly jostle the man's wallet pocket. The men on the wharves usually kept their wallets in one of the back pockets of their trousers, and when a man was jostled from behind, he was likely to think that someone was trying to pickpocket him and steal his wallet.

Invariably, the man who was jostled would turn around and accuse the closest person to him of trying to lift his wallet. More often than not, the accused person would become angry at the false accusation and an argument or even a fight might break out. As attentions would turn to the combatants, the hit would be made. Usually Frank and I would pick up a basket of peaches, jump off the curb, pass between the parked vehicles, sometimes right under the nose of snorting, excited horses, and we would dash out into the middle of the street. Then, with the basket of peaches carried between us, the two of us would run like hell out of the market area. We always made our escape by running in the street because running on the pavements with our stolen prize was out of the question.

Sometimes, as a man was bending over to inspect some basket of produce, one of us would goose him right in the crease of his ass. The offended party's reaction was sure to be quick, volatile, and accusatory. Norman did a number on this big fat man once, and the fellow turned to a little guy near him and said, "Are you a queer or something? You felt my ass."

"Look buddy, I didn't touch you."

"I'll bet."

"Is something wrong with you, goddamnit? Cause, I don't know what the hell you're talking about?"

"Are you saying I'm making this up?"

"I don't know what the hell ya doing, but you ain't no broad. So, why in the hell would I want to feel your fat ass?"

"Cause you're a fuckin' queer that's why!"

"Why you bastard," the little guy said. And he jumped up in the air and punched the fat fellow right in the face.

The punch made a slapping sound, and the big man rocked back. Then he leaped forward and grabbed the little guy. They fell to the ground and rolled underneath a wagon that was parked at the curb. The last I saw of them, they were tussling on the ground near the hoofs of a frightened horse.

Of course, those angry men could not imagine that the young, black kids they saw nearby were the instigators of the ruckus. And for all those many raids we made on the wharves, not once were we ever caught stealing a basket of peaches. We never knew if it was luck, or if mysterious forces were helping us. Mom had told me many stories about the spirits that helped poor black people in the South. Maybe we were getting help from one of those spirits—in particular, the spirit of our grandmother who was a Native American. And maybe our raids on the wharves was an extension of the old Indian wars, and we didn't even know it.

CHAPTER SEVEN

Every aspect of my family's lifestyle worsened in the wintertime. The cheap sneakers did not keep my feet warm. The lack of a sweater, a muffler, a warm coat, and gloves made the cold seem colder than it really was, especially in the morning when I went off to school. The wind seemed to blow right through those hand-me-down, Salvation Army clothes and smack right up against my skin. I remember those cold, fierce mornings. It was like facing icy winds and freezing temperatures in the nude, and I was sure that my brothers and sisters had the same experience.

To be sure, our food situation was absolutely dire in the wintertime. It was difficult to steal from the meat plant because the workers kept the building's doors closed, and the meat was kept off of the loading platform until it was being put directly in the trucks. On the wharves, the fruits and vegetables were kept inside sheds to keep them from getting spoiled and ruined by the cold weather.

One of the most worrisome aspects of our winter lives was the problem of trying to keep the drafty Noble Street house warm. The only source of heat the family had was the one medium-sized, wood and coal burning Franklin heater. It was shaped like a small barrel that sat on four legs, and it was made of wrought iron. It had a little door in the front through which we put the materials to be burned. Paper and wood were used to get the fire started. Once the wood was burning well, we would put coal on top of it, and after a time, the coal would start burning and glowing red hot. The coal would burn for a long time, but eventually more coal would have to be added and the ashes would have to be shaken down below the grating to the bottom of the fire chamber to a small compartment where it could be collected and disposed of.

It was a major problem keeping coal in the house so a fire might be maintained in the kitchen during the daylight hours when family members were up and about. It seemed that whenever the coldest weather would hit, the household was sure to run out of coal.

The Noble Street house became a one-room home for the family during the wintertime. We lived in that kitchen around that barreled-bellied heater. When we had coal, we had heat, but when we had no coal, we would still sit in the kitchen around that heater. My brothers, sisters, and I would put on our coats and wrap ourselves in blankets or anything that might keep us warm. Somehow we must have thought that we could transfer the heat from our bodies to the heater, and that would cause the whole kitchen to warm up. But, of course, that never happened. Also, during these heatless days, Mom would turn on the gas range and boil water in an attempt to heat up the air in the room with steam. However, frequently on these occasions, it was impossible to even boil water. Quite often, Mom was unable to pay the gas bill, and the Philadelphia Gas Company would terminate the family's gas service. No gas, no hot water.

But what was even more disturbing with the water, in the dead of the winter, the water pipes in the house would often freeze up. When this happened, Mom would go into the cellar and make a small fire under the water pipes to get the water flowing out of the kitchen faucet. If unfreezing the water pipes took too long, my brothers and I would have to go to a neighbor's house and get water in pots.

To be cold and hungry always made Norman, Frank, and I feel desperate, like we were backed up against a wall. We did not understand all the reasons for our poverty, but I believed that there had to be something working against us. All of the badness in our lives could not be happening of its own accord. I was even beset with the feeling that the badness was in my blood and that is why my skin was dark. I believed that all black people suffered from the same bad blood.

To me, that nonsense thinking was the only kind of thinking that made any sense when I tried to understand my circumstances. Why should my mother have to struggle so hard to make ends meet? My Mom was one of the hardest working mothers in the world. Her life was dedicated to her children, and she would do almost anything to keep them safe and happy.

This is to say that my Mom was a single-minded person; and in that sense, she was content with her life. That made her generally a happy person, even with all the problems she had to contend with on a daily basis. She was filled with pleasure and joy just being in the company of her children, and she felt excited when she held one of them close to her. Each time she did it, it was an affirmation of a dream she had when she was a young girl, that one day she would have her own child to love and care for. She loved to cook for her children and watch them enjoy a hearty meal, and she was fond of seeing them lounge around the pot-bellied, Franklin heater after they had eaten a good meal and they were brimming with childish contentment. She certainly had her favorite sons and daughters, but none of her children felt bereft of motherly love.

I often wondered if any white mothers had to suffer the way my Mother did. When thoughts like that crossed my mind, I could become angry as hell because it seemed as if God, fate, or whatever, played favorites.

For the Cooper family, God was always on an extended vacation in the wintertime. Thinking about Him always made me feel pushed aside and abandoned. What had we done to have Him punish us without heat in the dead of the wintertime?

I agreed with my brothers, Norman and Frank. They believed that we could not count on God to help us out of our poverty hole. They believed that we had to help ourselves. If there was no coal in the Noble Street house, and there was no money to buy it, then we had to steal it. Most of the factories and plants in the area used coal to heat their facilities. Train tracks ran right up to the commercial establishments, and train cars with tons of coal in them delivered the fuel to the factories and plants every week. Given the fact that there was coal nearby, it was unacceptable to me and my brothers that we should be sitting in our home, cold and without heat, while hundreds of tons of the black fuel sat in train cars not more than a block from our house.

In the dead of the night, Norman, Frank, and I, and sometimes Ducky, would raid those train cars and steal coal. We would use burlap bags or cardboard boxes to carry the coal away. The coal cars were never guarded, and our greatest danger was from the coal itself.

To begin with, the coal cars were these great, big black cavernous vehicles with open tops and funneled, trapdoor bottoms. They looked like mysterious beasts in the dim light at night. I always thought of them as being dinosaurs. To get the coal, we had to clamber up onto the creature's back and scoop out its guts. We did this by climbing the metal rungs of a ladder that was built into the side of the rail cars. The cars were about ten or twelve feet high, and they were always filled to capacity with coal.

Once we reached the top of the ladder of the rail car, we usually had to jump inside of it to get at the coal. Because the fuel was to be used in the huge furnaces of the nearby factories and plants, the coal was delivered in tremendously large pieces. To carry some of it off, we had to break twenty-five to fifty pound chunks of coal into smaller pieces that were more manageable. We carried ice picks, knives, and hammers to chip and bang the big pieces of coal into smaller ones. Sometimes the coal would be very hard. Nevertheless, the thought that the coal would bring heat to our kitchen was enough to keep us banging and chipping away at it until we achieved success.

Sometimes we would not break up a large piece of coal in the rail car. We would push it over the side and let it go crashing to the ground where it would shatter into many smaller pieces. We would then gather up the smaller pieces and carry them home. Once, a big piece of coal Frank and Norman pushed out of a railroad car almost hit me. The huge lump of coal just grazed my scalp. It probably would have killed me if it had hit me squarely on the head. Another time, when Frank was inside a train car, a monstrous piece of coal tumbled on top of him. A pile of coal would often shift when we would bang and chip away at some of it.

When the big piece of coal tumbled on top of Frank, and he started yelling for help, I almost panicked. My first inclination was to jump out of the train car before I became trapped, too. I had visions of being smothered and crushed to death, but I fought off the visions and helped Norman get the big chunk of coal off of Frank. That was one scary incident, and it reminded me of the time my father was standing precariously on the second floor windowsill.

Yes, in the early years of my childhood, my family had to struggle for survival and a little measure of household comfort. Stealing meat, peaches, coal, barrels, and shining shoes all spoke to the indomitable spirit of the Cooper brothers, but also we were being touched by the pervasive social motif of the time. The nation was being threatened by the Axis powers just as the Cooper family was being threatened by poverty. American troops were marching against Germany, Italy, and Japan, while the Cooper brothers were marching on the meat plants, the wharves, the barrel yards, and doing battle with the likes of Snotnose.

American troops were battling the enemy in both the European and Pacific Theaters, and it was a time of patriotic war movies and nationalistic fervor at every level of society. It was "Johnny Get Your Gun," victory gardens, and rationing stamps. There were air raid wardens and air raid drills. It was also the time of paper collections, tin can collections, glass collections, and supporting the war effort by buying victory bonds. Hitler, Mussolini, and Tojo had to be defeated and the world saved from fascism. I didn't know what fascism was, but I believed it to be bad.

America was at war, and I was for America. Still, there was I, very often hungry and shivering in my sneakers, never knowing one day to the next when the cupboard would be empty or the fuel bin without coal, yet I was more worried about this country's survival than my own. Was America worried about me? Probably not. If it was, I would not have had to steal food and coal.

I would go to the movie theaters on the weekend and see the Movietone news clips about the War, and I would cheer on the Americans. I believed the American soldiers and sailors were fighting a just war, even if they made me feel terrible when they wanted to rub my head for luck. Movietone said that God was on America's side. If that was true, God had to believe in the righteousness of America in the war against the fascists.

If I were old enough, I would have joined the armed forces, and I would have been proud to fight for my country. It would have been strange, though, because I would have been fighting mostly for white people in America.

I even laughed at the racial bigotry, epithets, and comic stereotypes of the enemy, the buck toothed, four-eyed Japanese, the rat-like characterization of Hitler and the Germans, and the swinish, pig figure of Mussolini that were portrayed in the cartoons and propaganda films that were shown at the movie theaters. The Axis enemies were abominable creatures. They were vermin like the little pests that infested the Noble Street house. As I would rid myself of the household vermin, so America and its Allies would rid the world of the fascist vermin.

There was no doubt that I was for America in the great world war, but even as I laughed at the cartoon stereotypes of the enemy, inside of

me, there was a certain feeling of kinship for the buck toothed Jap
because he was a racial caricature just like the black Sambo stereotype
of the negro boy. And what about the rat-like Hitler and the swinish
depiction of Mussolini? That was to say that the Germans and Italians
were low-life, subhumans. Those depictions were much like the grinning, "nappy-headed," subhuman nigger. I sensed, but I did not want to
believe, that if Hitler, Mussolini, and Tojo were the enemy, then those
stereotypes should have told me that according to white America, I was
the enemy, too.

To be sure, how could I argue with Movietone? God was on
America's side, and that made the Second World War a holy war. The
newsreels would show American fighting men, participating in religious services, kneeling and praying to God for strength and guidance
before going into battle. And the commentator would tell the movie
audience that the Japanese did not believe in God. They believed in the
Emperor. Japanese soldiers were not Christians, and God favored the
Christians. What I did not realize then was that my opinions about the
war were grossly shaped by Hollywood and Movietone.

And what made Movietone so effective, the newsreels knew how to
stage events. There were the pictures of the soldiers, dirty and bedrag-
gled, hiding in, and fighting out of, foxholes. They were seen covered in
blood and mud. And then there were the sights of those sinking
American ships, torpedoed by German U-Boats, and the squadrons
after squadrons of Japanese planes bombing Wake and the Philippine
Islands. It all had the desired effect. Those newsreel images made me
angry to see the enemy attacking America's troops. Those chink-eyed
motherfuckers, and those Nazi bastards. Who in the hell do they think
they were messing with?

I felt anger and hate towards the enemy that Movietone and the
Hollywood movies told me about, but I might have felt differently if I
had known the truth about how black members of the armed forces
were being treated during the war. In fact, Movietone and the

Hollywood motion pictures rarely, if ever, showed black soldiers, sailors, and marines fighting for their country. That in itself should have been a clue to me that something was wrong. But when it came to the Nazis and Japs, I had to believe in my country, America. What other country was I born and raised in?

I did not know that there were segregated military units just like there were segregated neighborhoods. I did not know that in the Navy and Army, black fighting men were usually given only menial tasks to do. Consequently, at the beginning of the war, very few black soldiers were able to become officers. That prohibition changed as the war ground on and the need for manpower became more severe. In any case, it was generally difficult for blacks to become officers in any branch of the service at any time during the War. Officers were considered gentlemen, and according to the mores of American society, black men were never to be classified as gentlemen.

I knew from my own experiences that whites thought black people were inferior to them, but I never imagined that that would affect the way blacks were used in the armed forces. To defeat the enemy, members of the American armed forces, of all races, would have to work together the way my brothers and I did when we had to get food or coal for the family. Nevertheless, whites in the military believed that blacks did not have the same fighting courage as they did, and that was why blacks were generally kept separated from the brave, white fighting men. Black members of the armed forces were relegated to performing support roles in the war as cooks, truck drivers, stevedores, and just generally being beasts of burden. Blacks were routinely sent into combat areas without sufficient ammunition, or no ammunition at all, for their weapons. Some white officers and noncommissioned officers, NCOs, did not trust blacks with bullets in their rifles. Perhaps those officers and NCOs were afraid that the blacks might turn around and use their weapons against them.

In the 1940s, the overwhelming social motif of the day was survival. The Coopers were trying to survive as a family, and America was trying survive as a nation. I did not really understand what the war had to do with my life the way I understood the nature of my poverty, but I knew there was a connection.

The Quakers were also caught up in the prevailing social motif of the day. While they were, by and large, pacifists, they would still help to organize the paper collection drives, the tin and glass collection campaigns that were used to help support the war effort. There was nothing unusual about this. The Quakers had a history of supporting America's social ideals. They were one of the first groups to come to the Delaware Valley area when the original thirteen colonies were settled. They had left Europe because of religious intolerance, and they had come to the "New World" to live by the dictates of their faith and hearts. They had a general humanist philosophy that said all men were equal in the eyes of God, and to fulfill that belief, they had dedicated themselves to a lifestyle that would pay respect to the brotherhood of humankind.

The Guild offered social services of all kinds to the people of the community, from family counseling and health services to educational and recreational activities. To the kids of the neighborhood, the Guild was primarily a center for fun and games. It was the place to go to play sports, participate in craftmaking, dancing, cooking, and reading classes, and many other programs. During the school year, the neighborhood children would go to the Guild after school, and they could participate in activities right up to six o'clock, dinnertime. In the warmer months, there would also be many field trips, to parks for picnics, the zoo, swimming pools, and museums. And, the summer was always topped off with a two-week camp vacation for the neighborhood children.

The main activities building of the Guild was a large red brick structure that was four stories high. In the basement, there were ping-pong tables. I loved the game, and over the years, I became quite good at it.

The most interesting thing about the basement of the Guild was not the ping-pong tables. The old Quaker Meeting House was once one of the stops on the Underground Railroad, and hundreds, if not thousands, of runaway enslaved people may have hidden in that building on their way to freedom. The walls and floor of the basement were honeycombed with hidden passages where runaways had found brief refuge from their pursuers. I used to go into those hidden passageways and try to imagine what it must have been like to be a black person on the run. The idea of that was most discomforting.

There was nothing religious about the Guild's activities. Social workers ran the programs, and fortunately for me, the Guild staff, in particular Francis Bosworth, took a strong liking to the Cooper family. I suspected that the Guild staff was interested in my family because they developed a tremendous admiration for my mother. She certainly was a woman to be admired, struggling as she did to pull her large family through the ravaging waves of poverty. Plus, Francis Bosworth thought it was just wonderful that my Mom taught her children to have respect for others, no matter what their ethnic background. Actually, there was nothing unusual about it. It was her nature. She could relate to people as individuals, whether they were white or black. She believed there was goodness in everyone, and she planted that same seed in all of her children, with the possible exception of Frank.

To say the least, I spent a great deal of time at the Guild. I really enjoyed the sports activities and the craftmaking, but I also went to the Guild because I liked the people there. I was especially fond of Mr. Bosworth. He reminded me of Gary Cooper. Bos, as we called him, was a tall, thin man who had very gentle manners, and he always spoke very softly. Even when he was angry, he would remain quiet and calm.

I also admired Bos very much because he wasn't like my father. Bos did not have an uptight, rough, angry, spiteful personality. My father was always physically and emotionally pushing me away. By the same token, Bos, emotionally, seemed to be always pulling me towards him whenever we were together. And that was something a boy needed, closeness with an adult male. I did not have a caring father at home, so I looked for one elsewhere.

Bos was also very fond of me. Indeed, after my mother, he probably liked me the best of all the other members my family. He used to say to me, "John, you have a good inner spirit that's going to show itself as you grow older." I did not understand what he meant by that, but I liked hearing him say it.

Bos invited me to visit him in his office anytime I had the need to, and whenever I was having some problem I thought he could help me with or when I was in need of some good conversation, I would often go to see him. He would sit me down at the head of his desk and offer me a prune. He always kept a bowl of prunes on his desk. "Now John," he would say. "How are you doing?" Then the two of us would begin a relaxed conversation. I never had any trouble talking to Bos. For me, it was like talking to one of my peers.

My relationship with Bos was, in a very definite sense, an oddity. Even though my mother taught me to be respectful of everyone, my experience had taught me that I should always be on guard around white people. Moreover, my brothers told me that if you relaxed around white people, you did so at your own peril. But I never felt uneasy or the least bit threatened by any of the white people at the Friends Neighborhood Guild, least of all Francis Bosworth.

To me, Bos was not a white person. He was Bos, and his person had no race or ethnicity attached to it. At the Guild, I was becoming aware that the importance given to skin color was a farce, an issue without substance. Perhaps there was something to that Quaker philosophy after all.

My relationship with Bos and other members of the Guild staff had a tremendous tempering affect upon my attitude toward whites in general. I was to have a fifteen-year association with the Guild, and as the years passed, I developed a deep affection for Francis Bosworth and other members of the staff. But it was Bos who stood head and shoulders above the rest. He was the first white person that I cared for as a friend. He treated me with respect.

Once Bos took me downtown to celebrate my birthday. We went to this expensive restaurant on Broad Street. When I entered the restaurant, all the white people there stopped eating and stared at me. It made me feel so uncomfortable. I had never been in a restaurant before, and I did not know how to respond. Bos calmed me down. He told me not to think about the people in the room with us. "Just think that you and I are here by ourselves." It worked. I was able to relax a little and have my dinner. However, I didn't care for the restaurant food all that much because it was not as good as my mother's cooking. But it was a new experience for me.

After dinner, Bos took me to the movie of my choice. I was surprised when he agreed to let me see "The Wolfman," starring Lon Chaney, Jr. It wasn't the kind of motion picture I thought he would be interested in, but as he said, "It's your night, John. I want you to enjoy yourself." It made me feel good inside to have someone give me his complete, undivided attention, and the outing was made even nicer because Bos was the financial provider.

There were two buildings that constituted the Guild establishment. There was the activities building, and across Fourth Street, there was the residence for the staff. Bos would often take me to the staff residence, and I enjoyed going there. The staff living-quarters were so different than my own home. Indeed, the difference was amazing. To begin with, the residence was big, roomy, and clean. As much as my mother tried, she could never keep the Noble Street house as clean as the Guild residence.

The living quarters of the staff had everything my home did not have, and being there made me feel even more like a poor person. Whenever I would visit the residence, I always wanted to stay there and never return to the Noble Street house. But this was just a random thought. I would never have been able to stay away from my mother for any meaningful length of time.

I first met Bos when I was three years old. When I reached the age of nine or so, he began finding work for me to do around the Guild establishment. I would do paperwork in the offices, like running the mimeograph machines, collating the Guild community newspaper, or shelving books in the library. I would do whatever small tasks the staff could scurry up for me. I would get a few dollars for my labors, but more importantly, I was allowed to go to the residence house for meals on the days that I worked.

When I first began eating with the staff, I felt uncomfortable and self-conscious about it. I found myself very much aware of every move I made, like the way I put the food on the fork, the way I put the food into my mouth, and the way I chewed it. I was also intimidated because there were so many eating utensils on the table, short knives and long knives, short spoons and long spoons, and short forks and long forks. It all looked like a bunch of silver metal to me, and no one told me anything about which utensils to use for the various courses of the meal. I learned by watching members of the staff, like Bos, use them.

After dining with the staff for a while, I learned how to eat according to the proper and best table manners. For instance, I learned that I should not put my face near the food in my plate, and I should not scoop the food into my mouth. Good etiquette required that I should always eat a square meal. When I began doing this at home, my brothers made fun of me and said I was trying to be a white person, but that didn't stop me from eating like the Guild staff.

Because I worked at the Guild, I was accepted as a junior member of the staff and that permitted me to visit the rooms upstairs in the staff residence. I would go up to the living quarters area with a staff member to relax after lunch, and that gave me the opportunity to see the bedrooms up there. I was really taken by the orderliness of the rooms, and there was such a nice homey feeling about them.

Nevertheless, it was unreal for me to be frequenting the Guild staff's living quarters. It was truly a mirage in comparison with the normality of my life. Visits to the residence house showed me living conditions that were so much better than what I had in the Noble Street house. Consequently, the visits always lifted and dampened my spirits. It was the world of haves, but I lived in a world of have-nots. A visit to the residence house was a trip into the intimate world of white people, and no matter how intellectually pleasing it was to me, it was always an emotionally wearing experience. Bos and the rest of the staff welcomed me enthusiastically to their quarters, but I could never shake the feeling that I did not really belong there.

Being able to see the lifestyle of white people, or, to be more accurate, seeing white people up close in their private, living space was quite revealing to me. There was a time, for instance, when one of the staff members was sick. He had the flu, and he coughed and spit up mucous just like I did when I had a cold. It may seem silly that such an observation should come as a welcome surprise to me, but white people were made to seem invincible and superhuman in legend, songs, history books, and Hollywood motion pictures.

It was true that I had white neighbors, white classmates, and many whites participated in the Guild activities, but on a close, intimate level, I knew very little about white people. Until Bos, and other Guild staff members, befriended me, whites were by and large strangers to me. I knew Freddy, my next-door neighbor, but that did not count because Freddy was not your average, everyday white person. Freddy was a breed all his own. If the truth be known, I was afraid of white people.

It was interesting to know that white people became sick like black people, but a much more shocking revelation came to me on a visit to the residence house. It was a day when I had worked in Bos' office, and I had lunch with the other staff members. It had been a wonderful lunch of glazed ham and baked macaroni, and I had gorged myself. Feeling full to the brim, after the meal was over, I went upstairs to play checkers with one of the younger staff members who was waiting for me in his room. I had reached the second floor, and I was proceeding down the hallway when the bathroom door ahead of me flew open and a female staff member who I knew very well, came out. She saw me, waved and went into her bedroom, which was next to the bathroom.

When I came up to the bathroom, the door was slightly ajar and a stinking, foul smell of defecation stabbed at my nose. The odor had been left behind by the female staff member who had just left the toilet compartment. The food gurgled in my stomach, and I had an attack of nausea. It was not that the smell was so unusual. After all, I had smelled shit before, but it was the fact that there could be such a foul smell at all left in the bathroom by a white woman. Just as I had the belief that white people, in general, were superhumans, something on the order of being perfect human beings, I had an even more intense belief in particular that white women were always clean, beautiful, luscious, and smelling like a honeysuckle rose. Until that bathroom incident, I had believed that all white women symbolized sweetness and light, sugar and spice and everything nice. They were Hollywood beauties and princesses in the storybooks I read in school. There was nothing stinky about a white woman. It was tremendously eye opening to become aware of the fact that white women also took a honest, healthy shit like even the blackest person I knew.

Over the years, I came to know many of the Guild staff members very well, and I became close to a number of them. But, of all the staff members I came to know very well, besides Francis Bosworth, the one who was dearest to me was Miss Margaret Lee. She was a lady, who was born in Kentucky, and who was reputed to have been a distant relative of the Civil War General Robert E. Lee. Miss Lee was the boy's cooking class teacher. The Guild's programs and staff were opposed to sexist role-playing long before Women's Liberation.

When I first enrolled in Miss Lee's cooking class, I was instantly impressed by her. She was tall and stately, and she had brownish-gray hair that was pulled tight around her ears. There were a few wrinkles in her face that suggested she was a woman well beyond fifty years old. At the same time, she had a wholesome face and pretty brown eyes. As I got to know her, there was always a nurturing glow in those eyes, and I was aware that she had the qualities Americans associate with the cultured, genteel southern woman. She was a lady of dignity, manners, and tolerance.

At all times, Miss Lee was a proper lady, which is not to say that she was snobbish or that she looked down on the rest of the world. She did not. But she was demure, soft spoken, and she behaved in a manner that was quite above the general comportment of most people.

There was something alluring about Miss Lee's lips. From the first moment I saw her, even though I was just a very young lad, I wanted to kiss her, and I never overcame my boyhood infatuation with her. She was old enough to be my grandmother, but that did not matter to me. Even in those old print, flowered dresses that she used to wear, she still looked better than any Miss America to me.

This thing between Miss Lee and I was not just a one-way street. She was attracted to me also right from the start. Perhaps it was because she recognized that I thought of her as being much more than a cooking teacher, and in a similar way, she was to come to know me as someone who was much more than just one of her students.

However, there was one uncomfortable aspect, at the very beginning, of my relationship with her, and it was something that I had to learn to disregard. Miss Lee had a heavy Southern accent. My older brothers had always told me to avoid white people with Southern accents as though they were the plague. White Southerners generally, my brothers emphasized, did not like black people, and below the Mason-Dixon line, blacks were treated worse than dogs. To be sure, most white Southerners were rednecks, and they were born and raised to hate blacks.

It was unsettling to me when I first heard that Southern accent coming from Miss Lee because I conjured up thoughts of her in the South abusing black people, but those were only brief thoughts that melted away once she spoke directly to me. I absolutely glowed when she took my hand and asked me to do something for her. Southern accent or no Southern accent, my instincts told me that there was no malice in her heart towards black people. I reached that conclusion even in the face of what my mother had told me.

My mother was born in Beaufort, South Carolina, and she was a very fair minded person who believed in judging people individually according to their merits. Still, having been born in the South and spending her childhood there, she had stories to tell about how the crackers, the bad white folks, used to mistreat, abuse, lynch, and kill blacks deep in the heart of Dixie.

Of course, in the end my inner feelings about Miss Lee proved to be correct. As our friendship grew, I found her totally free of prejudice. And, to my joy, she recognized my feelings for her, and she nurtured them. After a short while, I was elevated to be her assistant. That meant I got to work more closely with her in the cooking class, and then Miss Lee and I began getting together for a cup of tea when the class wasn't meeting. We would sit together and talk about life.

With great anticipation, I found myself arriving for cooking class early and leaving late just so I could be alone in the company of Miss Lee. I also had a romantic crush on her, but she probably thought of our relationship like that of a grandmother to a grandson. When we were alone together, she seemed to want to share her life experiences with me. She would talk a great deal about her childhood and growing up in Kentucky. Without complaining about it, she told me that she had known suffering and discomfort in her childhood. Unlike me, however, the harbinger of her problems was not poverty, but ignorance. It was shocking to her that the people she grew up with could be so ignorant of their humanity and have racist views.

Miss Lee would never ask me about my home life, which made me very happy because talking about it would have embarrassed me. She was interested in my future, and she was forever encouraging me to do well in school and get the best education I could. "A good education will probably not help you become rich," she would say, "but it will help you understand people and the confusion in the world a little bit better."

It was valuable to me for Miss Lee to express the importance of getting an education when she did. In my neighborhood, the kids I was growing up with, including my older brothers, did not place much importance on education. All the guys I knew thought that school was just something you tolerated until you were sixteen and old enough to leave it and get a job. And there was never any talk about college. Who even knew what a college was?

Miss Lee knew about college, and she talked plenty to me about it. She told me that I should set my sights on college, and she explained the relationship between a college education and higher paying jobs. Knowing next to nothing about college, I found it a bit annoying that she would talk about it so much, but little did I know that she was sowing the seeds that would send me off on a quest that would lead me to the highest honor that academia could bestow upon a student.

Miss Lee was also a globetrotter. She loved to travel in this country and abroad. It fascinated me to hear about her travels because I dreamed of going around the world when I grew up. Traveling went along with my sense of adventure, and Miss Lee stressed the fact that if I got a good education, and as a result, a decent job, I would be able to travel around the world some day when I became an adult.

Moreover, having traveled to every corner of America, Miss Lee wanted me to know that our nation was a big, wide country that was not the same all over. The South was different than the North, and the West was different than the East. The United States was unusual, she said, because it was divided into so many regional, subcultures. She liked to say, "We all call ourselves Americans, but from one section of the country to the other, the idea of being an American means different things to different people." She had also reached the conclusion that America may be too big for its own good, that true social togetherness might never be possible because the country and culture was just too diverse.

I was to know Miss Lee for a stretch of years, and in recalling the many conversations we had in that time, I came to realize that our talks matured just as I did from a child to a teenager. For instance, the quality of our discussions became more analytical and intense. Even though I did not understand many things she talked about in the formal sense, it was clear to me that she thought it was important for everyone to have a healthy skepticism about American society and its values.

In any event, while the basis for our conversations changed over the years, one thing never changed. She always encouraged me to fulfill my dreams, to set goals and strive for them. Education, she emphasized, would help me to succeed.

Being close to individuals like Miss Lee and Mr. Bosworth made me acknowledge the fact that there were certain white people I could truly and honestly come to love. But more importantly, I came to believe that Miss Lee and Bos could actually come to love me. That last notion gave me a strange feeling. I had that same black ass that those Park Guards and other white people didn't like, but the Guild people were different and special. They never once made an issue of my blackness, except to say that black people were mistreated in American society.

The Guild people made me feel that I was just as good as they were, even though I was ass-bottom poor and lived in abject poverty. And the Guild people never tried to get me to be like them. To the contrary, they encouraged me to be myself and follow my dreams in whatever direction it would lead me. Even in the face of my dire poverty, Miss Lee and Bos told me to keep dreaming and keep aspiring.

And I did just that, I dreamed, and I dreamed, and I dreamed. I made the mistake of telling some of my friends about my dreams, and they would laugh at me. "You're a damn fool, Johnny. You think you're going to travel to Europe? Only white people go to Europe. The only Europe you'll ever see is on the faces of white people."

Let them laugh, I thought. I was going to keep right on dreaming. However, my friends did point out an incongruity in my social life. I lived with both feet solidly in the in the world of poverty and insecurity, but I had one toe in the white world of affluence and opportunity. The Miss Lees and Mr. Bosworths were good people, but America seemed to be filled with more bad people. Miss Lee and Bos thought that the good people would win out in the end. That was why they encouraged me to keep on dreaming.

Once, Miss Lee went on a vacation to Europe during the summer, and she wrote to me from the Continent. That was a thrill for me. Most of the young kids in my neighborhood had never received a letter from anyone, and for me to receive a letter from someone in Europe made me the talk of the neighborhood for weeks. My mother was so excited about it, she couldn't stop herself from bringing it up in conversations with the neighbors, and I waved my newfound notoriety in the faces of all of my peers. If I could get a letter from Europe, then that meant, in my mind, that I was likely to go to Europe someday.

When the letter arrived, it was addressed to Master John Cooper. When I first held the letter in my hand and saw that it was pink with orange and red flowers printed along the border of the back flap, I was so taken by the beauty of it I did not want to tear it open. But then I straightened my backbone and told myself that a Master was required to open such a letter. A Master accepted the responsibilities that came with the title.

To be addressed as Master made me suddenly feel three feet taller because I thought that it had to mean I was somebody special. Consequently, it followed that Miss Lee called me Master because she recognized a certain uniqueness in me, a certain ambition that spoke of my masterful, high-minded intentions, and potential. Moreover, she probably addressed me as Master because she suspected that someday, in my adulthood, I would become a Master in one way or another.

Exactly what that would be, I did not know, nor did I really care. I was just thrilled by the suggestion of respect in the title of Master.

To be sure, I went overboard with the meaning and intent of Miss Lee's letter and the title she bestowed upon me. My reaction was an indication of how hungry I was for recognition and respect from the white world around me. That seemingly insignificant, archaic way of addressing a young boy was taken by me to mean something grandiose and elitist.

The truth was Miss Lee's letter gave me the first real chance in my life to distinguish myself. I was more than a black nobody. I was definitely a somebody, black ass and all. For a short period of time, her letter pulled my mind away from the poverty face that had blurred my individuality, my human distinction, and my self-worth since the day I was born. The whole world could see that I was Master John Cooper.

CHAPTER EIGHT

Bos and Miss Lee encouraged me to succeed in school. They said a good education would offer me the best chance for a happy life in the future, and I was inspired by their support. But I was up against that controlled, school environment, and it didn't help that I could be very headstrong and excitable at times. Such behavior almost ended my educational career just as it was really getting started.

My interest in school picked up considerably After my Gruesome Newsome scare and my contest of wills with Mrs. Riley. Indeed, I settled down to be a fairly good student, and I actually went more than a term or two without any bad incidents with my teachers. Then I moved up to the next grade level, and I got a new instructor, Mrs. Lockwood. Believe me, the first time I saw that woman, I knew I was going to have some kind of trouble with her. But I could not change my teacher, so I forgot about that negative feeling she gave me. Like Mrs. Riley, I can't remember Mrs. Lockwood's first name, but in my grade school days, I don't think teachers wanted students to know their first names. They wanted to be addressed in a formal way—Mr., Miss, or Mrs.

The first few weeks of my new class with Mrs. Lockwood passed quickly and without incident. And then, one bright cheerful morning, I was sitting at my desk, along with my classmates, listening to her discuss the government's nuclear weapons testing program. I was very interested in hearing about atomic bombs because I knew that it was those bombs that had put the final crunch on Japan and ended the Second World War. Few civilian people knew very much about atomic bombs back then, and I wanted to know as much about them as I could. There was all this talk that atomic bombs would bring an end to conventional warfare as it had been known in the past. That disturbed me because I had dreams of becoming a flyer in the U.S. Army Air Force one day. If atomic bombs became the weapons of the future, there would be no need for any hotshot fighter pilots.

After talking about the testing program, Mrs. Lockwood got up from her desk and began to write a list of points on the board that she wanted the class to write in their notebooks. Of course, she had her back turned to the class as she wrote on the board. I had noticed that throughout the lesson that morning a number of my classmates were not the least bit interested in the nuclear testing program, and when Lockwood turned around to write on the board, they started playing around, cracking jokes and generally making noise. Even Juanita and Shelton Pelzer were kibitzing.

Locky turned away from the board several times to tell the students making noise to be quiet and settle down, but as soon as she would return to the board, the noise would start up again. By the way, Mrs. Lockwood was not called Locky because of her name. She was called Locky, more by the boys than the girls, because of the way she crossed and locked her legs together whenever she sat down at her desk. She would twist up her legs like a corkscrew. I think she did that to keep the boys from looking up her dress because Locky was the only teacher I had in elementary school who had the front of her desk open which exposed her legs to the class. I wonder if she wasn't getting her kicks when she thought about the male students trying to get a peek up her dress.

Locky was a pretty woman if you liked them on the lanky side. She had blondish hair and somewhat of a nice face. She had small lips, and she liked to pucker them. When she did it, it made her look cuter than she actually was.

A sort of cute person she may have been, but she did not have good control over her temper. And when she exhibited bad temper, she became ugly. She could squint through one eye and curl up her bottom lip to such a degree that it made her look like Popeye. When that look came on her face, she was ready to take off after a student. It didn't take much to get her upset, and the fourth time she turned around to face the noisy students behind her she was steaming. In fact, her face had began to flush red.

Clearly, there had been a number of students making noise. Every child in class knew it, and Locky had to be aware of it, too. She spun around at the blackboard, and then she came dashing down the aisle right up to my desk.

"Didn't you hear me say to stop making noise?"

"What, Mrs. Lockwood?" I was taken back. "Me? I wasn't making any noise."

"Oh sure, that's what the culprit always says when he is caught. Now you get up to the front of the room where I can keep an eye on you."

"Me, to the front of the room?"

"Yes, you heard what I said. Get up to the front of the room, and I mean right now."

"Why do I have to go to the front of the room? I ain't done nothin'."

"Just get up and go. Now!" Her face was distorted into a frightening sneer.

My classmates were not making noise now. They were sitting as quiet as church mice. They did not seem to mind that I was taking their heat. My friends had gotten me in this pickle, but they wouldn't help me out. Even my lovely Juanita remained quiet, and she definitely knew I had not been making any noise.

"Go, I said," Locky shouted at me.

I gave her an unpleasant look. I didn't like her shouting at me, and I did not care for the silence of my peers. But, I got up from my seat, and Locky stepped back to let me go in front of her. I began to walk slowly to the front of the classroom. My slow movements were meant to annoy her.

"Go on, John. Move along." She poked me in the back with her finger. "I don't have all day with this." Locky did have a short fuse which caused her to get loud with students when they upset her, but I had never seen her poke, or otherwise use her hands when chastising a student until this instance with me.

When she poked me, I heard some students hissing under their breath. I thought the sound came from the corner of the room where my walking buddies sat, and I knew what the hissing meant. They were trying to tell me that the teacher was getting the better of me. That would never do. My buddies and I had reached the age where we felt compelled to defend and protect our masculinity against any and all challengers, especially if they were female. My buddies were saying that I'd better stand up to this teacher and not punk out or they would laugh me right out of the schoolyard, if not the entire neighborhood. Also, my brothers wouldn't like it if they heard I had let some teacher push me around. You had to set limits on what teachers could do to you.

I did not need my buddies' hissing signal. I was angry anyway because Locky had accused me of something I had not done.

"Go on, John. Move." She poked me in the back again.

That really upset me. "Keep your hands off of me," I growled at her over my shoulder. I stopped walking altogether.

"What did you say?"

"I said keep your hands off of me."

"Don't you tell me what to do, you insolent little brat. You're not talking to one of your little friends. You're talking to your teacher. Now move along this instant."

With that, she took hold of the back of my neck with a strong grip from her right hand, and that was not the worst of it. Locky had long fingernails, and they cut into the nape of my neck like sharp needles when she grabbed me. With that hold on me, she pulled me the rest of the way to the front of the room.

I screamed as I spun around and pulled myself away from her grasp, and as I did so, I caught sight of my walking buddies. The usually calm, mannerly Otis McAlily looked like he had fire in his eyes and he was transmitting that fire to me. He seemed to be saying that Locky's actions had chopped me down to kindergarten size and that called for an immediate response. Shelton Pelzer was biting his bottom lip because he seemed to be so upset with the way Locky had treated me, and his face cried out for retaliation for the sake of boys everywhere. Henry Washington actually stood up at his seat, and he started to raise a fist into the air. But he quickly lowered it again and sat down. It was a good thing that Locky had not seen what he had done. Threatening a teacher with bodily harm was an absolute no-no. It could get a student sent to a reformatory school, which was another name for a prison for kids.

Locky had now moved around me, and she was standing in front of her desk. "John, you just stand there because I want the entire class to know that you are a troublemaker, and to think you had the nerve to talk back to me. "Why young man, I'll have you…"

I turned quickly around to face her, and without realizing what I was doing, I took a quick step forward and buried a smashing right hand into her midsection. I felt her stomach give with the punch like something inside of her had gotten pushed around.

Gasps and moans of disbelief sprang from my classmates lips, and even my walking buddies turned their eyes away from me, not wanting to believe what they had just seen. That was not the kind of response that had been in their minds. I had gone too far. I had gone overboard, struck a teacher, and now I would have hell to pay.

When I withdrew my fist from Locky's gut, her knees went splat as she hit the floor, and she doubled over holding her stomach in pain. As I looked down at her, I could not believe what I had just done, but there she was, crumbled up like a rag at my feet. I had punched a teacher, and the likely consequences of my actions were just beginning to run through my mind. None of the possibilities made me feel good. In fact, I was quickly becoming sick to my stomach. There was no way I could justify punching Locky. Even my mother would probably not back me up on this one, and there seemed to be little doubt that I would be on my way to Madison, Boone, or the reformatory school, after Mr. Ross had his way with me.

My classmates were so shocked at what I had done, none of them even moved to help Locky back to her feet. I was in shock too, and I could only stand there with my mouth open. Locky was whimpering, and trying her best to keep herself from breaking out into a full-fledged cry in front of the class. But even so, she looked as though she was in tremendous pain, and I was beginning to think that she might die. If that happened, I would be charged with murder, and sent to the electric chair just like James Cagney in the movies. That thought made me lose it. I started trembling, sniffling and crying all at the same time, but I still could not bring myself to help her.

Minutes had passed, and I heard a girl crying in the first row behind me. Maybe she thought that Locky was dying, too. But then, Locky, holding her stomach, struggled to her feet. She gripped the corner of her desk for support as she glared at me.

"Get out." She waved her arm towards the door. "Get out and go down to the principal's office this minute." She barely finished ordering me out of the room before she broke down in tears.

I couldn't move fast because my legs felt like they didn't belong to me, but I wanted to get out of that room quickly. Looking at Locky was making my head swirl from guilt and shame, and I was certain that my classmates condemned me for what I had done. How would I ever be able to face Juanita again? She was probably afraid of me now because she couldn't be certain that I wouldn't hit her in the belly someday.

Somehow, I got out of that classroom without using my legs. I was in such a daze, for all I knew I might have floated out of the room. But once I was in the hallway and the classroom door was closed, I started crying uncontrollably, and I began to walk towards the stairs that led to the principal's office. I didn't want to go, and I was scared out of my mind because I could not remember the events clearly that led up to my punching Locky. The punch I remembered, but what happened to the atomic bombs she was talking about?

My mind was straining. I wanted to blank out the immediate past, and then my head started filling up with thoughts about Mr. Ross and that strap he was supposed to have in his office. If there ever was a time for him to use it, that time was now. I didn't want to get beaten. I wanted to go home and see my mother.

I was now on the first floor standing in front of the principal's office. I hesitated, but I knew I had to go in because if I did not, I would be suspended. I swallowed hard, shook my head to clear it, and entered the room. Once inside, I stepped up to a counter that split the room. The counter had a gate in it that would allow a person to get to an inner door behind it. I said to the school secretary that Mrs. Lockwood had sent me down to the office, but I said nothing more. The secretary directed me to have a seat on a long bench near the door. I crumbled myself in the corner of the bench and just pinned my eyes on the door beyond the counter. Written on the door was the title "The Principal." Mr. Ross was probably in there.

About ten minutes later, Hal Brophy, a fat white kid from my class, came into the office with a note from Locky for Mr. Ross. I could not look at Hal Brophy's face because I knew it would remind me of the awful thing that happened upstairs. Once he was gone, I watched the secretary rap lightly on the principal's door and then she entered the office. She came back out very quickly and sat at her desk behind the counter.

Before Hal Brophy had shown up in the principal's office, I had begun to calm down a little, but after the school secretary had delivered that note to the principal telling him about my terrible deed, I began shivering like I was cold. At the same time, I was sweating profusely. I did not want to face the man behind that door, but I knew I was going to.

Only a few minutes passed after the secretary returned before the principal's door open suddenly. Mr. Ross stood in his doorway and peered at me for a second or two, and then he shouted. "You, Cooper boy, get in here."

I got up from the bench and tried to gain some composure. I wiped the sweat from my forehead, and I held my breath to control the shivering. Nevertheless, as I walked through the gate in the counter to Mr. Ross' office, my legs were shaking so I wobbled when I walked. I was so scared the only thing I could think about was going to the Boy's Room to pee. Why was I so frightened of him? It was not because of his size. He was a small man, with a prominent baldhead. He could not have been more than five feet-three or four, and he was slight of build. But the truth of the matter was, the students were not afraid of him as a private person. We were afraid of him because he was the principal, the ultimate power in the school.

That ultimate power had ordered me to his office, and as I reached his door, Mr. Ross reached out and caught me at the back of the head. He roughly jerked me into his office. "Now get in here." He almost threw me to the floor. He closed the door as I tried to regain my balance. "Get over there." He pushed me towards a seat in front of his desk. I sat down, and he went around to the other side of the desk. He stood there a while before he spoke. "So you punched a teacher, you little hoodlum. You punched a teacher."

"I...I didn't mean it." My voice cracked as I spoke.

"I'll bet." He walked around to the front of the desk and came over to me, "You didn't mean it." He took a swipe at my head with his right hand, but I ducked and his hand just brush lightly through my hair. He stepped back. "Whether you meant it or not, I'm going to teach you a lesson you won't forget." He returned to the other side of his desk and he bent over to get something out of a lower draw on his right. When he stood up again, he had a thick leather strap in his hand.

It was true. He did have a strap to beat pupils with. But no, he wasn't going to hit me with that.

With his right hand, Mr. Ross began pounding the strap in his left hand as he came around the desk. "I'm going to light up your bottom boy. I'm going to give you the punishment you've probably needed for a long time."

He was closing in on me fast, and that leather strap looked so big. It would surely hurt me bad.

"I'm going to light up your behind, Cooper boy."

As Mr. Ross spoke to me, I had sat in front of his desk in a scared, frozen state. I was in his office, and I felt under his control. But when he advanced towards me, smacking the strap in the palm of his left hand, I began feeling like I was being pushed in a corner. And as the Cooper brothers always said, "When you're trapped in a corner, that is the time to go on the offensive and commit yourself to some action."

And just like that, my impulsiveness took over. I looked into Mr. Ross' face. "You're not going to beat me with that strap." I jumped up from the chair and ran to the door.

"Come back here. Come back here!" Mr. Ross shouted. Come back here and take your punishment like a man. Do you hear? And don't you leave this office. Don't you…"

But I was already out of his office door and on my way through the little gate in the counter. I ran into the hallway and stopped. I didn't know where I was going. I just wanted to get away from that strap. But then, I heard Mr. Ross coming up behind me and that made me take off.

Paxson School, like almost all urban, public schools I've been in, had those very long hallways that ran from the front to the rear of the building, and there were classrooms on both sides of the hallways. As I ran down the corridor on the first floor, I passed classrooms filled with students, but I felt as though I was no longer one of them. I was an outcast, and I had to escape the premises.

Mr. Ross was coming down hallway behind me, shouting for me to stop, but of course I did not. I knew he would not be able to catch me, but I made a mistake. I looked over my shoulder to see how much distance was between him and me. He was three classrooms behind me, and I was going to get away. But as I turned my head to the front again, someone opened a classroom door right in front of me. The doors to the classrooms opened out into the hallway, and I was running too fast to stop. I crashed headlong into the door, bouncing off of it and landing on my side in the center of the hallway floor. It was a nosey teacher who had opened her classroom door to see why Mr. Ross was shouting. Fortunately, I was not hurt in the collision with the door.

But before I could get up off the floor, Mr. Ross was upon me, and he took hold of me with his left hand. As soon as he had me in his grip, he started beating me with the strap in his right hand. "Try to get away, did you? Well, I got you now, and I am going to really teach you a lesson."

The strap banged on my shoulders and back, and I was surprised that it really did not hurt all that much. My mother could do a better job than Mr. Ross, and my father, if he used a strap on me, could light my body up like it was on fire. Mr. Ross' whopping was nothing like my parents, but I shouted and screamed anyway to make him think he was hurting me. I also made a lot of noise because I wanted to attract attention. I wanted the students in those classrooms to hear me and see for themselves. Mr. Ross did have a strap that he beat pupils with.

Well, to my satisfaction, I certainly did attract a lot of attention. Within seconds, every classroom door on the floor had been opened and teachers and students peered out of those doors at the scene of Mr. Ross beating me. To be sure that everyone took note of how brutal he was being to me, I fell to the hallway floor, writhing and screaming in the most hurtful voice I could muster. I was almost as good an actor as my mother.

Mr. Ross, for a time, was so caught up in delivering his punishment to me, he was not aware that he was being observed by staff and students alike. But then, suddenly, a teacher shouted down the hallway, "Mr. Ross. Mr Ross!" Do you know what you're doing?"

He had the strap held in the air above his head, and he was about to hit me again. The teacher's voice stopped him. He lowered his hand with the strap in it, and he looked up and down the hallway. He saw that all the classroom doors were opened, and teachers and students were staring at him.

He growled as he stood straight up, and he pulled me to my feet. He jammed the strap quickly into his pocket. "You're coming back to my office. I'm not finished with you yet." He looked up and down the hallway again. "Teachers, get your students back to their studies."

Then teachers up and down the hallway could be heard telling their students to return to their seats, and the classroom doors were closed.

He and I were now the only persons in the hallway. Mr. Ross had a hold of me at the back of my shirt collar. "You come with me." He began pulling me down the corridor toward his office, and he kept talking to me as he did. "You had the nerve to punch a teacher, and you punched her in the stomach. Did you know, you little hoodlum, that Mrs. Lockwood is going to have a baby? Did you know that?" He pulled me into the principal's office and slammed me up against the counter. He put his hand on the gate in the counter, and he was about to pull me with him through it. But the secretary stopped him.

"Mr. Ross, you have a telephone call from the Board of Education. It's important."

He stopped opening the gate, looked at the secretary, and then he pursed his lips tightly as he looked down at me. He growled under his breath, and I could see in his eyes that he wanted to haul me in his office and continue my ass-whopping. But, he pulled his head up a little. "You, boy, stay right here." He pushed me up against the counter. "Don't you move until I get back. Mrs. Mott, you watch this guy, and if he runs out again, call the police." He then went into his office and closed the door.

I stood there against the counter absolutely stunned and numb to the bone. I would not have been able to run if I wanted to, and I did not feel that way because of Mr. Ross. I felt that way because of what he said about Locky. He said she was having a baby, and I had hit her in the stomach where the baby was. I thought I felt something give way inside of Locky when my fist landed into her midsection. That was probably the baby's head, and it felt like I crushed it. I was a baby killer, one of the lowest of the low, a disgusting, and defeated human being. I thought about crying, but I was too numb to do anything but stand there like I was comatose.

When Mr. Ross came out of his office, he did not look at me. His mind was obviously on something else now, but when he caught sight of me, his memory returned.

"You, you little Cooper bum, you're suspended this very minute. Go home, and I want your mother here tomorrow morning. And if she is not here, I'm coming to your house to see her. Is that understood? Do you understand me?"

I could not talk, so I just nodded.

"All right, get out of here. Get out of my sight."

I left the office as ordered, and when I reached the hallway, tears ripped through my eyes. I had to run, run from the place where I had committed murder, and I ran down the hallway and out the street door. As the school door closed behind me, a hot, sweaty feeling came over me again, and I had to struggle to keep myself from emotionally coming apart. What a mess. What a vile person I was, and how could I ever tell my mother that I had crushed in a baby's head. When she found out, she was going to kill me.

I stumbled through the schoolyard and down Noble Street in the direction of my house. As I walked slowly along, not wanting to go home, I looked around at the factory buildings, the private homes, and the cobble stoned street, and I was thinking all that would not be my neighborhood for much longer. Being suspended from school was just the first step on the road to the death house. The cops would surely come and get me. They would certainly beat me, probably right in front of my mother, because I had punched a white woman and murdered her baby.

I pleaded for someone, anyone to help me. I could not face my mother. I could not, but I knew I would have to.

At that moment, I had reached Fourth Street, and I hesitated on the corner because once I crossed the street I would have only one block to go before I reached home. Then I heard a familiar voice cut right into my thoughts.

"Whatta ya doin' outta school?"

I looked to my left, and there was my father coming out of one of the neighborhood bars.

"I said whatta ya doin' outta school?"

I stammered. What could I tell him? The truth? No way. He wouldn't understand.

Actually, his question caught me by surprise. My father had never shown any interest in whether his children went to school or not, and now he was acting like a concerned parent. I didn't know what to make of it.

My father never finished grade school. To him, school was for smartass niggers who wanted to kiss the white man's behind. He believed that American society was set up to serve white people. Public school education was just another way white people controlled black folk. I would not have been surprised if he thought that by staying drunk he was preventing white society from controlling him.

He walked up to me and took hold of my shoulder. "I said why are ya outta school?" There was a familiar smell of whiskey on his breath, and it stunk. I recoiled from him because of that smell and because I thought he was going to hit me right there in street. I didn't want that to happen, and without thinking the words burst out of my mouth.

"I…I was beaten."

"Beaten."

"Yeah."

"By who?"

"Huh?"

"By who, I asked you."

"Mr. Ross."

"Who'n the hell is Mr. Ross?"

"The principal."

"The princybal. You mean the boss teacher? He beat ya?"

"Uh—huh."

"Well, whatda hell's goin' on here? He ain't got no right hitting you, boy. Your ma son, not his, the bastard. And is this a white man?"

"Uh—huh."

"Well, I ain't gonna have 'em beaten ma son." He took me by the hand. "Come on, boy, we're gonna go right to dat school and see this white man."

Off he went, pulling me behind him, back up Noble Street toward Paxson School. He staggered as he pulled me along because he was drunk and angry. He usually became violent and nasty when he was like that, and I did not want to think what he might do at school.

At the same time, I wanted him to go to my school. I wanted to see him confront Mr. Ross and stand up for me. It would certainly be a new turn for him if he did, and it would make me feel that I did have a father that cared something for me. But then, he was walking so fast and pulling me so hard, I was almost falling down trying to keep up with him. I wondered if he even knew he was holding my hand.

We reached the school, and he told me to take him to the principal's office. I did, and once we were in the office he released my hand and stepped up to the counter. "Can I help you?" Mrs. Mott said. And she gave me a curious look.

"Yeah, lady. This is ma boy, and I wanna see the princybal, Mr. Ross."

"Just a minute and I'll get him." She left the counter and knocked at the principal's inner office door.

My father leaned against the counter and watched Mrs. Mott go into Mr. Ross's office. She left the door open, and I could see Mr. Ross respond to her telling him that my father and I were in the outer office. He stood up at his desk and followed the secretary to the outer office.

My father waited until Mr. Ross was just opposite him on the other side of the counter. "You, Mr. Ross, whatta I hear 'bout you beaten my boy? Is that true, you little bastard?" He pointed his finger right into the principal's eyes.

Mr. Ross jumped back from the counter as fear suddenly smeared across his face. "Now just a minute, Mr. Cooper. You don't understand."

"Did ya beat my son, I asked you?" My father leaned over the counter towards Mr. Ross.

"Mr. Cooper," Mr. Ross was retreating backwards from the counter towards his office. "You don't…"

"Don't give me that shit. I can tell that you beat 'em, and now I'm gonna whop ya ass."

Mr. Ross spun on his heels and raced into his office. He slammed his door closed, and I could hear him locking it from the inside. Quickly, my father moved down the counter and started to go through the little gate, but Mrs. Mott shouted at him.

"Mr. Cooper. Mr. Cooper. Stop this! Stop it right now or I'm going to call the police."

He paused at the gate. "I don't givadamn about the police. That bastard beat ma son, and I'm gonna kick his ass." He started through the gate, and Mrs. Mott reached for the phone.

I was still standing near the door, transfixed. My father was really going after Mr. Ross. He was standing up for me, but it was still scary to see him like that because once he was turned on to violence, it was normally difficult to turn him off. I stood there, oscillating between a feeling of a new found respect for my father and fear that he would do something outrageously violent. But then I heard someone behind me. I turned around and there was Locky Lockwood. It made me feel good to see her standing there. She looked well, and maybe that meant the baby was also alive.

She looked at my father. "Mrs. Mott, John, what's going on here?"

Mrs. Mott put down the phone, and she came over to the counter to give Locky an answer. But my father shouted at her before Mrs. Mott could explain.

"Who'da hell are you? You gonna try and stop me from beaten up on that little bastard in there?" He stepped back through the counter gate and started towards Locky with a meanacingly look on his face.

"No Daddy! NO! She's my teacher." Spinning like a top, I turned about and threw my arms around her waist, and I squeezed myself close to her body. There was a baby in there. "Leave her alone, Daddy! Please leave her alone. She's my teacher."

My father stopped in his tracks. He looked at me wearily and with disgust. "You care 'bout these white peoples? Don't ya know they don't care 'bout you?"

"Leave her alone, Daddy. Leave her alone." I started to cry as Locky put her arms around me and pressed my face into her bosom. She had such nice perfume on, and it smelled so good.

"Ya crazy boy, crazy," he said to me. "Ya gonna let these white peoples walk all over you when ya grow up? Go on and kiss their ass, just like your goddamn moma." Then shaking his head with disgust, he left the principal's office.

I could not see Locky's face because her arms kept me tucked to her bosom. I assumed that she was confused about what had been going on in the principal's office, and I also thought she probably felt relieved now that my father was gone. After a moment or two, she pulled me from her sweet smelling body and held me at arms length. "Are you all right, John? Yes, you seem to be all right. And that was your father, huh? Well, stop your crying. Everything is going to be all right." She took me over to the bench and sat me down. Mrs. Mott tried to speak to her, but she waved the secretary off. She went through the gate and over to Mr. Ross' office door. She knocked at the door. "Mr. Ross, Mr. Ross. It is Mrs. Lockwood. I would like to speak to you."

Mr. Ross' voice came back through the door. "Is he gone? Is he gone?"

"Yes, John's father is gone."

Mr. Ross opened his door a little and peered out through the crack.

"He is gone, Mr. Ross, and I want to talk to you."

He opened the door wider, and Locky went into his office. He closed the door behind her.

I sat on the bench drying the tears from my eyes with my shirt sleeve until Mrs. Mott came over and gave me a tissue. She wasn't such a bad person after all. I had always thought she had to be a mean person because she worked for Mr. Ross, but she was even smiling a little at me.

I could hear Locky and Mr. Ross talking in his office. I could not make out exactly what they were saying, but I could tell that they were talking about some subject very excitedly. She was in his office for quite awhile, and all I could do was sit on that bench and fidget. What did Locky mean by saying, "Everything was going to be all right?" What did she mean?

When Locky came out of Mr. Ross' office, she said, "Please, sir, let it end here. I'm responsible for all this, and John is not to be blamed. His classmates told me he had not been making any noise. I accused him wrongly."

"All right, but are you sure about your health?" Mr. Ross said begrudgingly.

"I'm fine. The boy did not hurt me in any serious way. It was the surprise and the shock of his actions that stunned me for a time. I just want to forget the whole thing, and I would appreciate it if you would do the same."

Mr. Ross had followed Locky out of his office, and he stood near the door. He looked around the outer office, probably to make sure that my father wasn't there. "Mrs. Lockwood, if you really want to forget it, then I'll drop the whole matter."

"Thank you, Mr. Ross." Locky gave him a nod, walked through the gate and came over to me. "Come on, John." She put her arms around me as I stood up. "Let's go back to class. All is forgiven and forgotten."

As we were passing out the door of the principal's office, Mr. Ross stopped us. "Just a minute." He came over to the counter to take an angry look at me. "Don't you ever do anything bad like that again as long as you're in this school. Because if you do, you will be punished very severely for it. Do you understand me?"

I looked back at him, and I put on the most sheepish, repentant face I could muster. "Yes, Mr. Ross. I understand."

"Good." He smirked. "And be thankful that you have a wonderful, forgiving teacher like Mrs. Lockwood," he said, as he turned and walked away.

The crisis was finally over, and I knew I never wanted to go through anything like that again. The future I wanted required me to get a good education. That incident with Locky was a wake up call. I got away with near-murder, but I had to convince myself that such a stroke of luck happens only once in a lifetime.

And as things turned out, Locky Lockwood was truly a forgiving person. She and I became good friends, a friendship that went beyond the teacher-student relationship. It was a friendship that was a little like the one I had with Miss Lee. I felt I had to like her because I just missed hurting her baby, and I think she felt she had to like me because I caused her to become physical with a student. She and I began getting along so well after our run-in, my walking buddies called me teacher's pet, but I didn't care. I was not going to get myself into any more trouble in school, if I could help it.

When my father came to school that day, it was the only time he ever did anything to help me, and to be sure it was somewhat misguided on his part. If he had gotten to Mr. Ross and beaten him, the incident with Locky would have been a complete educational and criminal catastrophe. Both my father and I would probably have gone to one type of prison or another. At the same time, Mr. Ross' decision to accept Locky's request to excuse me from my bad deed, was likely to have been influenced by the threats my father made.

My father never spoke to me of his visit to my school on that eventful day, and he never told my mother about it, either. Eventually, I told her about it some weeks later. At first, she thought I was joking, but after I convinced her that I was telling the truth she just shook her head and said how lucky I was that the situation turned out so well. She gave me hell for hitting the teacher, but she did not beat me. I don't know if she discussed the Locky affair with my father. My guess is she probably did not. In any case, a few months after the incident, my mother and father separated permanently. I was never to live with him again, nor was I to even see him for many, many years.

CHAPTER NINE

Along with Miss Lee, the Guild and its staff opened up a whole new world for me. Through the Guild, I had some unique experiences. Given my poverty background, I could never have had them on my own. For example, there were times when the rich people of Philadelphia, the white people who lived in the Mainline section of the city, millionaires row as it was sometimes called, would invite some of the poor children from the inner city out to their fancy, extremely well-kept, mansion-sized homes for a weekend party. Children from the Guild would often be included in those weekend affairs, and the Guild staff was sure to take only the best-behaved youngsters to the Mainline.

I must have gone to those Mainline parties six or seven times over the years, and I was always absolutely dumbfounded by the experience. In just about one hour, the Guild's station wagon could take me from a world of poverty to a world of ultimate affluence. I would be taken from the dirty, back streets of a socially stricken neighborhood to communities of large white homes with sparkling glass windows, where all the houses were set well back from the roads amidst acres and acres of green grass, trees, and sights of conspicuous wealth like tennis courts and swimming pools.

When I saw those white houses, on my very first trip to the Mainline, I immediately imagined them to be clouds, and I thought the Guild station wagon had somehow taken me up into the sky. There were no houses like them in the Philadelphia that I knew. Even the houses along Frankford Avenue did not come close by comparison.

With my imagination, they were not just mansions out on the Mainline; they were palaces. Of course, the only palaces I had ever seen were in the movies, and these Mainline mansions seemed to be like them. And as I was to come to understand it, the people who lived in those palaces were not just rich, they were Philadelphia's nobility. For me, nothing spoke of our society's inequality more than when I went to a weekend party on the Mainline. While I enjoyed the experience, I was always shocked by it. It was very difficult for me to accept the fact that some people should live in such spacious surroundings and luxurious residences, while others like myself should live in rundown, dilapidated hovels. It took only one visit to the Mainline for me to realize that whatever life was, it was not fair.

The picnic parties were held on the lawns and around the swimming pools of those big white houses. The activities were kept decidedly on the outside of the mansions; but, nevertheless, I did get the opportunity to visit the inside of some of those great palaces. Upon entering them, I was struck by the beautiful tile or hardwood floors that sparkled with cleanliness, and there was usually the smell of flowers in the air. And the ceilings were so high; it was like looking up to the top of the sky where the sun lived. Such a view seemed to confirm the fact that I was visiting clouds in heaven. And then there were the sitting rooms and dining rooms, with all manner of furniture—divans and couches of all sizes, long mahogany dinner tables, covered with beautifully patterned table cloths, and many different kinds of chairs, bookcases, and electric lamps.

It was the lamps that caught my attention the most, along with the ceiling lights. Many of those electric lights were on, even though the picnics were always held during the daylight hours. That was an indication to me of just how rich the Mainline people were. In the Noble Street house, we would never put on the kerosene lamps until it was quite dark. We did not have money to burn like those people, and how nice I thought it must be, to flick a switch on the wall and have electric light everywhere. It certainly beat carrying kerosene lamps.

All the mansions I went into had loads of household appliances. I looked at all those things, and I wished my mother could have them. It would make her life a hell of a lot easier. But then, I had to remind myself that I was only visiting heaven. Under no circumstances would I be allowed to stay there. If God were white, then I was sure that no black asses would be allowed to pass through the pearly gates. Did that also mean that my mother could never have any of those wonderful household appliances? And yeah, I know, life was not fair.

Another thing that impressed me very much about those Mainline palaces was their bathrooms. They were so clean and shiny, I became inhibited, and I could not pee or defecate in them. The bathrooms were also very large, and they had both a shower and bathtub. I thought it was strange to have both a shower and bathtub in the same bathroom. Couldn't rich people make up their minds as to whether they liked taking showers or baths? And the toilet bowls were clean enough to eat off of them. The porcelain was so white, it made me think of newly fallen snow, and I thought it was quite funny to imagine the rich people of the Mainline sitting on large snow toilets.

Parked in the driveways of the Mainline palaces were automobiles, limousines and little sports cars. That was impressive, but what truly startled me was that one of the Mainline families I visited had their own horse stable, and I was completely floored when the young girl of the house told me that she had her own horse. She even offered to let me ride the animal, but I declined because I did not know how to ride a horse at that time. When I got back to Noble Street, I told all my friends, "Just think about that. Havin' ya own horse to ride anytime you chose to. Dammit! White people sure got it made."

Whenever I went out to the Mainline, it was always like entering a dream world. I found I could stare at myself going through the motions of being a guest among Philadelphia's elite just the way I stared at the motion picture screen when I went to the movies. It was I who ate the meals, played ping-pong, and swam in the swimming pools, but at the same time, it was not the real me doing those things. They were activities that I was having in a movie-dream. The real me lived in a poor neighborhood where no such affluent lifestyle existed. But, more sadly, why were all these movie-dream houses I visited only owned by white people? Did any blacks own such houses?

And of course, it was always a let down for me to leave my dream world and return to Noble Street. But then, I would always tell myself that no one could live in a dream. Dreams had time but no space. In the end, I would ask myself why had I ever gone out to the Mainline in the first place.

During the Christmas holidays, the Guild would always find parties to take the neighborhood kids to. Children would be taken to parties at the department stores downtown on Market Street, to Gimbel Brothers one year, Lit Brothers another, and Snellenbergs yet another year. Our host would dish out the ice cream, cake, candy, and cheap gifts, and there was always a white Santa Claus "Ho, Ho Hoing" all over the place. I liked the parties well enough, but I hated the Santa Claus. Almost all of the poor kids at the parties were black, but the Santa Claus, as fake as he was, was always white. What difference it might have made to our young impressionable minds if just one of those Santa Clauses were black, I'll never know.

I also remembered a time near the end of the Second World War when some of the neighborhood kids were taken to the Philadelphia Naval Yard to have Christmas dinner with the sailors. The great thrill of that event was the fact that I had dinner on an aircraft carrier that had fighter airplanes aboard. The warplanes were Hellcats and Avengers. After the dinner party and the gift giving was done with, the children were allowed to go up to the flight deck and sit in the fighter planes. I sat in a Hellcat, and I was zonked out of my mind with excitement. Those were the kind of airplanes I saw in the Movietone newsreels at the motion picture theater. The pilots stood on the wings of the planes while we sat in them, and they explained how a flyer used the stick and rudder pedals. I felt like an ace in that cockpit.

When we were riding home in the bus from the Naval Yard, my mind was up in the clouds again. I thought of how wonderful it would be to fly an airplane, to be a fighter pilot. I wished that I had been a naval pilot in the Second World War, fighting the Japanese in the air above the South Pacific Ocean. During the war, I wanted to be an Army Air Force pilot. But, whether it was the Army or Navy, it did not matter to me. I just wanted to fly, and my experience on that aircraft carrier told me that flying had to be in my future.

I could always recall the odor of that ship, and for many years I believed that I would have a professional military career. I remember how comfortable I felt aboard that aircraft carrier, and I remember the sound of my feet on the gangplank when I went on and off the vessel. The most exciting thing of all was when I sat in the cockpit of the Hellcat. The joy rippled through my body as I imagined myself flying with John Wayne in "The Flying Tigers" movie. I sat in a real airplane. God bless America and all the ships at sea.

As always in the midst of that joy, there was something bothering me. All of the pilots I saw were white. I saw no black pilots, no black officers, and only black mess men and cooks. Thereafter, even though I kept my dream of becoming a flyer alive, I was bothered by the question of whether a black person such as me could become a pilot in the Army Air Corps or in the Navy. I guessed that I might possibly have been able to become a pilot in the Army but never in the Navy. The problem, as always, was my black ass. It always seemed to upset white people. I wouldn't find out until years later, after I had given up on my flying dream, that my guess about my chances of becoming a military pilot was right on the money. Of course, I could have asked Miss Lee or Mr. Bosworth about it, but I never did.

Of all the activities that I became involved in under the auspices of the Friends Neighborhood Guild, the most memorable experience had to be my meeting with Mrs. Eleanor Roosevelt. It was a brief meeting, but it left a most indelible impression on my consciousness. She was one of the most noted, admired, and respected persons of the twentieth century, all around the world. She gave to me, in one handshake, the realization that no matter how high a person might go up the social ladder, he or she is still nothing more than common human flesh and blood. It is not the title that makes the person, "Master John," but it is the person who gives meaning to the title.

Francis Bosworth liked me a great deal, and that is why I came to meet Mrs. Roosevelt. The encounter between she and I happened in March of 1950. It was on the occasion of the celebration of the Guild's 70th year as a neighborhood community center. An anniversary banquet was planned and Mrs. Roosevelt was to be the main guest speaker. The gala function was to take place in a large hotel ballroom downtown on Broad Street, and many politicians and social dignitaries were also invited.

Bos, who was then Director of all Guild programs, decided that it would be appropriate to have two boys from our neighborhood escort Mrs. Roosevelt through the ballroom to the speaker's table. One young lad would be white and the other black. I was chosen to be the black escort. Moreover, parents from the Noble Street area were also invited, and my mother received an invitation.

I was working at the Guild one afternoon when Bos came over to me with the news. He had just come out of his office, and he was smiling broadly. Two other staff members accompanied him.

"How are you doing, John?" he said. He stopped next to the mimeograph machine I was operating.

"Okay, Mr. Bosworth. Okay."

"Good," he said, with a twinkle in his eye. He leaned back, shifting most of his weight to one leg, and a closed mouth smile spread across his face. "Now John, you know we're going to have a big anniversary banquet next month, and I wanted to ask you if you would like to go."

"Yeah, I guess so," I said nonchalantly. I wasn't crazy about going out to dinner. I recalled that restaurant experience a few years back.

"Good," Bos said to me. "And John, Mrs. Roosevelt will be our principal guest speaker."

"Mrs. Roosevelt?"

"Yes, the former First Lady, President Roosevelt's wife."

"Oh yeah, FDR." I remembered I had heard the teacher in school call President Roosevelt that.

"That's right, FDR, and his wife will speak at the banquet, and you know what? We want you to escort her through the ballroom to the speaker's table. That means you will get the chance to meet one of the world's great ladies."

"Me?"

"Yes, you, and that means you are a very lucky fellow." He shook my hand before returning to his office.

Throughout that entire afternoon, staff members going in and out of Bos' office stopped to congratulate me for being chosen as an escort for Mrs. Roosevelt at the banquet. They were all more excited about it than I was. At nearly fourteen years old, I knew it was somewhat of an honor for me to meet and escort the wife of Franklin Roosevelt, but what I did not understand was the fuss everyone was making about her being a great lady. One staff person tried to explain to me why everyone was so excited about Mrs. Roosevelt coming to the banquet. I was told that she was a great humanitarian, who almost single handedly pulled all the countries of the world, including America's biggest political adversary, Russia, together to form the United Nations. She had a reputation of standing up for human rights.

Another staff member told me about the time that Mrs. Roosevelt defended Marian Anderson against the bigoted Daughters of the American Revolution. She demonstrated that she was for equal rights for all Americans and all the people in the world. She fought for Marian Anderson because she cared about black people. She was not just a white lady. She was a human lady who cared about the plight of fellow human beings.

By the end of the day, my feelings had been whipped into an emotional frenzy. I was not going to meet just another titled lady. I was about to meet a saint, a woman who was helping to transform the world and bring all people closer together through the United Nations. After listening to the various staff members extol the virtures of Mrs. Roosevelt, I realized that I had been blessed. If Mrs. Roosevelt was helping to change the world, then I thought for sure she could help change my social circumstances. Perhaps she could help change my perpetual state of poverty. Perhaps she could relieve me of my feelings of anxiety when I was around most non-Guild white people. Perhaps she could even relieve me of my blackness. The Guild staff members spoke of her as though she was a miracle worker. Why shouldn't I expect her to perform a miracle for me?

When I got home that evening, I cornered my Mother next to the kitchen gas range to tell her the news. I did not want the rest of the family to hear my conversation with Mom because some of my brothers and sisters didn't like the fact that Bos was always showing favoritism towards me.

"Yeah," Mom said. "I know about the banquet, John."

"Well, Mrs. Roosevelt is gonna be there."

"Mrs. Roosevelt? Mrs. Roosevelt."

"Yeah, Mom. She's gonna be the big guest speaker."

"You mean the wife of Franklin Roosevelt is gonna be at the banquet?"

"Yeah, yeah, that's what I mean. And Mom, Bos asked me to be one of the two boys that's gonna escort her to the speaker's table. I'm gonna have to walk with her through the ballroom."

"You're kidding…aren't you?"

"No, Mom. No. You can ask Bos yaself the next time you see him."

"Oh Johnny, Johnny you're gonna meet Mrs. Roosevelt, the President's wife. What an honor. What an honor. They say she's a great lady, a very great lady. And…and I'm gonna be there to see it, too." Mom hugged me. "My son is gonna meet Mrs. Roosevelt and escort her to the speaker's table. Whatta honor. What an honor!"

I got more of the same from my mother. She, too, made me believe that Eleanor Roosevelt was indeed some kind of special person in this world.

The banquet was still weeks away, but I never stopped thinking about it for long on any of those days prior to the event. I had determined that something wonderful, even magical, would happen when I met Mrs, Roosevelt. I firmly believed that my world would be changed. I wasn't just sure how it would change, but I did believe that it would change for the better.

As the day of the banquet drew near, I found myself taking on a haughty air. If my life, my world, was to suddenly change, it would mean that the lives of the other members of my family, my friends, and just all of my neighbors, would change also. It was inevitable that that would happen because I believed it was no accident that I was chosen to be one of Mrs. Roosevelt's escorts.

After all, I was Master John Cooper, a black boy who received a letter from Europe. I was a lad who sat at the Guild's staff lunch table, and I frequently went up to the staff members' bedrooms. I had been privileged to visit the Mainline, and I sat in the cockpit of a Hellcat. Was that not an indication I was someone special? I was not just a common, everyday black-ass nigger. John Cooper was following destiny's call. Fate had chosen me to be the instrument of social change, to bring a new way of life to my family and to my neighborhood. I was going to be a catalyst as a consequence of my meeting with a saint.

My family and my friends noticed the difference in me, too.

"What's wrong with you Johnny?" Frank said. "You've been acting damn bossy lately."

"Yeah, I've been noticing it too," Norman said. "You been telling off the little kids like everyday now. Ya know, you been acting like Ma-Daddy."

"Get off that shit, Johnny," Frank said. "Ever since you heard you were gonna get to meet the President's wife, you been acting like ya betta than everybody else, and you been going 'round here like you think you have the right to tell us what to do. Goddamit, you been actin' like you're white."

"I ain't been doing nothing," I said halfheartedly.

I did not know I was acting any differently, but if I was outside with my neighborhood friends, they noticed the difference.

"Come on Johnny, let's play some ball."

"No," I said. "I don't want to play any ball."

"Why? Ya never play with us anymore. Ya just come out here and stare at us like we're some kind of monkies or somethin'. What's da matter with you? Are you sick?"

"Oh, there ain't nothin' wrong with me. I just don't want to play any ball."

"Okay, so you don't want to play any ball, but you don't want to do anything anymore? You've become a real drag. A real, real drag."

What did my friends know? I couldn't afford to play with them as I used to because we played so recklessly on those glass strewn, rocky lots. Suppose I got hurt, fell down on a piece of sharp glass, cut myself, and then I had to go to the hospital? I might then miss my meeting with the saint, and not only would that be bad for me, but it would be bad for them, too. As I saw it, I was about to be a part of a divine mission, and no one but me knew about it.

Finally, at last, the day of the banquet arrived, and there was much excitement in the houses in the Noble Street neighborhood because many of my friends' parents were going to the banquet. I was the only youngster from Noble Street who was going, and for that occasion, my mother had no trouble getting me to take a bath in the washtub in the kitchen. I wanted to be sparkling clean from head to toe. I was even given Ivory soap to scrub myself with; the soap that was top of the line for poor and working class people.

Neighbors and friends flocked to my house throughout the day to talk and laugh about the new excitement and notoriety that had descended upon us. The adults looked at my Mom with such envious eyes. She was obviously pleased by all the attention, and I felt enormously proud that I was able to help make that wonderful occasion possible for her.

After what seemed like an eternity, even though it was only hours, the moment of departure at last arrived, and Mom and I had to go the Guild. It was from the Guild that the contingent of neighborhood folk and staff members would be leaving by car and station wagon for the Broadwood Hotel downtown.

As my mother and I stepped onto the stoop, we were amazed to see the sidewalk and the street in front of our house crowded with people who had been waiting quietly so as to surprise us when we emerged. Once we were outside, the crowd of friends and neighbors began shouting and waving.

I heard people saying, "We're so proud of you! We're so proud of you!"

I did not know what they had to be proud about because I had not done anything yet. If everything went as I imagined it, the magic would come later.

I was surprised to see all those people at our doorstep, but I was even more surprised when I noticed that there were a number of white people in the crowd—Freddie, the Schwartz family, and some white people from Buttonwood street. It was unusual to see Buttonwood Street people on Noble Street. For whatever the reason, they thought they were of a higher class than the likes of the Coopers, Freddie, and the Schwartz family. Nevertheless, the crowd was giving us a rousing send-off, and I was very pleased.

My mother and I stood on the stoop for a while listening to the well-wishers. There were shouts of, "Say hello to Mrs. Roosevelt for me, and tell her we love her." The longer I stood there, the more I felt like a celebrity. Even Mom was caught up in the moment. She began blowing kisses to the crowd. It was wonderful to receive such adulation, but we had to leave. We did not want to miss our ride.

As we stepped off of the stoop, my brothers and sisters came to the front door. They gazed out over the crowd and smiled. Even Frank had to let himself go, and he smiled so broadly I thought he was going to rip the corners of his mouth. At that moment, if I had it in me to speak, to my family, friends, and neighbors, I would have said, "You ain't seen nothing yet." The best was yet to come. I wished I could have told them all, "Just wait until I return. Just wait until I rub elbows with the saint. Things are going to be different in this old neighborhood as soon as I get back."

Upon reaching the Guild, the staff gave my mother and me a round of applause, and then there were more individual congratulations all around. At some point, we all got into the various vehicles and started for the hotel. When we reached the Broadwood and stepped into the lobby, newspaper reporters bounded over to the people in the Guild banquet party. In particular, they wanted to speak to Mr. Bosworth about the evening's festivities, and he gave them a full accounting. When he told the reporters that I was going to escort the Great Lady to the speaker's table, the reporters then wanted to talk to me. I was suddenly in the spotlight. Joseph Thomas was the white kid who would also be escorting Mrs. Roosevelt, and the reporters interviewed him as well. Joseph and I were not friends, although we did know each other by sight because both of us were active Guild members.

The newspaper reporters wanted to know how it felt to be given the honor of escorting Mrs. Roosevelt. I tried to give good answers to their questions, but in the end, I did not know what I was really saying. I was intimidated by the questions and the flash bulbs that kept going off, but

I did my best as my mother stood nearby watching the interviewing and smiling with glee. She must have been wondering how did her son suddenly become a celebrity.

The reporters had their angle on the story before they started talking to me, and they asked me nothing but leading questions. In effect, I let them put words in my mouth. Being interviewed was all so very new to me. The reporters wanted some quotes and padding for their human-interest story of poor boy meets Great Lady. They had the substance of their story long before I ever arrived at the Broadwood Hotel.

After the reporters completed their interviews, Bos led the Guild group to the north wing of the hotel and into a large banquet hall. There we discovered a monstrous room, ornately designed and filled with rows and rows of tables all covered with white dining clothes. Upon each table was the ususal clutter of knives, forks, spoons, plates, bowls, and glasses of water. But I was ready for all that silver metal this time.

In front of the banquet hall, there was a raised platform upon which sat a long table. At the center of the table, there was a podium with microphones situated on it for the speakers. Mrs. Roosevelt would be up there on the dais, probably close to the podium. That was where she would speak from, but first, Bos told me we would meet her at the door, which was some two hundred feet or more from the speaker's table. Joseph Thomas and I would then escort the former First Lady through the banquet hall to the platform.

The Broadwood Hotel was an elegant establishment. It had thick carpeted hallways and rooms, and chandeliered lighting. There were marble stairs with golden handrails and ceilings fifty-feet high. There was gold, silver, and glass shining and sparkling from every wall, nook and cranny, making the hotel look like yet another real palace, something straight out of a fairy tale. The decor in the hotel was so lavish, I could not imagine how the Guild came by the use of the place, if only for a few hours. But more importantly I thought this was a proper setting for me to meet Mrs. Roosevelt, who I now thought of as being my white fairy godmother.

I fell into conversation with Joseph as we, and everyone else in the banquet hall, waited for Mrs. Roosevelt to arrive. Joseph seemed to be a nice enough kid, although I found him very nonchalant about meeting with Mrs. Roosevelt. In fact, he seemed to be mystified about his own presence there. He was not excited about meeting her, and he told me if he had had his way about it, he would have stayed home. His mother had insisted that he come.

I could not believe what I was hearing. Didn't this knucklehead realize who he was about to meet, the Great Lady, FDR's wife, a saint, my white fairy godmother? Didn't he realize that magic was going to strike our community and nothing would be the same again? The truth was Joseph didn't have a clue as to what was really going on. He didn't seem to have the ability to grasp the momentous nature of the occasion.

I felt angry. I wanted to grab Joseph Thomas and shake the hell out of him. He could spoil everything. I knew enough about magic from the movies and story books, that, for it to work, people had to believe in it. Joseph Thomas obviously did not believe that magic would be occurring at the Broadwood Hotel that night. Indeed, he probably did not believe in magic at all. Goddamit! He was going to mess up everything!

I started thinking that I had to get rid of Joseph. Maybe I could hide him in a broom closet or drop him down an elevator shaft, like they always did to unwanted guest or intruders in those Hollywood B-movies. I told myself I would commit murder if I had to in order to keep the magic alive. There was too much at stake to let an unbeliever screw it up; and that made me wonder, why was this great responsibility dumped on my shoulders?

Joseph and I had stopped talking, and he turned away from me to gaze out across the banquet hall at the rows and rows of tables that were filled with poor and working class people dressed to the hilt in their Sunday clothes. The men were all in their double-breasted suits with white shirts, and most of the women had on inexpensive, print dresses, the kind that are bought in the bargain basements of the big department stores. Some of the women were also wearing corsages.

Most importantly, Joseph Thomas had his back to me, and I thought that was the opportunity I had been waiting for. I took a quick glance around the room. The people in the dining hall were not paying any attention to the two of us. Everybody was talking and jabbering among themselves at their tables. Now was the time. I could grab Joseph about the neck sudden like and choke him until he fell unconscious, and then I could drag him off to an elevator shaft and drop him into it. If someone asked me why I was dragging a body along the carpet, I would tell them that Joseph had fainted from all the excitement; or I could say that Joseph had fallen asleep from drinking too much punch.

Just as I was about to snatch that unbelieving booby about the throat, someone tapped me on my shoulder from behind. I turned around to find Bos standing behind me, and next to him I saw a very tall woman who was wearing a long mink coat that seemed to touch the floor. She had arrived—my white fairy godmother, the Great Lady.

"John." Bos smiled. "I want you to meet Mrs. Roosevelt."

"John." She held out her hand and smiled. "I'm glad to meet you."

I stared at her, and I trembled as my hand reached out to meet hers. "She is so tall," I thought as I looked up to her face. "Gee whiz." I smiled awkwardly and thought, "she does not have a good looking face." I would have thought that a fairy godmother would be stunningly beautiful, like the good witch of the North in The Wizard of Oz. But this Saint, this Great Lady, was not beautiful. Even with those expensive pearls hung around her neck and the mink coat she wore, she looked drab, wrinkled and simply like any old, ordinary, un-magical, human white woman.

She was next introduced to Joseph Thomas.

"John and Joseph will escort you to the speaker's table," Bos said.

"Oh, that will be very nice." Mrs. Roosevelt smiled. "It will be a pleasure to have such fine young men walk with me."

Perhaps she did not have the nicest face to look at, but her voice was beautiful, so soothing, like music. And when she also patted me on the cheek, I knew I was with a very unique, special person. Although she did not look like Miss Lee, Mrs. Roosevelt, in a certain way, reminded me of my cooking teacher.

When I reached out and shook Mrs. Roosevelt hand, I knew from the first second of contact with her that the jig was up. Her hand was cold, shriveled by age, and covered with little brown spots. Maybe her hand was not warm because she had just come inside from a cold winter's night or maybe she had tired blood. I did not know why her hand felt so cold, but I did know there was a message in its coldness, a message that I could not deny. It was a message that told me that my fairy godmother was not going to have chicken and mashed potatoes at the Broadwood Hotel that night. She had decided to stay in fairyland, wherever that might have been, and without my fairy godmother, there would be no magic happenings for Johnny and his community.

It would seem that I had set myself up for a fall. I had let my imagination run wild, and now I was due for a reality check. Moreover, reality can bite like a rattlesnake. Even though I was an immature kid, I should have known that the cold hand of reality would pull me out of the fantasy I had created about meeting Mrs. Roosevelt. In the real world, magic did not prevail. It had nothing to do with my poverty or my blackness. If I was so naive and stupid to believe that magic would release me from my difficulties, then I deserved the disappointment that was coming my way. Appealing to magic as the means to reorder my dismal life was like appealing to the Klu Klux Klan for help to alleviate racism and white supremacy.

Mrs. Roosevelt brought no magic with her to the Broadwood Hotel. She may have been the ultimate humanitarian, and she may have believed deeply in the oneness of humankind, but in the end, she was no Merlin the magician. Consequently, there would be no great changes in my life because of my meeting with Mrs. Roosevelt, and her speech was to say as much.

To be sure, the air was already fizzling out of my fantasy balloon when Bos lined us up, one on each side of Mrs. Roosevelt, Joseph to the left and me to the right. I felt a certain irritability when the sign was given to the main table and a hushed silence fell over the large banquet hall. At that moment, the three of us marched off, Mrs. Roosevelt slightly in the lead, and Joseph and I parallel to each other, walking just behind her.

As we walked down the aisle towards the dais, I was overcome with this feeling that I was out of place being next to Mrs. Roosevelt. She was not dressed in clothing befitting the audience she was going to speak to, nor was her attire suitable for the occasion of the banquet. She dressed like a rich lady of means, even if she did look somewhat drab overall. Although her dress was simple, nothing ostentatious and showy, she did arrive in this full-length mink coat, and she wore an expensive pearl necklace. What do you think the bargain basement ladies thought of those expensive items?

There was yet another reason why I felt uncomfortable walking behind Mrs. Roosevelt. The dinner suit I was wearing was made up of a sports jacket donated by my brother Frank, a white shirt loaned to me by my brother Allen, a pair of pants rented to me by Norman, and lastly a pair of shoes that Abie begrudgingly allowed me to use for the evening's affair. If my brothers had descended upon me at that moment and told me to return their clothing, I would have suddenly been naked. I wondered what Mrs. Roosevelt would have said about that? The Lord gave His first children leaves to cover their private parts with, and I guessed that the Great Lady would have done no less for me.

I did catch sight of my mother's face, among the many guests, as I walked Mrs. Roosevelt down the aisle to the dais, and I could see that she was definitely pleased. That happy look on her face meant a lot to me. On that basis alone, the evening could be considered a prized success.

As Joseph and I arrived at the speaker's table with Mrs. Roosevelt, a flurry of photographers' flash bulbs went off, and the three of us paused for a moment to let the news people take some snapshots. Then, Mrs. Roosevelt ascended to the dais, and Joseph and I went to our table nearby.

The guests then ate their dinner while they waited for the main speaker, Mrs. Roosevelt. However, there were many other speakers at the podium throughout dinner. Many of them were politicians, businessmen, and religious leaders. Even Bos said a few words, and it was he who introduced Mrs. Roosevelt when it came to her time to speak. When she got up to the podium, a respectful silence fell over the room,

The topic of Mrs. Roosevelt's speech was "The American Neighborhood, A Laboratory for World Understanding." The subject immediately turned me off. Here she was speaking with pride about "the social vitality and benefits of the American neighborhood," but she could not have been talking about the neighborhood I lived in. Of course, she was generalizing about neighborhoods in America, but I kept thinking, "Come on. Lady, let's get real."

She talked about people living together in neighborhoods where the individuals were like partners working toward a common end of peace and tranquility. That was not the neighborhood I lived in, and chiefly because of the race issue. Mrs. Roosevelt did not get into discussing race problems, but she should have. That was the thing that divided American neighborhoods. If she were to walk down Noble Street, she would immediately become aware of that. The only understanding she would likely find in my community, among the majority of the residents, would be a belief in segregation.

Mrs. Roosevelt spoke as a Great Lady that evening, a Great Lady with a vision, but that vision was far from reality. When she left the banquet hall, she took her vision with her, back to Hyde Park or the United

Nations or wherever she went, and she left me with my pests and bigots. In fact, she could not have done any more or any less than that. After all, my fairy godmother wouldn't have been white, would she?

I cooled it with magic for a while, after my meeting with Mrs. Roosevelt, but I still held on to my deep belief in it as my savior. At the same time, as I matured into an adult, I came to realize that America's black people put too much faith in one kind of magic or another in the hopes that it would relieve them of their poverty and "niggafication." There was a belief in the magic of government policies and welfare programs that would somehow make them socially equal to white people. There was the belief in jobs and money as a panacea that could prevent racism, and then there was the ultimate magic that blacks believed in, religion. As the church told them, believe in Christ and everything will be all right. The "all right" doesn't come about until your dead of course, but what does that matter when your life isn't worth living anyway?

My mother and I did receive a great deal of attention from our neighbors and friends after the banquet dinner with Mrs. Roosevelt. We were the closest thing to a celebrity that the people of the Noble Street community had ever seen, and for a few weeks the community basked in the spotlight that Mrs Roosevelt's visit had brought to the area. But in the end, the people of the Noble Street community returned to their daily struggles for survival, and Mrs. Roosevelt's visit became something that was talked about like a folktale or a bedtime story.

Chapter Ten

My experience with Mrs. Roosevelt may have been a bust in the name of magic and fairy godmothers, but it had been an important, revealing experience all the same. From my meeting with her I began to become aware of the social force known as power.

Mao Tse-tung may have said that "power comes from the barrel of a gun," but that was power based on brute force. My encounter with Mrs. Roosevelt showed me that brute force was not the most effective form of power. A quiet, nonaggressive form of power is much more effective because people fall under its control willingly and with smiles on their faces. Perhaps that was why Uncle Tomism was so insidious. Imagine, how Snotnose would have reacted if he had been given the honor of escorting Mrs. Roosevelt through the ballroom. I don't think he would have danced or shuffled his feet, but he might have put a broad grin on his face and rolled his eyes up to the top of his head. It would have been a good show for the photographers. I didn't act like a clown when I was walking with Mrs. Roosevelt, but I was under her spell just the same.

The Quakers had power in the Noble Street neighborhood—the power of dispensing favors and controlling the social programs that they offered to the people of the community. The Quakers had the power of largesse, particularly over the neighborhood children. The Guild staff decided which children would go to summer camp, the Christmas parties, the trips to the Mainline. And there was another kind of power staff members of the Guild had; they gained power from the respect they received from the people who participated in Guild programs.

Mrs. Roosevelt had power that came with her image as a Great Lady, and that image demanded more than respect. It demanded devotion. The idea of devotion is love in its most mystical sense, and it bespeaks of the power one individual can have over another. So then, Mrs. Roosevelt did have a type of magic after all.

I grew up in a socially powerless environment. Consequently, I became very sensitive to the uses, abuses, and symbols of power. Growing up in Philadelphia, I learned at a very early age that there were social lines of demarcation that black people should not cross, be it in white enclave neighborhoods, the public parks, the public schools, the department stores, or in the midtown area of the city where white people liked to shop.

When I was only six years old, I began taking long walks around the city by myself. I would do that when I wasn't palling around with Norman and Frank. I was a streetwise kid, and these long walks of mine did not disturb my mother or older brothers, just as long as I told them where I was going and when I was coming back. My mother knew that I would be careful.

I would begin my trip the way Norman and Frank had taken me downtown. I enjoyed walking down Third Street from my house to Market Street. Once I reached Market Street, I would turn West and walk to Nineteenth Street, and then I would return home by a different route, often taking back streets, small alleyway-like streets, that still remained from Philadelphia's past.

When walking down Market Street, I would be immersed in the atmosphere of the modern age, but when I traveled down those alley streets, I would be taken back in history to the time of the lamplighters and the era when horse and buggies were the chief means of transportation. Many of those streets, with their historically old houses, like

Elfreth's Alley, had a past that went back to Colonial days when the city was a village, and more than once I thought I saw George Washington peeking at me from behind closed shuttered windows. I was very fond of making up stories about those old houses, particularly about the people who might have lived in them. I had a great interest, even as a small child, in social history.

I would walk down Market Street and look at all the nice things in the store windows, but I could not go inside most of those department stores like I did with my brothers. Still, I would stroll along Market Street, gushing with envy, staring painfully into the showcase windows at the clothes, toys, and household goods that I did not have. I would think that my life would be happier and more meaningful if I had all that store stuff. How nice it would be if I had a pair of new skates or a scooter.

I did not have the courage to go into those department stores like Lit Brothers, Gimbel Brothers, and Snellenberg's, but the John Wanamaker's Store was different. John Wanamaker was the most expensive department store on Market Street, and it also had the best window displays. I was always drawn to that store at Thirteenth and Market Streets. The Wanamaker building was a good many stories tall, and its facade was dark, craggy and mysterious looking. Indeed, to me the establishment appeared more like a fortress than retail store, and it was even more impressive because it sat right across the street from City Hall.

The items that were displayed in the windows of Wanamaker's, the clothes, the fishing rods, the radios, and even the lawn mowers, always looked so attractive, appealing and even beautiful. At times, there would be food displayed in the windows, sausages and meats, or cakes and cookies, all extremely appetizing and luscious looking. The enticing appearance of everything in Wanamaker's windows made it almost impossible for me to pass that store and not try to go inside of it.

The Wanamaker's Department Store was yet another house of dreams to me. When I looked at those window displays, I could imagine that everything I ever wanted was inside that building. I also made myself believe that any establishment that had so many fine things on display in its windows had to be a house of magic. If I could go inside, I was sure that somewhere in the bosom of Wanamaker's there was a Wizard, like Merlin or the guy in Oz, who could turn my life around and make everything perfect for me. No more bedbugs, and hungry days. The answers to all my family and social problems was just beyond those glass display windows. That had to be the reason why I was drawn to Wanamaker's.

On Market Street, John Wanamaker's was the department store for wealthy people, and if there was one thing the management of the store did not like to see was a poor-looking black boy coming through the door. The management must have thought it was not good for business, and the floorwalker or one of the sales people would chase me out of the store whenever I would dare enter it, but that did not stop me from coming back on another day and invading the premises again. The wizard was in there and one day I would track him down.

Across the street from Wanamaker's, there was a Horn & Hardart nickle restaurant, an automat. It was called an automat because most of the food was self-serviced and kept in rows of little glass compartments that were placed in encasements built into the walls of the restaurant. The compartments were put together in a series of six, like stacks of glass blocks, one on top of the other. To buy any of the food, first a selection was made. Then the right amount of nickels for the price of the food was put into a coin slot next to the container with the item chosen. Lastly, a little knob below the coin slot is turned, and the front door window to the food section would pop open. The food is taken out, and it can be eaten at one of the many tables in the restaurant.

On my trips up Market Street, I always passed through the H & H at Broad Street because there was so much food to see in those rows and rows of glass compartments. Moreover, the restaurant was always so clean. It had such pretty marble counters, and there were silver etchings around the doors to the food compartments. The silver was always shining like sunlight. It was a very nice place to visit, and best of all no one bothered me. No one ever tried to chase me out of the eatery, and when I was in the automat, I always thought how nice it would be if I could have a restaurant like that in my home with all its varieties of foods. It would be like being in food heaven. Of course, I would have my mother put some special things in my automat, like fried chicken, peaches and shortening bread, and gravy-soaked hamburgers. My stomach would always growl with joyous anticipation when I went into H & H.

After leaving H & H, I would cross Broad Street and pass through City Hall Courtyard. On top of the City Hall Building, looking out over the City with a pensive stare, was a statue of William Penn. Penn always seemed out of place to me up there on his perch. Penn was the symbol of Philadelphia's motto. Philadelphia had the reputation of being known as the city of brotherly love. What a joke. That statue symbolized a lie.

In those days, the Northern side of Market Street, west of City Hall, had the Chinese Wall running above it. The Wall ran from Broad Street to Thirtieth Street. The Wall constituted an overhead bridge and track-way that carried trains and passengers right to the doorstep of City Hall from Thirtieth Street Station and other parts of the United States. I would frequently go into the Broad Street Train Station to watch the travelers coming and going, and I would dream of the future when I would go traveling around the world. Broad Street Station would be my starting point. Just like Miss Lee, I would take a train all the way to California, and I would see the Pacific Ocean. Heaven knows, it had to look, and smell, better than the Delaware River.

The station was a gloomy looking place. The interior was made up of dark walls and oxidized metal beams. The only relief from its shadowy nature was the skylight windows high above the huge waiting room area. Tucked in the middle of the waiting room, there were rows and rows of benches where incoming and outgoing passengers could rest, and across the waiting room from the entrance to the station, there was a wide stairway that people used going up to and coming down from the trains on the upper tracks.

The Broad Street Train Station was always cool, even on the hottest of days. It must have been those shadows that kept it that way. The coolness of the building was an added reason for me to go in. On my long walks across Market Street, the station was a good place to stop and rest, especially on hot summer days, and I would sit down on one of the long benches inside. I was never allowed to rest in the station for very long because just like my visits to Wanamaker's, some attendant was sure to come along and tell me to move on. I was never specifically chased out of the place, but I was told to keep moving. The people in charge of running the station apparently did not like seeing a ragamuffin-looking black boy sitting on the benches in the waiting room. But I would never stay in the area for very long. I never wanted to. Just being in there for a short while was always enough to stimulate my imagination.

After leaving the Train Station, I would wander by the Fox, Stanton, and other movie theaters that lined the south side of Market Street. There was a group of movie theaters that stretched from Fifteenth Street to Nineteenth Street. Each one of these theaters had blazing, colorful, neon marquees that called to the passerby to come in and immerse himself in a Hollywood fantasy. There was nothing I enjoyed more than going to the movies. It didn't matter to me that there were no black people of any significance in these motion pictures. It was the make-believe nature of Hollywood motion pictures that I enjoyed. When I was in the theater, my imagination would take over, and my poverty and blackness would just dissolve into the characters and story line of the movies. I found relief from my social bondage in the make-believe stories on the motion picture screen.

The string of movies on the west side of Market Street ended at Nineteenth Street, and there on the northwest corner of the intersection was the last of the downtown, center city first run movie houses. The name of that movie house was the Mastbaum Theater, the most elegant and largest motion picture theater I had ever been in.

The Mastbaum Theater was one of those magnificent movie houses that were built in the 1930s. It was built in art deco style and looked more like a symphony hall than a movie theater. It had the finest acoustics, and plush carpeting covered the hallways and staircases. There were box seats for the elites, and very nice upholstered seats for the masses, the working class and poor kids like me. It had a big stage, the center of which could move up and down like an elevator. The Guild took a group of Noble Streets kids to the Mastbaum once for a special show, not a movie, and on that occasion an, entire orchestra came right up out of the floor of the stage. That was one exciting day for me. To see that orchestra come from below like that was pure magic, and as a consequence, the Mastbaum always held a special place in my heart.

In my mind, a visit to the Mastbaum Theater was for me a visit to wonderland. Its movies were always the best, like Errol Flynn in Objective Burma, and the popcorn and candy was supreme. When I entered the lobby of the Theater I came face to face with a huge fountain that spouted arcs of colored water into the air, and there were marble walls, golden banisters, and tremendous sparkling chandeliers hanging down from the ceilings very similar to the Broadwood Hotel. The decor of that lobby was right out of the palace in the Cinderella story.

Given the fact that the Mastbaum Theater was the incarnate of wonderland for me, it was perfectly located as the final base for me to touch before starting back home from my long walks downtown, and it helped to focus the fact that my walks were all about wishes, dreams, and fantasy. The items in the department store windows, the food in H

& H, the train station with its promise of future travel and adventure, the movie marquees; they all stimulated my imagination in the belief that one day I would have a better life, a better life like the characters in the movies.

I could not believe that Hollywood was wrong in telling its tales of success on the movie screen. More often than not, the poor guy, the downtrodden guy, made it to the top of the social heap in the end, and invariably the movies had happy endings. The good guys always beat the bad guys, and the staunch hero always got the girl. And to be sure, love conquered all, from hunger to deadly enemies. I firmly believed that if these scenarios were not true, for white people at least, then Hollywood would not be allowed to make movies with such story lines. And even though I was black, I thought I was special. If I tried real hard, I believed, I could be successful, too.

As the years went by, I must have made that trip down Market Street more than a couple of hundred times. I liked visiting Market Street a lot, but I knew that the people who worked in the stores downtown didn't like me very much. They were always chasing me away like I was an infectious disease or something. Keep moving black boy. Keep moving.

The shop owners, the sales people, and the floorwalkers of the department stores were like gatekeepers to me, but they were not the most troublesome people I encountered on Market Street. The police officers bothered me most of all, even though they rarely, if ever, spoke to me as I walked along the sidewalks. But, it was that gun they carried and the air of authority that surrounded them that caught my attention. There were plenty of cops on Market Street. They would be standing on corners or strolling between blocks. Whenever I was near a police officer, I had the distinct feeling that I was being watched and that the cop suspected me of being involved in some nefarious activities. I would frequently imagine the police officer saying to me, "Hey boy! Whatta you doin' down here on Market Street? You don't belong here." At those times, I always remembered my long walk down Frankford Avenue.

Because there were always many police officers on Market Street, I came to the conclusion that they worked for the shop and department store owners. I saw the cops as the foot patrol of the business establishments. They were just extensions of Wanamaker's and H & H, along with other stores. And, why didn't I see any black police officers down on Market Street? The only time I ever saw a black uniformed cop was on Columbia Avenue, which was in North Philly. Columbia Avenue ran right through the heart of the city's largest black ghetto.

Maybe it was against the law for blacks to work as sales people and floorwalkers on Market Street. Also, maybe it was against the law for black cops to patrol Market Street. I was not sure about the law as it related to black people and cops, but Market Street, with all its shops, stores, and restaurants was a street for white people.

If the truth be known, I was scared of cops. Police officers had a great deal of individual power and authority, and I knew that. I had seen them use their power in my neighborhood. I remember a hot summer day back in 1942. It was in the mid-afternoon, and Norman, Frank, and I were returning home from the Guild after spending a day playing softball with the Green Street Monarchs. We had decided to go home by the Fourth Street route, and as we neared Buttonwood Street, we found a great deal of commotion going on. Traffic was held up, and cars and trucks were backed up Fourth Street for a number of blocks.

At the intersection of Fourth and Buttonwood Streets, crowds of people had gathered on each corner, and they were all staring out into the center of the cross streets to where a policeman stood. It was a hot day, and the gathering of people seemed to draw even more heat to the stuffy, humid air. The crowds of people on each corner, adults and children, were jockeying for position near the pavement's edge to get a better view of the police officer. He, in turn, was looking down into a large hole at his feet that was right in the middle of the intersection.

When my brothers and I came upon the scene, we immediately pushed our way to the front of the crowd on the northeast corner. I did not notice it at first, but to one side of the hole in the ground there was an empty wagon, the type that a single horse would pull. There was excitement in the air, and we were not about to let the moment pass without trying to discover what was the cause of it. Now at the front of the crowd, we stared out into the intersection at the police officer, and I noticed standing near the police officer were a number of men in blue coverall, work uniforms. The coveralls were covered with dirt and clay, and I recognized them as Philadelphia Gas Company employees. They had probably dug that hole in the street to fix a gas leak. It was common to see them in the neighborhood because the old gas pipes under the ground were forever bursting, and then the street would have to be dug up so the pipes could be repaired. Whenever there was a gas leak, an evil smell would fill the air in the area. But, if this was a gas company dig, why was the policeman there?

Then my attention focused on the wagon. There was no horse to be seen, and just as I was thinking about the wagon, I heard a loud whining and snorting sound of a horse. I knew immediately where the sound was coming from. It was coming from the hole in the ground at the policeman's feet. I took a deep breath as goose pimples tickled my arms and back. Now that was excitement, real excitement, the kind of excitement I experienced when I went to the movies. And it sure beat playing softball in the hot sun all day.

I turned my attention to the police officer. He was a strong, stocky looking person, with very hairy arms. I had seen many white men with plenty of hair on their arms and legs, and it always made me feel creepy. Thick hair made some white men look as though they had fur like an animal.

The police officer was engaged in a very loud, gesticulating conversation with a scruffy looking, medium built man who had very dirty hands. The scruffy fellow was shaking his head as the officer talked to him. The cop seemed to be trying to convince the man of something he did not want to hear.

The whining and snorting from the hole had now changed to horse screams of agony and pain. The animal in the hole was obviously in great difficulty. The agonizing sounds from the horse caused the crowds on the pavement to push out into the street toward the hole where the policeman and the scruffy man were standing. My bothers, me, and all the people on the pavements wanted to get a view of the horse and to see what condition the animal was in. Everyone wanted to know why the animal was making such painful sounds, but when the police officer saw the people inching toward the center of the intersection, he quickly ordered us back to the pavements proper in no uncertain terms. "Get back! Get your asses back! This is a police matter!" But, my brothers and I were not about to pass up the opportunity to see that horse in a hole on Fourth Street.

A din had now arisen and mingled with the hot stuffy air. Along with the horse's whining shrieks from the hole, there was the noise of car and truck horns blasting as impatient drivers wanted the police officer to clear the streets of the people and the horse and wagon so they could be on their way South down Fourth Street. At the same time, more and more individuals were arriving, and it was becoming very difficult for the crowds to stay on the pavements because the volume of people was overloading the area. People were being forced into the street because there was no standing room on the sidewalks.

Between talking to the scruffy looking man and trying to keep the crowd on the pavements, the police officer was becoming very agitated. He crossed his hairy arms, and then he banged his fist into his left palm as he tried to make an emphatic point to the man with the dirty hands. But, the shorter man kept shaking his head.

At one point, when the officer had turned his back slightly to the us, Frank decided it was time to make a dash out to the hole and take a peek into it, and we did just that. We ran from the pavement to the center of the street, right up to the edge of the hole. It was hardly a pleasant sight that awaited us. There, at the bottom of a ten foot hole, lay a big reddish brown horse. Its front legs, twisted and mangled, were under its body, as was one of its back legs. Bones were clearly seen protruding from beneath the skin of both front legs and the rear leg that was doubled underneath the poor creature's body. The horse had three broken legs. No wonder the animal was in such agony and pain. The hole was more or less rectangular in shape, and the horse had fallen into the hole across the width of it rather than the length of it. The animal was wedged in the hole in a most awkward position so tight it could not move its head. It was quite an ugly sight to see.

We had just enough time to take a quick peek before the police officer spotted us and chased us back onto the pavement with the rest of the crowd. But, we had gotten a look at the animal, and we would have much to tell when we arrived home later.

Soon thereafter, a police van arrived on the scene and a half dozen policemen or so got out of the vehicle. The newly arrived uniformed officers gathered in a huddle with the cop who been talking to the man with the dirty hands. They talked among themselves for a short time, and one after another they went over to the hole to take a look at the horse's predicament. They talked in low tones, obviously not wanting the onlookers to hear their conversation. Clearly they were trying to make a decision, and finally they broke up the huddle and told the scruffy looking man to go over to the pavement and join the rest of the crowd.

"No," the man with the dirty hands said. "I want to stay with my friend."

"You can't," the hairy-armed police officer said. "There is nothing you can do, Mister. The animal is suffering. You know what we have to do."

"I don't care what you say. I still want to stay with my friend."

"Well, you can't." The officer's voice was firm. "It's against regulations. You have to go over there with the crowd, and I mean right now."

The policeman led the man with the dirty hands over to the curb and pushed him gently, but firmly, into the front of the crowd on the southwest corner. Then, all the police officers ordered everyone to back away from the intersection. The cops made me and my brothers move back for about twenty feet or more, but we still managed to stay near the front of the group. We wanted to see what the police were going to do.

After the crowds had been pushed back, the police officers took up positions in front of them on each corner, and a signal was given to the hairy-armed policeman. He then took his pistol from his holster, and I felt my heart begin to beat fast. It was the first time I had ever seen a real gun drawn for action. I remember how dark and deadly the weapon looked. It gave me the shivers. It was one thing to see Buck Jones, the cowboy movie actor, draw his trusty six-shooter to take care of some bad, black hat guys in a flick, but it was another emotion all together to see a cop pull out a real gun among real people on Fourth Street in my neighborhood.

The cop with the drawn gun took one look around at the groups of people knotted on each corner, as though he wanted to be sure that everyone saw that he had his pistol out and in his hand, and then he walked up to the hold where the horse was. The animal could still be heard whinnying in snortful, painful sounds.

The hairy policeman raised his arm and aimed his pistol into the hole. A dead silence fell over the crowd. Was he aiming at the horse? Where was he going to shoot him? I could not see into the hole. And, the policeman seemed to be taking a long time aiming his weapon.

But then, a cannon went off in my ear. The cop with the hairy arms had fired his pistol. My brothers and I flinched, as did most of the people around us, from the sound of the pistol blast, and the screaming from the hole stopped. The officer had shot the horse, and I assumed that the animal was dead. I suddenly had a short spell of nausea at the thought of the dead horse in that hole. I had a gruesome image in my mind of the horse's head having been shot off.

"All right, everybody. All right. It's all over. Now you can go about your business," the policemen said.

But my brothers and I, and most of the people in the crowd around us, could not move. The noise of the pistol shot must have still been ringing in everyone's ears, and we all seemed to be in a state of mild shock.

And then, the police officers shouted again. "Let's move it, everybody. Go on home. There is nothing left here to see."

After a moment or so, the crowds of people on the various corners began to move, and my brothers and I then took off for home, anxious to tell the tale of death in the afternoon to other family members and friends. And once we started home, I didn't have that same feeling of shock anymore. All I felt was excitement. I was sorry that the horse had to die because I liked horses, but then I did a lot of killing myself. I killed rats, mice, roaches, and bedbugs. Probably all the people in my neighborhood had to contend with, and kill household pests. Consequently, I lived in a neighborhood of killers. That cop was just another one of them.

I do not mean to suggest that the policeman's actions were in any way comparable to the killing of household pests. The policeman did not act because he was under attack. He shot that horse as an expression of his legal power and authority to take control of public situations, for the common good of all, of course.

The killing on Fourth Street was a great conversation piece for days among members of my family and friends. One of the most lasting impressions I had from the experience was the sound, like a cannon, of that shot from the policeman's pistol. Sounds have a way of staying in my head for a long time. Music, church bells, the siren sound of an ambulance, and human voices that bark at me in anger, like those Guards in Pennypack Creek Park; they all play over and over again in my head, long after the event has passed.

The man with the dirty hands, who obviously was the owner of the horse, had kept shaking his head. I concluded, and my brothers agreed, that the horse was killed against his wishes. The man kept saying, "I want to stay with my friend," but an officer had pushed him away, into the crowd. The police had decided to put the horse out of its misery, and once they had reached that decision, there was nothing the man could do. I didn't understand it then, but I was learning that the police had tremendous discretionary power, and that was one of the essential reasons why I saw only one black police officer in the North Philly black ghetto and no black, uniform policemen on Market Street.

My neighborhood was made up largely by the lowest elements of the working class: unskilled laborers and the day workers. Most of them were people who worked but did not earn enough money to cover their living expenses. Normally, they had to skimp from paycheck to paycheck, usually borrowing from Peter to pay Paul. The people at the bottom of the neighborhood class system were the paupers like my family, which lived off of welfare. Taking the working group of the community as a whole, they held such jobs as stevedores, mill hands, factory workers, and meat packers and loaders. They worked with their hands, and it was muscles rather than machines that got them through the day. The men, both black and white, worked a hard eight hours a day for little pay and a meager lifestyle. I suspect many of these men were happy when the Second World War came along. It gave them the chance to earn more money because of the war industries, and it also allowed many of them the opportunity to join the military services and thereby have a legitimate reason to leave the humdrum, repetitious lifestyle of working and supporting a family in civilian life.

On the weekends, the working class men, and some of their women, would drink a lot. Too many of them would get downright nasty, stinking, fighting drunk. I was never in a western frontier town back in the nineteenth century, but thanks to the images I got from Hollywood, there were times when I thought my neighborhood was a frontier town because there were so many drunks staggering around, and so many arguments, one on one fights, and group brawls, in the streets. Perhaps that was part of the pattern by which the men of my community released their tensions after a long week of doing backbreaking, aesthetically unrewarding and unfulfilling work. But, whatever the reason, the neighborhood bars would usually be filled to the wee hours on Friday and Saturday nights.

Friday nights, in particular, were special. Friday night was Gillette Fight Night, and the men enjoyed sitting in the bars, listening to the prizefights on the radio. There was always a series of bouts, and while they drank their beer and hard liquor, there was always a lot of betting going on. The bar crowd had great affection for the fighters because prizefighters were recognized as working class stiffs like themselves who were just trying to get the big break, a shot at the championship title.

It was summer, and one Friday night my brothers and I were out late roaming through our neighborhood. We were allowed to stay out later in the summer months because there was no school and because our bedrooms could become stifling in the humidity of a hot, dry summer's night. As we were coming down Third Street, we came upon a confrontation that was taking place on the sidewalk in front of one of the many local beergardens.

A burly man and a rather small woman were facing each other, screaming and cursing at one another at the top of their lungs. They were both reeling around like they had had plenty to drink throughout the evening, and they reeked like a couple of winos. The vocal din and racket that surrounded the pair was ear-shattering. It was difficult to believe that two drunken individuals could make so much noise. They sounded like an army of people shouting all at once. My brothers and I stood about ten feet away from them to see where the argument might lead. For instance, maybe the woman would get knocked down, and we might get a chance to peek up her dress. That would be worth waiting for.

But, before the woman's panties could be exposed, someone called the police. A red police cruiser soon arrived with two officers in it. They got out of the vehicle and stood up straight. They were tall and both of them were big-boned and muscular. They looked somewhat young to be wearing policemen's uniforms, but at the same time, they were both more than six-feet tall. That was the norm for our neighborhood; big, tall white police officers that were invariably on the young side. Norman used to say he believed that the biggest cops were always assigned to black communities. "And you know why? They want to scare us."

The first thing that the cops did was to separate, and get between, the feuding pair, and they then tried to find out what the two were arguing about. As it turned out, it was a marital dispute, but the reason for the couple's disagreement was never ascertained. To tell the truth, I did not care what caused the argument. I was just interested in seeing if they would start hitting each other and rolling around in the gutter like dogs. It was a black couple, although that did not matter much. I had seen many white men and women mixing it up in the streets on the weekend in my neighborhood.

With the arrival of the police, the couple quieted down. That always seemed to happen in situations like those. I had seen the police intervene in street arguments and fights, between drunken people, and usually the officers would just tell the individuals involved to go home and sleep it off. These two cops must have had a slow night because they interrogated the couple, wanting to know specifically what started the argument.

Neither the husband nor the wife wanted to talk about what started the argument. The two cops then concentrated their attention on the man, and they insisted that he tell them what had started the ruckus. One of the officers began pushing the man by banging the heel of his hand on the drunken fellow's shoulder. "You are gonna tell us what started this, aren't ya?" The cop continued banging the man's shoulder and pushing him backwards on the pavement until he had him up against the wall of the beergarden. "You are gonna tell us, aren't ya?" The police officer pushed the man into the wall again.

Finally, the drunken man couldn't take it any longer. "Keep ya fuckin' hands to yourself!" he shouted at the cop who had been pushing him into the wall.

That kind of statement seemed to be just what the pushing police officer had been waiting for, and without any hesitation, he took his nightstick and smacked the man over the head with it. The drunken man immediately fell to his knees.

I was so close to the police officer wheeling the nightstick, I distinctly heard the squashing of hair and flesh when the nightstick smashed into the drunken man's head. Blood began flowing down his face. I took a step back from the sight of the blood, and I cringed because I thought the cop might hit me next. Norman and Frank did not move. All their attention was on the action before them, and they were probably not even thinking about themselves.

It was then that the other police officer spoke to his partner. "Come on, let's take this bastard down to the clink."

The man's wife ran around the officer who had just spoken, and she quickly moved to the spot where her husband was on his knees. Taking hold of his right arm, she tried to help him to his feet, and as she did she screamed at the cop who had used his nightstick as a weapon. "Ya didn't have to hit him. He didn't do nothin'."

The partner of the nightstick-wheeling cop moved quickly to his fellow officer's side. "Lets take this bum to jail." He then pushed the woman away from her husband and took hold of the man's right arm. His partner put his nightstick back on his belt, and he then grabbed hold of the man's left arm. The two cops began to drag the man toward their vehicle, but the woman, drunk and wavering on uncertain feet, put herself in the policemen's path, blocking their access to the squad car. With the woman in front of them, they stop dragging the man, and they told his wife to get out of the way before she was charged with interfering with an arrest. But, the woman would not move.

"Get outta the way lady," the cop said, "'fore you get hurt."

The woman refused to move. "You shouldn't be arresting my husband. He didn't do any…anything wrong."

"Just get ya ass outta the way lady, right now," the cop said.

"No, I…I ain't movin' till you leave my husband alone."

The police officer that ordered the woman out of the way snarled, and he let go of her husband's armpit. He then walked up to the woman and pushed her roughly away from the squad car. "Get out of the way, bitch." He pushed the woman again. This time, the push was so strong she fell down, sprawling on the sidewalk with her poontang showing because she did not have on any panties.

My brothers and I stared with delight at the woman's nooney. She was stinking drunk, but it was still exciting to see her snatch. The three of us, Norman, Frank, and I, looked at each other and grinned with delight. This kind of police action we would like to see everyday if it meant that we would see the poontang.

With the woman on the ground, the cops again started with the man toward the squad car, but, to the surprise of the police officers, the woman jumped to her feet, and moving quick as a cat, she attacked the police officer who had pushed her down by jumping on his back. The cop quickly responded to her pouncing. He bent forward and took his right hand and reached back over his shoulder, catching the woman about the neck. He then swung the woman right over his back with a powerful, jerking thrust of his arm. The woman did a cartwheel in midair landing on her side and arm with a loud thud. She was stunned from the fall and did not move for a time.

Norman and Frank scurried back from the area of the action. The woman almost landed right where they were standing. Norman did not like what the police officer had just done, and an angry, disgusted look spread across his face. But he knew there was nothing he could do. Frank had a look of excitement on his face, and I thought he was thinking that in flipping the woman over his back, the cop had done something nifty. Frank liked the show of strength, no matter who exhibited it.

Looking at his fallen wife, the man now became enraged. He broke loose from the police officer who had been holding him under the armpit, and he jumped to his feet. He seemed to have lost his drunkenness. He then charged the cop who had thrown his wife to the ground, and with a strong blow, struck the policeman in the mouth. In receiving the blow to his face, the cop spun halfway around and almost fell down. But, when he regained his balance and turned around to confront the man who had hit him, he had his nightstick in his hand, and there was a terribly angry look on his face, a face that was turning bluish red as blood also dribbled down his chin from a cut on his bottom lip.

With a growl like that of a dog, the bleeding cop jammed his nightstick into the stomach of his attacker. The man groaned in pain as he doubled over at the waist, but he stayed on his feet. Then he began retching, and I thought he was going to vomit. That made me move further away from the fighting. There was nothing as nasty to me as vomit. My brothers didn't move. They were staring at the action with slight smiles of joy on their faces.

If the drunken man was going to throw up at that point, he never got the chance. The cop that jammed him in the stomach then whacked him right across the face with his nightstick. There was a crunching sound, and the front of the man's face seem to flatten from the blow. I thought I saw teeth go flying out of the man's mouth, and he stumbled backwards, catching hold of a street light pole to keep himself from falling. The other cop, who had done a number on the woman, then moved swiftly over to the man clinging to the light pole. The man's face was now beginning to balloon out and blood fell to the pavement in huge drops, but that did not stop the second cop from leveling a series of punches to the man's face. The policeman continued to punch him until he released the pole and fell unconscious to the pavement. As he lay there, a huge puddle of blood formed around his head. I began cringing from the sight of the blood. The color was the strangest looking red.

"Black motherfucker," the cop said.

"Yeah," the other cop said. "Let's take these two shits down to the can."

I did not like what the police officers had done to the man and woman, and I wished I could have helped them. But, along with everything else, I found myself staring at the pistols the officers were carrying, and every time I did I remembered the loud bang on Fourth Street the day that horse was killed. I didn't want those cops to shoot me, but I suspected that they had the authority to do so if they wanted to. So I had best stay out of their way.

I glanced at my brothers. They, too, looked very angry about what was going on; but like me, they did nothing. What could they do?

The two police officers grabbed the man by his arms and dragged him to the squad car. They then picked him up and threw him into the backseat of the vehicle. Next, they took hold of his wife, by the arms and legs, and they threw her into the backseat of the car directly on top of her husband. One of the officers locked the rear doors of the vehicle. For the arrested pair, there would be no escape.

While the fighting had been going on between the couple and the police officers, a number of black men came out of the beergarden and stood at the door watching the fracas. They watched with anger on their faces as the cops subdued the man and woman and threw them in the squad car like sacks of garbage. They obviously knew the couple, but like me, they did not want to become involved with the police. However, when the two officers got into the squad car and drove off, the men in the doorway of the bar began to shout names at them. "You rotten bastards."

"You sonafabitches."

"White trash."

"You red neck motherfuckers!"

The police car had gone half-of-the-way down the block when it stopped with a screech, and then the car backed up rapidly towards us. With the cop car coming towards them, the men in the doorway quickly disappeared into the bar, and I knew I should get away from the front of that bar, too. I had a bad feeling about what was going to happen next, and I did not want to get caught in the middle of it. My brothers must have had the same feeling, and the three of us ran across street, just as the squad car stopped in front of the bar.

We stood on the opposite pavement, waiting to see what was going to happen next. At that moment, the front doors of the patrol car snapped open, and the two officers jumped out. They drew their guns from their holsters, and they hustled into the bar. Seeing those guns in their hands, again I heard the sound from the shooting on Fourth Street in my head. Those white cops might shoot those black men in the bar. I held my breath in anticipation.

"They're going to shoot those guys," Norman said.

Frank nodded in agreement, and I waited for the bang. But the sounds of gunshots were not heard, and I was about to relax a little when all hell seem to suddenly break loose in the bar.

First, there were loud shouts of anger and cursing. Then, there were sounds of objects smashing together, accompanied by sounds like that of a bat hitting a softball. The shouting went on for a number of minutes before it stopped. But as soon as it did, then there were sounds of breaking wood and glass, as best as I could make out.

About ten minutes had passed before the two officers emerged from the bar. They came out smiling as they reholstered their guns. They nodded to each other, obviously pleased about what they had just done, and without taking any notice of my brothers and me standing across the street, they got back into their squad car and drove off.

With the cops gone, we could not resist the temptation to take a peek in the bar to see what had happened. Running back across the street, we stood on the steps of the beergarden and peered inside. I was shocked at what I saw. The bar had been devastated. Tables and chairs lay broken and strewn across the floor. Some broken chairs were even on the serving counter, and behind the counter a dazed bartender stood silently shaking his head in disbelief. As well, broken bottles and glasses stained the floor with beer, whiskey, and water.

But what really caught my attention was the sight of five black men lying on the floor amidst the debris. They were crying and moaning in pain, and blood was flowing down some of their faces from wounds on the top of their heads. I could not believe they were the same men that had been standing in the doorway. They now looked so much like pieces of broken furniture splattered with blood, and I wondered how those two cops were able to reduce the bar and the people on the floor to such rubble, in such a short period of time. Did white cops have the authority and power of superman?

"Woo," Frank said. "Those cops really tore-up some heads in there."

"Yeah," Norman said. "They really wacked some skulls."

On the way home, I listened to my brothers chattering about what the cops had done in that bar, and as we walked, I was thinking about cops in the movies. They were always the good guys, but movie cops did not have black people to deal with. There were very few of them on the big screen. The black actors that I knew, like Bill Robinson, Billy Best, Eddie Anderson, and Mantan Moreland, they never played important roles in the movies. Therefore, I never saw them have any confrontations with the police. They were usually grinning, dancing, shuffling their feet and saying, "Yeasirr, Mr. Boss." Now, why would a movie cop want to beat up an Uncle Tom?

CHAPTER ELEVEN

I once had a revealing incident with Mantan Moreland. Of all the black actors in Hollywood movies, it was Mantan Moreland I knew best. He played in the Sidney Tolar Charlie Chan movies. It was said that he was playing the role of Charlie Chan's chauffeur, but in reality it was his job to act as a dim-witted clown for the amusement of white movie goers. He was presented on the screen as a dumb black man who was afraid of his own shadow, and in every movie of the series, he was sure to be seen rolling his eyes around in his head in a blank, unfocused stare, while he screamed in fright, "Mr Chan, Mr. Chan!" That was the image of a black buffoon, who was afraid of the dark and constantly calling for Mr. Charlie to come and protect him.

I met Mantan Moreland one warm summer's evening. It was the first time I saw a real movie actor, and it was such a thrill. I couldn't believe it was really him until he spoke. Norman, Frank, and I came upon him standing in front of the Earle Theater, where live comedy shows were performed, at Eleventh and Market Street. It was late, and he was taking a break between shows. When we recognized him, he was reposing next to a car, smoking a cigarette while he was having a conversation with a companion.

I started grinning as I followed my brothers, and without any hesitation they walked right up to Mantan Moreland. The closer I got to him, the widder my grin became. I was always going to the movies, but now the movies had come to me.

"Hi, Birmingham." Frank poked himself right into Mr. Moreland's conversation. Birmingham was the name he used in the Charlie Chan movies.

Mantan Moreland turned away from his companion, and he looked down at Frank. "Yeah, hi kid," he said. He went back to his conversation with his companion.

"Hi Birmingham," Norman said.

Mantan Moreland did not turn to look at him. The actor only nodded his head to acknowledge the second greeting.

I didn't say anything. I was still finding it hard to believe that this was a real movie person right in front of me. Perhaps he could appreciate my grin.

Then the three of us just stood there listening in on the conversation between Mantan Moreland and the other guy. They were talking about the audience in the theater. The audience was not responding well to his performance, and the actor was saying that some nights are just like that.

The next thing that happened surprised me. Frank tapped Mantan Moreland on the arm. "You know, Birmimgham you're kinda funny in those Charlie Chan movies. You act just like someone we know."

That comment stopped Mantan Moreland right in the middle of a sentence, and he turned to look at Frank. There was not a pleasant look on his face, and he growled. "Aw forget that stuff. That's just acting." He then put out his cigarette and went back into the theater.

Frank shrugged, and we started towards home. Norman was saying that Mom would never believe us when we told her we had met Mantan Moreland. The Charlie Chan movies were favorites of hers. But, I wasn't thinking about Mom. I was trying to make some sense out of what Mantan Moreland had said about his appearance in the movies. "It was just acting," he said. What did he mean? The Hollywood motion pictures were important to me, and I believed that they were telling stories about the real world. But he had said, "That's just acting." I wanted to know what he meant, but I was too young to understand the sublty of what he was trying to convey. Nevertheless, it was still a major thrill for me to meet Mantan Moreland, and I soon forgot about what he said.

All the kids in my neighbhood, when they had the money, would go to the movies on the weekends back in the 1940s. The Saturday matinee at the Bijou, the Fairmount, or the Girard was a weekly ritual. In fact, Saturday was the time when children and young people all across America, would collectively nurture their fantasies and worship the celluloid heroes that Hollywood had packaged for them. It was a time, in our collective consciousness, when real life took a back seat to make believe.

The program for a Saturday afternoon matinee was always the same. First, there were a couple of comic shorts with Bugs Bunny, Daffy Duck, or Woody Woodpecker. Next, there would be a chapter picture with a cliff-hanging ending, followed by a cowboy movie that would be filled with horseshit and gunsmoke, and finally a mystery, monster, or horror flick. We were able to see the whole program for a mere thirteen cents.

The cowboy pictures were a particular favorite of my brothers and me. In those B-class Westerns, we knew what we were going to get every time. It was always the case of the good guys, the white or brown hats, against the bad guys, the black hats, with the good guys winning in the end. And the good guys were always tall, strong, forthright, moral, and rugged individualists. They were protectors of the little fellow and the underdog, and they were always ready to lay down their lives for the Caucasian woman. As people, the behavior of these movie cowboys was always larger than life and more akin to the activities of Greek Gods than mortal men. And these hero-cowboys were always white.

The one movie cowboy that Norman, Frank, and I admired the most was Buck Jones, one of the three Rough Riders. The Rough Riders were fast-drawing, hard-punching former Texas Rangers who lived apart but reunited to fight bad guys whenever law and order was threatened in any frontier town. They would get a cabled message that they were needed somewhere, and they would sally forth from their ranches to beat back the hands of the bad guys. When they had accomplished their task, the Riders would then separate again, riding off in three different directions, as their theme music thundered in the background, "When the Rough Riders ride, beware!" and the movie screen darkened.

We liked Buck Jones the best because he was the coolest of the Riders. With his penetrating eyes, he could stare down and scare away most baddies, and if he did not scare them away, he could out punch any black hat with his flashing fists. Also, he could draw his gun as fast as lightning. And when Buck Jones put his chewing gum in his mouth, "look out Mr Baddy 'cause your time has definitely come."

Buck Jones was a he-man, an example of the best of what any man could be. He was seen as being a powerful person in body and mind, which was consistent with the fact that he was a white man. White people had the power in society, in and out of the movies. Buck Jones was just one example of it.

There was a series of Rough Rider movies, and in each one Buck Jones did his he-man thing time and time again. Even Allen had to admit that Buck Jones was one of his favorite cowboy movie stars, although he liked Tom Mix just a little better.

And then one day, it came out of the blue, the surprise of all surprises. Buck Jones would appear in, and be the star attraction at the Gimbel Brothers 1942 Thanksgiving Day Parade. He would ride his horse down Philadelphia's Broad Street, and we would have the opportunity to see him in person. Going to the Thanksgiving Day Parade to see the clowns, the celebrities, and the Mummers' Bands was a yearly ritual for the Cooper boys. There were times when even some of the girls would go to the parade, but if it was a very cold Thanksgiving Day, usually only Norman, Frank, and I would be there. And now we had a special reason to go to the Parade. It was going to be a day to remember, a delicious event.

On Thanksgiving Day morning, my brothers and I arose very early. In fact, none of us had slept very much the night before. The Parade was not to start until 9:30, but we had gotten up long before that time to be sure that we would get to Broad Street before the crowd arrived. With Buck Jones in the Parade, we wanted to have good curbside seats. It was only seven o'clock when we went downstairs from our bedroom. It was the usual three of us, and after a quick breakfast of cereal, we decided to play a game to pass away the time until we left for the Parade. Since the rest of the household was still in bed, we went back to our room to play. Naturally, we played cowboys and Indians.

Norman and Frank wanted to be cowboys, and who do you think was the Indian? My brothers wanted authenticity that morning. They borrowed some of my mother' rouge and lipstick, and they painted up my face to look like Hollywood's conception of an Indian Brave on the warpath. We were going to the Parade to see a real cowboy. So, my brothers wanted to play cowboy to a real look alike Indian.

With my bee-bee gun and make up on, we played a most energetic and engaging game of cowboys and one Indian for over two hours. With our hoots and hollers, we soon had the entire household up, and we raced from one room of the house to the other, firing bee-bees and throwing broom handle lances at one another. We became so wrapped up in the game, we completely lost track of time until Mom told us that it was a quarter to ten. "My God," Norman screamed. "The Parade has already begun."

Without a moment's hesitation, we grabbed our coats and raced from the house. Only the three of us were going to the Parade that day and to reach the route of the Parade, on Broad Street, we had only to go straight up Noble Street. Noble Street intersected with Broad Street, but that connection occurred eleven blocks from our house. We took off running as fast as our feet would carry us, and we did not stop until we reached Broad Street. I was willing to bet we set a world's record for the mile that morning.

When we arrived at Broad Street, huffing and puffing, the Parade was in full swing, and we pushed our way through the large crowd that stood between us and the curbside. We were not going to be denied. Some mothers' children would just have to give way and make room for us.

When we reached the curbside and immediately looked northward, the direction from which the Parade was flowing, we realized that we had not arrived a moment too soon. There, coming towards us, just two blocks away, was a white horse with a cowboy on it. Although we could not make out the face of the rider, we knew it had to be Buck Jones, our hero. Who else could it be? And what was even more exciting, Buck Jones wasn't just riding his horse down the street and waving to the crowd like previous celebrities I had seen. He had his rope out, and he was throwing it into the crowds along the curbsides.

He would use his rope like a cowboy did when he was roping steers on the range. He would throw his rope into the crowd and lasso a little kid, and then he would gently pull the young person from the curb to the foot of his horse where he would say a few words to the boy or girl before he removed the lariat. Buck Jones was going from one side of the street to the other, lassoing kids as he came down Broad Street.

As the Hollywood cowboy neared us, the familiar face of our steely-eyed hero took form. It was really he, Mr. Buck Jones, and he looked just the same as he did in the movies. He had on the same big ten-gallon hat, the same form fitting clothes that never got rumpled in a fight, and the same shiny, brown boots. I was so pleased and thrilled to see him that I started giggling uncontrollably.

And then, Buck Jones was right in front of us, not more than ten or twelve feet away, and he was staring in my direction with those pene-trating eyes. "I'm not a bad guy, Mr. Jones," I wanted to say, but I was too excited to speak. Before I realized what was happening, just like that, he threw his rope in the air and it came down over my body. The Rough Rider had lassoed me, and he began pulling me from the curbside.

My brothers watched me being pulled from the curb, and there was a look of astonishment on their faces. Buck Jones had actually lassoed their kin, and at the same time the people who had been standing near to us began shouting and cheering. "You caught one, Buck! You caught one!"

I was scared as he pulled me toward the horse he was sitting on. Then the pulling stopped, and right in my face was the silver spurred boot of Buck Jones. The spur rested in a stirrup that was pressed against the body of the white horse. The horse jiggled his feet a little, and I looked up into the face of the Rough Rider. He looked down at me, unsmiling and with a serious purse to his lips. He studied my face quickly and leaned down form his saddle toward me. "What ails ya boy? What ails ya?"

"I ain't no bad guy, Mr Jones." My voice trembled. "I ain't no bad guy."

"Yeah, I know, son." His voice was firm and reassuring. "I know." He then took his lariat off of me, wrapped it up in cowboy lopes and rode off down the street without saying another word.

I did not watch him go. I just ran back to my brothers and the crowd at the curbside. The people in the crowd stared at me as I returned, and some of them began to laugh. "Buck Jones caught an Indian. He caught an Indian just like in the movies"

"Hey," Frank said. "You still got that lipstick and stuff on your face. Everybody thinks you're an Indian."

Is that what it was? Suddenly I felt safe, and I wasn't scared anymore. Buck Jones did not thinik I was "a niggah" or one of the bad guys. He wanted to know why my face was all colored with rouge and lipstick. He had no mean thoughts for me, and now I could look down Broad Street after him. There he was, still lassoing young people from the curbside. And now I felt good about the way he drew me to him when I had been roped. There was such power in the way he had pulled me from the crowd. When I looked up to him, he looked so big, tall, and strong sitting on that white horse, and there was power in his voice when he asked me, "What ails ya boy?" Yes, Buck Jones was everything the movies portrayed him to be, and there was nothing fake about him. He was a real genuine Rough Rider.

For the next few days, as best as I can remember, I was feeling very happy and secure in myself. I had been hog-tied by Buck Jones, and I believed that he had become my protector, the same way he protected those frontier people in the movies. He was the white man on the white horse, and I had a right to feel proud that he had picked me out of the Thanksgiving Day crowd. I surmised that it could not have been an accident. With my faith in the power of the movies to stimulate my imagination, I believed it was something that had to happen. I was sure it meant that under Buck Jones' protection my life would most definitely get better. Things were always better on the frontier when the Rough Riders came to town. I missed out on a fairy godmother, but now I had a fairy godfather. "Ain't I the lucky one."

Not quite, because fate had other plans for me. It was a lesson I would learn over and over again throughout my life.

Two days after I had been lassoed by Buck Jones, the movie hero was dead. He died in the Boston Cocoanut Grove nightclub fire on November 28, 1942. From all accounts, he died as a real life hero. When a fire first started in the nightclub, it was reported that Buck Jones got out of the nightclub safely, but he then returned to the smokey premises to try to save other trapped patrons. That was a fatal mistake. He died with 490 other people.

Buck Jones' death was a hard blow for me to take. In my childish way, I generally understood that people died, but not Buck Jones. He had made a commitment when he lassoed me, and therefore he had an obligation to protect me until my life got better. Death put an immediate end to that flawed, immature logic. Death had caused the man to forsake his movie image, and I worshipped the movie image because I did not know the flesh and blood man.

That's what Mantan Moreland was trying to tell me. "It's just acting, kid. Just acting."

CHAPTER TWELVE

Upon completing the sixth grade, my educational sojourn at Paxson Elementary School came to an end. It was time for me to move on to Junior High School, and as such I would be leaving friends I had spent six years with. For the first time in my life, I came to realize that friends come and friends go. I was certainly going to miss Juanita, but in any case, my kindergarten friends and I had reached a parting of ways. Other significant changes were set to occur in my life. I spent some time at Stoddart-Fleisher Junior High School, and then my family moved uptown to Kensington. Leaving the Noble Street neighborhood was one of the hardest things I ever had to do. My family had lived at the 238 address for many, many years, and even with all the problems we had there, it had been a special place for us; a place where we could put down roots and become a member of a community. There were times when we had been hungry and without heat in the dead of the winter, but as Dorothy discovered on her visit to Oz, as bad as things may get at home, there was still no place like it.

When Mom told us that we would be moving uptown, I don't think any of her children believed her. It didn't seem like we had the right to move. The 238 address was not just a house, it was an atmosphere, a unique environment that put our stamina to the test. It was a house that had taken us out of the twentieth century, back to a time when people had to be more family oriented and more self-reliant. The night before

we packed up and moved, I walked around the Noble Street neighborhood, and I was feeling more than just nostalgic. I did not cry, but as I
looked at the meat plants along Third and American Streets, and I
walked down near the coal cars on Willow Street, I knew I was leaving
something behind that could never be recaptured again. That made me
feel sad, but I could also accept, without quarrel, that if Mom said it was
time to leave Noble Street, then it was time to go. I would say goodbye
to friends and neighbors and that would be that.

There were also practical and emotional inducements that encouraged me to accept my departure from the Noble Street house. We were
told that the new house on Hope Street would have electricity, central
heating, hot running water, and no outhouse. We were coming back to
the twentieth century. Perhaps some of the good things in life would
finally be heading our way.

Our new house was a half a block from the Frankford El trains. I
knew that El line well, and being close to it meant there would be easy
access to transportation up and down town. I would have little difficulty in visiting Noble Street whenever I felt the need. My mother had
gotten a job as a nurse's aide in one of the city hospitals. She would have
to use that El line to get to and from work. The nurse's aide position was
a civil service job, which meant that after her probationary period, she
would have a permanent job. When my mother got her first paycheck,
she took the family off of welfare, It was the first time we had been off of
public assistance in over a decade. To mark the occasion she gave a party
just for her children. It was a party like no other. We ate delicious food
and reminisced about the life we had lived on Noble Street.

From Friday to Sunday, Mom spent the days in the kitchen cooking
every manner of food that her children liked. With twelve children, that
was a lot of likes to satisfy. She cooked chicken, roast pork, pot roast, meat
loaf, hamhocks and greens. She cooked sweet potato pie, apple pie, blue-
berries and dumplings, shortening bread and peaches, coconut cake, and
bread pudding. My mother cooked endlessly, and my brothers, sisters, and

I ate endlessly. That weekend was never to be forgotten. No welfare for the Cooper family ever again!

"Johnny isn't it fun to have a party like this." Marion said.

"Yeah, it's great."

"I've never seen Mom so happy." Dotty said.

"Well, she feels free."

"Why is that?" Dotty said.

"Oh, don't you know?" Marion said.

"No."

"She is making her own money."

"Didn't she do that before?" Dotty said

"Not when you're on welfare." I said.

"Why?"

"Welfare money comes from public assistance."

"So it was given to Mom."

"Yeah. And you know sometimes the check didn't come."

"I'll say," Marion said.

"But now she is working, and she's getting paid. Mom says that's better, and that's why she is happy." I said.

"I'm glad. Now Mom can have her own money." Dotty laughed.

"That's right, and I am going to go and get some more bread pudding."

Getting off of welfare was a happy experience in my young life. It was true that as a child I never had to fight with caseworkers or the welfare bureaucracy as my mother had done, but I had known the degradation of living on public assistance. It was something about which I never made a point of telling my friends. If they knew about it, we never discussed or acknowledged the matter. Families on public assistance were the poorest of the poor, and even in the Noble Street neighborhood, I had occasionally been made fun of for being on welfare.

I did not know it at the time, but there had always been a danger for me in growing up on welfare. I may have wanted to deny it, but I was slow in maturing. I was afraid to grow up. I wrapped myself in the fantasy of the

movies and the persona of celebrated personalities, and I would probably
still be waiting for my fairy godmother or godfather if my mother had not
changed the family's social context by getting a job and moving us out of
the Noble Street area. I believe she knew our move to Hope Street would
be more than just a change in location.

Our new home was in a different environment than the neighborhood of Noble Street. The houses were much more up to date, and
commercial buildings were conspicuous by their absence. There were
no dilapidated buildings on our new street, and no signs of deep, abid-
ing poverty like in my old neighborhood. All the homes on the street
were flat-faced, rectangular row houses with narrow windows and
doors. At first glance, it was a monotonous view, but what gave the individual houses some distinction were their colors. They were painted in
light, bright, living colors. The view was somewhat tacky, but not
unpleasant. The house we were moving into had a light, brown facade.
The Noble Street neighborhood had been drab and colorless, but Hope
street looked bright and colorful. I felt good about that. And even the
sun seemed to shine brighter uptown.

Our new home was smaller than the one on Noble Street. There were
only two floors to the house, with three small, compact bedrooms
upstairs. It would be a tight squeeze finding living space for the entire
family, but that was worth it because we had stepped forward into the
modern era. The house also had a very nice, clean cellar, and the floor of
the cellar was covered with linoleum. The basement was a good, safe
place for the young kids to play. And, one of the most pleasing things
about our new Hope Street home was the fact that it was not overrun
with rats, roaches, and other vermin. However, the chinches had moved
uptown with us.

Initially, on the surface of things, it appeared as though our move to
Kensington was entirely in the family's best interest, but I soon learned
that my new neighborhood had a much darker side. Blacks lived within
two adjoining blocks on Hope Street, but the surrounding community

was all white. The whole of Kentsington was a much more segregated community than the Noble Street area had been. I can only speculate as to the reason why. The whites who lived closest to Hope Street, and the ones that I came to know the best were largely second generation immigrants from Eastern Europe who had achieved the status of skilled, blue collar workers and lower class professionals like electricians and plumbers. These individuals had made it to the ranks of the lower middle-class, but they wanted to go further up the social ladder. They saw themselves as achieving greater upward mobility through their children. Using education as a springboard, they wanted their children to become doctors, lawyers, and teachers in the future.

The upwardly mobile whites in the Hope Street neighborhood did not want to look back or down the social ladder. They wanted to forget where they came from because they were only interested in where they were going. Black people were a reminder of the places at the bottom of the social system. Therefore, they wanted little or no contact with us. The blacks could live in their neighborhood just as long as they stayed in their place, on their street, particularly after dark. There was to be no socializing between whites in the neighborhood and the blacks on Hope Street. Contact between black and white kids in school was unavoidable, but other than that the taboo remained in force.

Some months after I moved to Hope Street, a friend of mine from the Guild came uptown to see me. He rode his bike all the way. My friend's name was Nelson Reyes. Nelson was Puerto Rican, and he did not look like he was a black person. He had a full head of straight, jet-black hair and a Castilian complexion. He came uptown to show off his new Schwinn bicycle, and he took me for a ride. We went up Dauphin Street through an all white block.

It was a warm day, and many people were sitting on their porches and stoops. As we rode down the center of the street, the whites began name-calling.

"Goddamn, salt and pepper riding together."

"Hey you nigger. Get the hell out of here!"

"Yeah, get the hell away from here, nigger, and take that gypsy with you. We don't want your kind around here."

Nelson sped away from Dauphin Street as fast as he could go, and when we got back to Hope Street, he said to me, "Why didn't you tell me not to go up that street?"

"I didn't know how those people would act." I said. " But why didn't you tell me you were a gypsy?"

"I ain't no gypsy."

"That's what they called you."

"They're crazy."

"If you say so."

Now don't misunderstand me. Kensington was not like the Deep South. There were no signs saying where blacks could or should not go, but there was a pervasive attitude among the white people about it.

Kensington Avenue, right underneath the El train, was a business district. There were all kinds of stores and restaurants running northward, block after block up that street. Of course, blacks could go shopping on Kensington Avenue because white people, who owned all the stores, were never bashful when it came to taking black people's money. Still, it was an odd thing to see white and black people shopping together in the stores. The two groups rarely communicated to one another in the process, and they would seem to go about their business like ships passing in the night. I felt most uncomfortable whenever I had to go to one of the stores on "the Avenue," and that was particularly true whenever I went into the Woolworth Store. A salesperson or one of the assistant mangers would follow, from counter to counter, any black person who came into that store. Apparently, all black people were thought to be potential thieves, man, woman, or child.

But what was even more disgusting was the fact that just about every single store on the Avenue generally treated blacks like they were unclean aliens. When blacks went into the supermarket to buy food, they were watched very closely by the store's personnel, and they were not allowed to touch food, like vegetables, fruits, bread, packaged meats, and boxed products unless they put it directly into their carts to be purchased. However, blacks were permitted to look at canned goods and put them back on the shelves. I guess the whites thought that the tin can would protect the food inside from the uncleanliness.

The clothing stores were also a mess. Black patrons were not allowed to try on clothing before they made their purchases especially women's dresses and men's pants. Moreover, the black person had better know his clothing size correctly if he purchased such items on the Avenue because there was no return, exchange, or refund policy for blacks. The white shop owners assumed that if a black person bought an item of clothing and took it home, then he must have tried it on. They would not take it back.

Apparently, in renting the house on Hope Street, my mother did not know she was moving into a white, enclave neighborhood. The house we now lived in was better, more modern, and the surrounding environment was cleaner, more appealing, and more colorful. But we had been swallowed up by a white community just like Jonah had been swallowed by the whale. We were semi-prisoners in the whiteness of the Kensington community, and we had to learn to live with that situation. But, there was a limit.

There were three movie theaters in a five block walking distance of our Hope Street house. One of these theaters was only a half a block from my new home. Two of the theaters, I was to discover, including the one nearest to my house, had Jim Crow seating arrangements. That was something I had never been confronted with back in the Noble Street neighborhood. My brothers and I knew what Jim Crow was because our Mom had told us about it.

The first time I went to the theater nearest my house, I went with my brothers Norman, Frank, and Ducky. When we arrived at the theater, we walked up to the movie booth and brought our tickets, and started into the theater. As we were handing our tickets to a white man at the door, he said, "Are you new around here? I've never seen you before at this theater."

"Yeah," Frank said. "We just moved in down the block."

"I thought so." The man smiled. "Cause I know all the colored people around here."

"You do," Norman said.

"Yes I do," the man said. "And I wanna tell ya that in this theater you have to sit over on the far side in the last four rows, all right?"

"Whatta ya mean?" Frank said.

The man looked at him strangely. "Don't ya understand English? I said you haveta sit over on the right in the last four rows."

"And why is that?" Norman said.

"Yeah," I said. "Why is that?"

"Tell us," Ducky said. He cocked his head inquisitively to the side.

"Whatta ya mean about what I mean?" The man was becoming flustered. "You gotta sit over there cause that's where the colored sit."

"You're telling me this place is Jim Crowed?" Frank put his hands on his hips to emphasize his question.

"Jim Crowed?" The ticket taker looked truly confused. "I don't know anything about Jim Crowed. I only know that coloreds sit over there."

Frank kept his hands on his hips and looked the man straight in the eye. "Why do I have to sit over there? Is my money different than anybody else's money?"

"Naw, your money's the same, but ya suppose to sit over there."

"Well, we're not gonna sit over there." Frank took his hands off of his hips, as he curled his lips back into a nasty snarl.

The ticket taker became uneasy. There were four of us and only one of him. We were not little boys anymore. We were all teenagers, and Frank in particular had strong, powerful looking arms.

The man backed away from us a little ways. "If you don't want to sit over there, then you gotta leave the theater. Here's ya tickets and you can get ya money back."

We did not go into that movie house that day, and the four of us fumed about its Jim Crow seating policy for the rest of the afternoon and evening. And the more we thought about it, the angrier we became. We now saw ourselves as living in Red Neck Philadelphia.

We decided that we were never going to go to the two Jim Crow theaters because we believed that no ticket collector had the right to tell us where we could or could not sit. We kept our promise for a number of months, and we only went to the theater that did not practice Jim Crow, or we went to the movie houses downtown. However, eventually, a new movie came to the theater up the street from our house that my brothers and I had to see. It was the 1951 movie version of The Thing.

"We're gonna see that movie," Frank said. "And we ain't gonna sit in no corner of the theater, either."

The four of us, Norman, Frank, Ducky, and me, discussed what we were going to do when we got to the movie house. We would buy our tickets, give them to the ticket taker at the door, and we would let him tell us where the colored people were supposed to sit. But once we were in the theater, we would sit wherever we damn well pleased.

That's what we did, and when we were inside the theater, we sat down in the middle of the center row of seats. The theater was rather crowded that day, filled with many young people, almost all of them white. Our seats were a couple of rows in front of a group of white boys, and as we took our seats we could hear them grumbling.

"What are they doing over here?"

"They're not suppose to be in this area."

"Let's make 'um move before they spoil the picture for us."

Neither any of my brothers nor I said anything to the white kids in back of us. And they were not the only whites that were disturbed by our presence sitting in the center row of seats. We heard murmurings and a few ethnic slurs slashing the air all about us, but most of the young white people were too timid to speak directly to us.

When the picture finally started, the majority of the moviegoers immediately became involved in the drama of the film, but not the group of boys to the rear of us. They started throwing popcorn and Juicy Fruit candy at us. At first, the popcorn and candy only hit me and Ducky, but then a hard piece of Juicy Fruit candy hit Frank right in the back of the head.

What the hell?" he shouted. He stood up.

We all knew where the candy and popcorn was coming from, and Frank turned around and jumped over two rows of seats in a crowded theater, landing right in the middle of the five white boys who had been throwing at us. Frank stood over them as they sat in their seats, even as a chorus of people was telling him to sit down. He ignored the other white kids. "Now who's throwing candy down there at us?"

One of the white boys, a tall stringy looking lad, who I guessed was the leader of the group stood up and said, "I threw that can…" Before he could finish the last word of his bold admission, Frank hit the boy with a right uppercut. The fellow screamed, and he went over the back of his seat, coming to rest with his head down and his face right in the middle of a teenage girl's crotch, or so Frank told me later. He had hit the boy just at the point in the movie when The Thing was seen clearly for the first time. The creature screamed at just that moment, and in the theater, the boy that Frank punched also screamed. The two screams seemed to coincide, and some of the young people in the movie house, mostly girls, especially the girl who had the punched boy's face between her legs, looked up and saw this black figure, Frank, standing against the background of the motion picture screen, and they started shouting, "The Thing is in the theater. The Thing is in the theater, and he is beating up some kid." A couple of girls actually jumped up and ran back to the lobby.

Most of the kids in the theater had not even seen what Frank had done because they were too busy looking at the action on the motion picture screen. Those individuals who did see Frank's whopping punch got the shit scared out of them, but Frank wasn't the blame. The tall stringy, white boy, and the rest of his bunch, were responsible.

Frank jumped back over the two rows of seats and sat down next to us, and a short time later the ticket collector, who also doubled as the theater's usher, came walking down the aisle, followed by two frightened girls. He came up to the row of seats we were sitting in, and he flashed his light in our faces. I don't know what he was going to say, but he never got the chance to say it. Suddenly voices began flying through the darken movie theater.

"Hey, turn that flashlight off! You're spoiling the movie!"

"Hey bonehead, no lights!"

"Put that light out! I paid my money to sit in the dark!"

The ticket collector quickly turned his flashlight off, and he went back up the aisle followed by the slouching, frightened girls. He never came back to bother us again, nor did he say anything to us on our way out. The white boys in back of us did not throw any more popcorn and candy during the movie. I guess they were afraid that The Thing would come back and get them if they did. And, after that day, we never concerned ourselves with Jim Crow seating arrangements in that movie house. Some black people from Hope Street continued to sit in the segregated section of the theater for a time, but eventually the word got around that blacks and whites could sit anywhere they wanted in the movie house.

With our success in desegregating the movie theater up the block, my brothers and I decided soon thereafter that we would defy the Jim Crow policy at that other movie house, which was three blocks away. That time, we got seven other Hope Street kids to join us, and we descended upon that bastion of Jim Crowism one afternoon and sat down right in the middle of the theater. No one in the movie house, the white patrons or management personnel, contested our right to sit wherever we chose. Jim Crow had gotten its neck wrung at that second theater without a whimper. To this day, I wonder why. Could it have been that the management of the second movie house had heard that there was a Thing loose that looked like a black person, and it was attacking white people in the neighborhood movie theaters? Like Birmingham in the motion pictures, white people do not like messing with things they don't understand either.

CHAPTER THIRTEEN

The move to Hope Street thrust my family into a new social environment, and it had consequences that could not have been anticipated. It would seem that our movement up the social ladder, even though it was only a half-step from the bottom, had a bad effect on our family as a unit and, in particular, the relationships between my older brothers.

Mom's job did not pay much, but from her Noble Street experience, she still knew how to stretch a dollar. And even though the family just got by from paycheck to paycheck, there was no longer any need for us to be thieves as before. The family could now survive without our use of the stealth and cunning that had given rise to a special kind of camaraderie between my brothers and me. Battling hunger, cold and ongoing deprivation, we had developed the attitude of soldiers who were fighting in a war against poverty. But now that we lived in Kensington, all we had to do was just wait for Mom to come home with her paycheck.

In very quick succession, our male-dominated family structure began to come apart. A few months after we moved to Hope Street, Abie joined the Army, and he was to later fight in the Korean War. Some months after Abie joined the Army, Frank joined the Army, and a few weeks after Frank joined the Army, Norman joined the Marine Corps. Around the same time, Allen, who began working as a messenger for the Western Union Telegraph Company, got his own apartment in our old neighborhood downtown. Consequently, in less than a year after we had moved to Hope Street, all my older brothers had left home.

Strange as it may seem, I was not unhappy to see my brothers go out into the world on their own. They would be striving to make a better life for themselves, and I had the feeling that they would have a better chance at it if they separated themselves from the family. Also, their leaving made life better for those of us who were left at home. There were four fewer mouths to feed, and there was less household congestion. More than anything else, when my older brothers left home, my role in the family changed considerably. I was the senior male in the household and big brother to all my siblings, except Marion.

Moving uptown also brought a change in school for me. I was assigned to a new school, Penn Treaty Junior High School, which was located quite a distance from Hope Street in one of the most segregated communities in all of Philadelphia. Penn Treaty was located in Fishtown, a neighborhood that sat to the east on the southern most border of Kensington. Fishtown was made up almost entirely of blue collar, working class people whose culture and lineage went back to Ireland. The people of the area were famous for their ethnocentric attitude, which said that the best people were the working class Irish.

Fishtown was almost entirely a residential neighborhood. Street after street was lined with porch fronted houses that were old but very well kept. All the houses seem to be painted with the same color, a rustic brown. There was nothing obtrusive about the houses, and the people were not very friendly. On the many occasions that I walked through Fishtown, never once did anyone say a greeting like, "Hello," or "Good morning." I was to learn later why these Fishtown people kept such a distance from me.

Given the character of the neighborhood that surrounded it, Penn Treaty was a white school. Of the hundreds of students who went there, only a handful of blacks were in attendance. The black students like me were all from neighborhoods far from Fishtown, and being a student at the school occurred more as an accident than on purpose.

My first day at Penn Treaty was a memorable one. After taking care of the administrative business of my transfer in the main office, I was taken to my assigned classroom, and as I walked through the door, a barrage of white faces leaped at me from all over the room. Those white students stared at me so sharply, I felt as though I was being cut to ribbons with razor blades, and that was to be my homeroom class. I would be with most of these white kids for the entire school day. Moreover, I found no comfort in the fact that there were no other black students in my homeroom class, and that situation would remain that way for the year I spent at Penn Treaty.

Because of my good scholastic record at my previous junior high school, I was placed in the top academic class, the number one section for my grade level, at Penn Treaty. I was to sit with the best and brightest of my age group, and apparently that was very disconcerting to many of my new classmates. As I was to learn, there had never been a black student in the number one section before, and the white kids in the class did not know how to handle it. The way they would usually fend me off was with forced smiles and cold stares.

My number one section classmates were not alone. Throughout that first day of school, I was slapped and punched by dead smiles, taunting smirks, and looks of incredulity and amazement from white students. Could a black kid really be smart enough to be in the number one section of his grade? Of course not. Someone must have made a mistake. It was bad enough to pick up that message from white students, but the few black students I saw gave me the same looks.

I do remember the coolness of my reception that first day at Penn Treaty, but there are great gaps in my memory about the rest of that year I spent there. I don't remember the teachers, the subjects I studied, or any of the daily activities of the school day. I do not specifically remember students as individuals, but I have recollections of them as a group with indistinguishable faces. I have no feeling or memories of anything warm, good, pleasant or happy happening to me as a student at Penn Treaty.

After my first few weeks at Penn Treaty, I became aware of the existing tensions between black and white students. It was there, but it usually did not get out of hand. I give tremendous credit to the teachers and the school administration for that. The principal and his staff members were dedicated to creating an excellent learning environment for the students, above all else. Everyone worked tirelessly to keep the students focused on learning. However, there was an incident at the school that almost reversed that situation.

The incident occurred in the Spring Term of my year at Penn Treaty. It was just another day at school until a fight broke out in a gym class between a white and black girl. The fight lasted only a few seconds, with none of the principals involved obtaining even a scratch, but afterward word spread throughout the school that a black student had knifed a white girl student. The false report spread like a communicable disease, and it became a call to combat for the Fishtowners.

I first heard the news of the incident as I was passing through the halls between classes. Soon thereafter, white students began shouting, "Niggers get out of school! And you betta get on the boat! Go back to Africa before we cut your throat!"

Over and over again, I heard calls for niggers to get out of school. The white kids didn't say it to my face. They said nasty things when I was not looking at them or they would shout out racial slurs from behind me. I did not want to get into a verbal confrontation with any student, nor did I want to get into a fight with one. But I was not going to let any white kid call me a nigger to my face.

Fortunately, no white student actually made any physical advances toward me. I believe it was because I was in the number one section, but if the whites wanted to attack me or any other black student at school, there would have been no contest. I heard no nasty racial remarks from the white students in my immediate class, the kids I was with every day. But, by the same token, they did not give me any support either. They remained neutral.

A couple of my classmates gave me sympathetic looks of support, but they would not stand by me openly. The teachers, however, were very supportive and protective of me. Many of them went about the school trying to keep everyone cool, and time and time again they explained that no one was stabbed.

Along with the name calling in the hallways, epithets and graffiti began to appear on the hall walls and in the bathrooms.

"Monkies go back to Africa."

"Niggers should still be slaves."

"Fishtown is for whites and not baboons."

"Negroes are not people. They are coons."

In the lunchroom, food was thrown at black students, and the lockers of black students were broken into. One black girl, a little mousy kid, was pushed down a flight of stairs, but luckily she was not hurt badly.

By mid-day, the school administration and the teachers knew they were sitting on social dynamite, but they could not control the situation. Things were happening too fast. Of course, it was clear to me that these prejudicial feelings that the white students had for blacks had been inside of them all along like an accident waiting to happen. The fight in the gym sparked the racial tension, but it didn't create the racism.

As the name-calling and racial incidents increased during the day, I found it impossible to concentrate on the subjects in my classes. Indeed, there was only one subject being taught in school that day, and it had little to do with the three R's. I was further struck by the fact that the white students were enjoying what was happening. Calling me and other black students niggers seemed to give them a new vitality, a certain type of self-actualization. They were not simply angry. They were happy-angry.

As time wore on, word got around the school that the black students would get their asses kicked when classes were over for the day. I did not like the sound of that because I knew the black kids at Penn Treaty were not likely to get help from the people in the Fishtown area. I thought I might have to fight my way home, and that was a long way to go.

Being in school all day, I did not know that by noon the false news of a stabbing had spread through the surrounding community, and the Fishtown residents were calling for revenge. By the time two-thirty rolled around, Penny Treaty was surrounded by an angry mob of white adults who were calling for street justice for all the black students. The angry mob did not care about truth. They were nigger hunting.

The police were called, and the principal asked every black student to report to his office and not to leave the premises when the final bell sounded. When the white students left the school, the mob outside quickly realized that the black students were not being allowed to leave, and they began to hoot and holler. Someone threw a brick through the principal's window.

I remember peering out of the schoolhouse windows at the angry mob, and thinking, "Would those people really hurt me? I mean, like lynch me?" I saw women in the crowd. Some of them were holding little babies. Would those women attack me with their babies in their arms? Did they hate black people that much? When a second brick whistled through the glass windowpane near me, I got the answer to my questions.

All the black students were huddled in the principal's office, and we were scared as hell. The principal tried to calm us down, but he was not having much success. No matter what he said, we knew that there was an angry, racist mob waiting for us outside. There were about eleven of us black kids in the principal's office, and there were hundreds of Fistowners outside. When the principal tried to tell the crowd from his window that there had been no stabbing, he almost got his head taken off with another brick. And then a voice shouted, "Give us those little niggers, and let us give them an ass kicking."

From the principal's window, I could see police squad cars and maybe a dozen or more uniformed officers moving about the angry mob. The police ordered the people to go home, but the people ignored the cops. The mob even shouted back to the police, "You go home. You don't live here. This is our neighborhood, and we know how to protect our kids from boogies." They could defy the cops because the officers were so few in numbers, and the police were not very anxious to use force against the Fishtowners.

As we waited inside the school, the mob would quiet down for some minutes, but then they would get loud again. "Bring the boogies out! Bring the boogies out!" The people in the street said it over and over again, and the looks on their faces were like the looks I saw on the white students faces earlier that day in school. They were not just angry, but they were happy-angry.

It was a stalemate. The black students were not coming out, and with the police at hand, the mob was not going in. After about a half an hour or forty minutes, a police sergeant came inside the school and told the principal that the officers would escort the black students out of school and to the nearest public transportation system. Even the police knew that none of the black students lived in the immediate school area of Fishtown. They would escort us to Girard Avenue where we could get a trolley going west. That was good enough for me. I just wanted enough room to run. No one was going to get me if I could just get up a head of speed.

Most of the black students did not want to leave the school because they were too afraid of the mob. But the police obviously wanted to resolve the situation so that the Fishtowners would cool off. And then there was the practical matter. We could not stay in school forever. We had to go home sometime.

The sergeant told us to wait there until he came back, and he left the principal's office. The little mousey girl who had been pushed down the stairs began to cry. She was sure she was going to be murdered when she left the building. Other black students had similar concerns, but they did not cry. I think, like me, they were too scared to cry, and that was good. In that kind of situation, Frank would be the first one to say that crying would not do you any good.

The police sergeant returned, and we were all led down to the front exit of the building. When we emerged from the school, angry white adults tried to converge on us, but the police kept them away. Using their bodies and their police cars, the officers surrounded us and led us down the center of the street, away from Penn Treaty and towards Girard Avenue. A number of teachers walked with us, keeping their bodies between the mob and us.

Having been rebuffed, the white people screamed at us, and angry voices began exploding in my ears like cannon fire.

An old, grandfather type person shouted, "Get those niggers."

"Beat those black bastards," a twisted face man said.

"Animals, that's what they are," a woman screamed.

A man with a bat in his hand was jumping up and down. "They're not fit to be around white kids."

"Which one of you boogie's stabbed that white girl?" A teenager said. "Who did it?"

"Just let me get at one of those nigger kids and we'll never have any more trouble with them."

"Yeah, and you betta not come back to this school tomorrow!"

To look at the faces in the mob made me think those people would surely kill us if they could get to us. However, the police and the teachers kept them away. Half of a block from Penn Treaty, the police used their cars to cut off the entire street leading from the school, sidewalk to sidewalk, curbside to building walls. They stopped the mob from walking on the pavement along side of us. Half of the contingent of police held back the mob as other officers and teachers led us for another long block to Girard Avenue.

With the Fishtown mob behind us, we reached Girard Avenue, and as we did, I broke away from the police, the teachers, and the rest of the black students. I ran as fast as my legs would carry me and then some. I had no intention of waiting for a trolley car. I had more faith in my running ability than public transportation, and I was confident that no adult Fishtowner could catch me if he was on foot.

I ran for blocks and blocks. Just like my brothers, I was an excellent long distance runner. As I was running that afternoon, I thought about the Thanksgiving Day when Norman, Frank, and I had run from the Noble Street house all the way to Broad Street to see Buck Jones. Being excited or scared can seem to put wings on my feet. I was running like Mercury. I did not stop running until I was completely out of Fishtown, and by a long way around, I eventually got back to Hope Street.

When I got home, I was exhausted. I was tired from the running, and I was tired from feeling frightened and threatened. I had seen some ugly and scary white faces that day, and when Mom came home from work, I excitedly told her all about it. She listened to my every word, and when I was finished telling her about everything that had happened, her first reaction was to become very angry. Then she cried, and then she hugged and kissed me. "Don't worry, John. Those people are not going to hurt ya."

The next day, Mom told me to stay home, and she took the morning off from work. She said she was going to my school. "Let me go with ya, Mom. Those people over there are crazy. Let me go, too."

"No, John," she said to me coolly. "You stay home. I'll be all right. I'm just going over there to talk to your principal."

"But Mom, it's the people 'round that school that you have to be careful of."

"I know. I know, John. Now you just stay here till I get back. Stay here." She patted me on the cheek, and then she was gone.

She left me home by myself. My younger brothers and sisters had gone off to their school. As time went by I began hearing noises in the house, noises that sounded like someone in agony. First the sound was upstairs, then in the kitchen, and finally it was in the front room with me, all around me. It pawed at me, mocked me, and made me feel miserable. I was beginning to think that the sound was coming from my mother in Fishtown.

I was frightened out of my mind as I thought about my mother being in danger. I thought those crazy people over in Fishtown might attack her. I missed my older brothers at a time like that. They would not have let Mom go to Penn Treaty by herself. They would have gone with her, but I had let her go alone.

I let my mother go alone to Penn Treaty because I was afraid. I did not want to go with her because I did not want to face those wild-eyed racists that I had seen the day before. If I went into Fishtown, I was sure I would be recognized as a black Penn Treaty student, and those angry people might conclude that I had something to do with the alleged stabbing. Then, before you know it, they might lynch me.

Finally, I could not stand the waiting anymore. The noise in the house was growing louder, and I was sure I heard my mother cry out in pain. Those bastards were beating her. "Let my mother go," I said to myself as the fear swelled up in me, and I realized that she had been gone too long.

Then, I could stand it no longer. I was going to Penn Treaty, into Fishtown, to get my mother. I charged out of the house and raced down the block to Dauphin Street. At the corner, I turned east towards Fishtown. I crossed Kensington Avenue on the run, and the more I thought about my mother being attacked by an angry mob, the faster I ran.

I was into Fishtown, and three or four blocks ahead, I thought I saw a familiar figure coming towards me. It was Mom. Like a flash, I raced the remaining blocks that separated us, trying to see if she was beaten or hurt in any way. When I drew close to her, she looked perfectly well, untouched, and as we met I threw my arms around her.

"Mom, Mom, You're all right?"

She did not answer right away, but she took my face in her hands and just smiled for a second or two. "Yes, I'm all right, Johnny. I'm all right."

"I'm so glad, Momma. I'm so glad."

She put her arms around me. "Come on, son. Let's go home. I'm gonna cook you a very good lunch."

I'd never been more proud of my mother than I was of her that day. Not only had she gone to Penn Treaty to find out about the trouble, but she had walked to and from the school, right through the heart of Fishtown. The angry mob I told her about did not stop her. I was truly taken by what she did, and to be sure, it had quite an emotional impact on me. In confronting the danger in Fishtown, she taught me to never let white people scare me. They might beat me. They might even kill me, but I should never let them scare me, again. If I let them do that, I would forever walk in their shadows.

Mom did not insist upon it, but I went back to school the next day. If she could stand up to those Fishtown white people, then I could do no less. There was one thing I found very strange about the entire affair. There was no mention, to my knowledge, of the incident in the Philadelphia press or in news commentaries on radio or TV. Except for the people involved, it was almost as though it did not happen. There had not been a race riot, and only a few black students had been frightened and intimidated. However, the situation had nearly turned into something extremely dangerous. I couldn't see how keeping the incident out of the news reports served the public interest except that it helped to keep a placid face on the racism that lived in Fishtown.

After I met Mom in the street returning from Penn Treaty, we walked home together, arm in arm. She cooked me a very good lunch. She cooked fried sweet potatos and pork sausages, and it was absolutely great. And as I ate that delicious meal, I thought. "God, I am really lucky to have such a wonderful mother, and she is the best cook in the world."

All my young life, I had been looking for magic, waiting for a fairy godmother to save me from my poverty and make my life better. But I didn't need any magic or fairy godmothers because I had my real mother to love me and take care of me. No one could have given me a better start in life than she did. And movies? What did they know about real life? It was all just acting. Now, it was time for me to face the real world.

And then it came to me like a flash, and I asked Mom to come into the front room for a moment. When she was standing before me, I dropped to my knees. "Mom," I said in a very serious, solemn voice. "I will never be ashamed of you again, and If I ever have any children I hope that I can be as good a father to them as you were a mother to me."

With a curious eye, she looked down at me. I was sure she was wondering what I was up to. "Didn't you get enough to eat?"

"Sure, Mom."

"But, I bet you want something else."

"Well…"

"What about some peaches and shortning bread?"

I smiled. "Now that you asked…"

EPILOGUE

There you have it. We've revisited my past. It has been cathartic, which makes me wonder about the belief that you can't go home again. Surely, the past must remain behind us, but that does not mean it dies. It survives in our memory. Yes, the Noble Street house is gone, but it is not forgotten. In reverie, it will always be a part of me. In that sense, I live in the past, and I am happy to do so. Because, the simple truth is, without the past, there can be no present. One builds upon the other.

When I was growing up on Noble Street, shame and anger were my constant companions. The house I lived in was hardly fit for human habitation. My family was on welfare. We were often cold, hungry, and without basic necessities. In a community of poor people, we were the underclass, and frequently my situation embarrassed the hell out of me. But today, I recall that experience with pride. My life had meaning then. It had a clear, unmistakable human purpose, survival. I might have wished for a fairy godmother or divine intervention to right the social wrongs I experienced, but my brothers and I were always willing to stand up to harsh reality and seize the day.

Like my mentor, Miss Lee, I have traveled widely and taken up residence in many different states and foreign countries during my adult life, but that Noble Street house stands out in my mind as the only real home I have ever had. It may sound strange for me to say that, since I lived there during the worst time of my life. But, on the other hand, it makes a lot sense. A home is more than material things. It's family and feelings of togetherness. It's a place of spiritual and emotional comfort, of parental love and sibling support. No other social environment is like that, and, as Dorothy discovered in the Wizard of Oz, there is no place like home, because home is an affair of the heart.

Speaking of what is in the heart, there is truth in the saying you never know what you have until it's gone, or you outgrow it, or you move away from it. Specifically, I don't know the reason for this, but I do know that when I was a young boy, I felt cheated and denied. This caused me to concentrate on the things I wanted rather than the things I had. I took for granted the ongoing love my mother gave me and her extraordinary, creative, cooking ability. More often than not, I let the negative influences in my life guide me. I even used my friendship with the Quakers to gain social recognition. I wanted white people to like me. At times, I realized I was taking a one-sided view of my life, but I could always rationalize that I was acting out of necessity. Nevertheless, as Mr. Negativity, I probably allowed myself to be more bitter than I had to be and less happy than I could have been. It was my mother who remained steady and upbeat. She was the major source of energy in my life. I have a feeling that this is generally true of all mothers everywhere.

Sadly, my Mom has departed this earth, and I miss her hugs and cooking desperately. If I could turn back the clock I would. Believe me, I'd bear almost any burden if I could just hear her say one more time, "Are you all right, Johnny?" Those words had a way of putting me at ease, no matter what the crisis or situation, because I knew that it meant she would always be there for me. When you're growing up black and poor in America, a loving, supportive mother is an absolute necessity.

My mother never encouraged me to think badly of white people. She taught me to respect each person for being him or herself. Social status aside, being white or black, rich or poor was mere happenstance. It took a while, during my maturing years, for me to come to understand this. Indeed, I resisted believing it. The opposing evidence was everywhere.

White people had everything, money, power, central heating and electricity in their houses. They were cops, teachers, and Presidents, and they were beautiful in the movies. It seemed that whatever they did, they could do no wrong. They appeared to be superhuman. But it was all a fantasy. I had to go among them to find that out, and I learned I was envious of an image. When I got to know the flesh and blood person, white became just a color of the rainbow. Like my mother said, you must take each human being one at a time.

My Mom was not a bossy woman. She rarely raised her voice to her children. Of all that I knew about her, I can say honestly she was born to be a mother, to nurture, to comfort, to lead. Given her social situation, a dozen children, an alcoholic, brutal husband, living on public assistance, I often wondered why she had such a good outlook on life. The answer was obvious. She enjoyed being a mother. Children were a blessing to her, and no amount of hard times could make her feel differently. She was filled with the spirit of motherhood, and that was satisfaction enough. If you want to be religious about it, she thought she was fulfilling a holy commandment.

Of course, my mother was no saint. She was a flesh and blood person like the rest of us. But, Mabel Marie Cooper was an emotionally strong woman, and I grew up being very dependent upon her. She stood for all that was good in my childhood, a goodness I can still feel sometimes wrapped around me like a warm blanket, but in truth, she is with God now. However, I have my memories, as bittersweet as they are, and they tell me life is very much like two sides of a coin. There is always the good and the bad of it, and you can't have one without the other. To be sure, the two sides help to give meaning to one another. Let's face it, there can be no day without night. Similarly, if there is an up, there has to be a down. And where would heaven be without hell?

In the same fashion, there are also good and bad people. My father was a terrible, bad man. My mother was a very good woman. Mr. Bosworth and Miss Lee were very good people. Like my mother, they had a tremendous influence on my life. When I met them, I was a frightened, introverted little boy, and they opened up the world to me. They helped me gain a measure of self-worth, and they taught me about love beyond family and color. It was remarkable that they had the same belief as my second grade teacher, Miss Levin. She said that love was good for everybody, and no one can ever get too much of it. Therefore, love should be given freely. I understood this to mean that love is definitely colorless.

Outside of my family, Bos and Miss Lee were the first real, absolute friends I ever had. The two of them accepted me just the way I was. They didn't want me to act black or to try to be white, and when I was with them, I felt relaxed and in good company. This took some doing on their part because when I met them I was loaded down with bigoted baggage. I was on my knees, living in the shadows of white people, but they gave me a helping hand and stood me on my feet. Because of them, I was able to step out of the dark and into the light.

Once I stepped from the dark, my Quaker friends saw right through me. They knew I was embarrassed about being poor and black, but they never allowed it to become an issue between us. From the very beginning, they appealed to my inner spirit, and they turned my emotional head around. Bos told me there was something unusual about me, and it would show itself as I grew older. Miss Lee treated me like I was someone special. The two of them built up my self-esteem and gave me the strength to challenge the white world that I believed was oppressing me. In no uncertain terms, they let me know that I was not born to be a loser. There was power in the art of positive thinking, and in many respects, life is what you make of it.

Bos and Miss Lee strongly encouraged me to seek out a better life. Get a good education, they said, because it could be the road to a more secure lifestyle in the future. I didn't realize it at the time, but they put an inspirational charge into me that became a driving force. It would send me to college and graduate school, to eventually become a college professor. It was not an easy accomplishment. In fact, I had to jump through scads of emotional hoops, scurry through many hells, and lay low in a series of purgatories before I reached the Olympus of academia. It seemed I had to take the long way around, and if there wasn't a mountain to climb, I tried to climb it anyway. Time and again, I had to fall back on the inner spirit that Bos had identified in me. If I had not come to terms with it, I would have definitely failed in my scholastic endeavors.

I've now been teaching for many years, and I am pretty good at it. But, the import of what I do is not in the classroom. I savor the role of mentor. In that regard, I find myself drawn to students who lack self-worth and a meaningful sense of self-identity. I bring these individuals into my office. We talk one on one, and may even have a cup of tea together, just like I used to do with Miss Lee. I try to help them the way she helped me. I say to them, "You are the master of your fate, and the only losers are the people who stop trying."

It would have pleased me very much if my Quaker friends knew how my life turned out, but this was not to be. They knew I went off to school, but my first attempt at getting a college education was a disaster. I dropped out in my second year, and I was so ashamed by my failure, and the hurt it caused my mother, I ran away to the Army. I wanted to hide from my family and friends, and I was too embarrassed to stay in touch with Bos and Miss Lee. I did not want them to know that I let that great college opportunity slip by me, and as my Army years dragged on, I lost contact with them. Nevertheless, I kept myself informed about the fortunes of the Friends Neighborhood Guild. Under the directorship of Mr. Bosworth, the Guild became involved with the government's urban renewal and renovation program in celebration of the nation's Second Centennial Anniversary. It is ironic that Bos was, in part, responsible for the destruction of my old Noble Street neighborhood.

I don't know what happened to Miss Lee. Did she stay at the Guild? Did she go on to another settlement house? Or, did she return to

Kentucky? I become sick and angry with myself when I think about my negligence. I had no right to abandon our relationship. I loved that woman, and I wanted her to think only the best of me. But, that is exactly why I could not face her after my court-martial in the Army. I did not want her to know that I was a jailbird. It would have broken her heart, and I would have never forgiven myself. I preferred to remember the good times we had together, sipping tea in raptured company.

It really was a happy day when Mom got her nurse's aide job. She kept it for many years, until she retired. But, she told me, a happier day for her was the time I left home for Penn State University. It was a dream come true. She had a wish that at least one of her children would graduate from college. I was the first to go, but it would be ten years before I received my undergraduate degree. Allen, Ducky, and Midge, my youngest sister who was born when I was twelve years old, also went to college level schools. Allen was the first family member to graduate from an institution of higher learning. He graduated from Curtis Institute of Music in Philadelphia as a classical composer, and for some years he gained a reputation as one of America's top, black composers. He was even friendly with Leonard Bernstein. During the 1960s, the music establishment was grooming him for stardom, but his sexual escapades got him into trouble. Suddenly those doors of access closed in his face, and Allen's classical music career ended immediately thereafter with a bang.

When we moved uptown to Kensington, the character of my family changed completely, and it was never the same again. On Noble Street, on many a day, our fate was in our hands. But on Hope Street, we became just another family living off wage income, and there was nothing unique or unusual about that. Indeed, we had risen above the underclass, but something was lost. For my brothers and I, our new lifestyle took on a mundane quality. There was no longer any destitution to challenge. Uptown, we now lived in dullsville.

Given the less venturesome nature of our lives, it should have come as no surprise that my brothers would want to leave Hope Street. They were probably trying to recapture the vitality they had on Noble Street. Where might they find the excitement that could revitalize them? In the military, however, this only seems to have worked for Abie, and he surely got more excitement than he bargained for. He joined the Army one month and the Korean War began in the next. He fought as a paratrooper in that war, and he gave a good account of himself. When he returned from Korea, he was silent about the experience. That surprised me. Abie was the weakling among my brothers, and as a kid he was always trying to prove he was as strong and brave as Norman and Frank. Having been in mortal combat was certainly proof that he was brave. In fact, he was a war hero. I wanted to know about the action he participated in, but he would give me no details. He would only say, "War ain't no fun."

I found Abie's remark rather striking. The war abroad may not have been any fun for him, but the war I fought at home had many interesting, enjoyable moments for me. For instance, it gave me pleasure winning the standoff with Snotnose, outsmarting the workers at the meat plant, and planning diversionary tactics for a raid on the wharves. But, if Frank and Norman thought they were going to find this same kind of fun in the service, they were sadly mistaken.

Frank went into the military before Norman. He joined the Army, and I know he did it because he wanted to outdo Abie. It was no surprise that he also joined the paratroopers. After basic training, Frank had had enough of the Army. Of all my brothers, he was the most arrogant, undisciplined, and disrespectful of authority. In a word, Frank did not like to take any shit from anybody. By his very nature, he had an insubordinate personality, and that was not going to work in the military. Consequently, when he entered the Army, he was a court martial waiting to happen. It was just a matter of time.

The showdown came when a sergeant gave Frank an order he didn't like. He turned on the sergeant and threatened to beat his butt. Since this was unacceptable military behavior, his commanding officer filed court-martial papers against him, but before the trial, Frank went AWOL. While he was absent from his duty station, he committed a crime. He was convicted and sent to prison. As a result of all of this, he was given a dishonorable discharge from the Army. but he did not regret anything that had happened. He said, "The Army was just a lot of bullshit."

No one was more surprised than I when Norman joined the Marine Corps. I could not imagine him submitting to military authority. He was too intelligent, and too single-minded. Norman believed that he was always right, and he liked out-smarting people. What kind of soldier could he be in the command structure of the Marine Corps? And, the Corps was the toughest branch of the services. Honor and obedience were everything in the Marines, but such standards were laughable to Norman. He went into the Marine Corps solely to do Frank one better. He did not think that military life would be so demanding of him. He thought he would be able to slick his way through it, but the Parris Island basic training set him straight. It was much harder than he could have ever imagined.

Norman joined the Corps in the early summer. After basic training, he came home on leave, and he told me that he was not going to stay in the Marine Corps for four years. He said, "I'll be home for Christmas." He had a plan, and he kept his word.

Back at his military base, Norman was assigned to a workstation in a machine shop. Every day when he would report for duty, and the machines were turned on, he would immediately go into a fake frenzy. He would call out, in a loud agonizing voice, that the noise of the machines was attacking him. "I can't stand the sound! It's getting into my head! It's killing me!" He would go on in that manner until he was taken out of the shop. He continued faking these symptoms for a couple of weeks, but then one day, after bellowing about the noise, he collapsed on the floor and began frothing at the mouth. He was rushed to the base hospital.

Norman was kept in the hospital for a month, and he was given a number of physical and psychological examinations. The doctors could find nothing specifically wrong with him, but still they came to the conclusion that he was mentally unfit to serve in the Marine Corps. He was given a medical discharge and informed that he could never join any branch of the military services again. That was okay with Norman, and he told me that on his way home from Camp Lejeune in North Carolina, he could not stop laughing. How stupid could those military doctors be? They fell for that phony frothing at the mouth trick. "Those guys in the Marine Corps are dumb," Norman said.

As one of my brothers was getting out of the Marine Corps, another was going in. Ducky joined the Marine Corps soon after I went off to college. We were very close, and I believe my leaving home influenced him. He was another brother I never thought would go into any branch of the services, least of all the Marine Corps. He did not fit the "few good men" mold. He seemed to have no ego, and he did not play bravado games. He was such a nice person; I didn't think he could hurt anyone even if he was in a real military battle. I just knew he would be out of place in the Corps because Marines are known for being killers. Moreover, because Norman told me how tough basic training was on Parris Island, I thought my little brother would never get through it.

Man, was I completely off the mark. Ducky not only finished basic training, but he went on to serve in the Corps for four years. Moreover, he obtained the rank of sergeant, and he received many commendations. He became a model Marine, and that absolutely amazed me. I thought I knew him better than anyone else in the world, but I came to realize that I did not know him half as much. That got me thinking. If I really did not know my own brother, could I ever really know anyone? Probably not. Too much of what we think we know is simply a function of what we believe. I thought Ducky would be miserable in the service, but after his discharge, he said to me, "I had a good time in the Marine Corps."

When I joined the Army, Ducky had been in the Marines for over a year. It was a foolish move on my part, but I thought I could handle service life with ease. As a younger person, I had wanted to make a career out of the military if I could become a pilot, but after three days in the Army, I knew I had made a mistake. Basic training fell on me like a ton of bricks. I had problem after problem after problem. It was a horror, but I was able to get through it by reminding myself that my younger brother had graduated from Parris Island. If he could take that shit, I could handle bootcamp, too.

Leaving Noble Street did have a profound effect upon me and my brothers. If I did not know better, I could have easily thought we were fleeing the homefront. To be sure, in succession, Kenny and Ronnie, as they came of age, also joined the Army. They served uneventful tours of duty. During this same time, in their own way, my sisters Marion, Dotty, and Jeanny, were also moving away from the family nest. When I returned from the Army in 1959, Marion and Dotty were married, and they both had a child. A few years later, Jeanny got married, and she had two children quickly, one right after the other. In age, they were less than a year a part. All of my sisters became mothers and homemakers. It seemed to be their destiny.

My mother was not disappointed with the career her daughters chose. Modern feminist philosophy aside, she probably thought they were doing the right thing. They were assuming the duties and responsibilities of motherhood. Nothing was more important, if not liberating, than that. Unconscious as it might have been, I think my sisters patterned themselves after Mom. They all had similar relationships with their husbands, and they were nurturing, loving mothers.

My sisters grew up in a household that was dominated by males. That background may have been an influence on them when they chose their mates. Marian's husband was a bad guy. He was a man who liked to take chances and live dangerously. For his effort, he paid the ultimate price. He died tragically at a young age. Dotty's spouse was a reserved, insecure, self-effacing man, and she had been drawn to him because of his weaknesses. But, he changed, and their situation became one of tyranny of the weak. Dotty stayed with him for over a decade, but eventually they separated. In Jeanny's eyes, her husband was a man of stature and power. Her attraction for him was probably a natural transition from childhood. When she was growing up, she had seven older brothers to look up to, and they took care of her. Undoubtedly, that gave her a comforting feeling, and I believed it carried over. In any case, Jeanny still lives with her husband today.

Once my brothers and I left home, we were never to be a part of Mom's household again. There would be visits, but our fledgling days were over. When I went off to college, I had no idea how momentous the occasion was. For the first time, I was going to be tested as an individual, and I was not prepared for the ordeal. I failed miserably. I missed my mother, my brothers, the comfort of the family, and the Noble Street house, but I had to learn that once you leave the nest, you can't fly back again. The winds of change won't let you. This was a lesson that was hard for me to learn, and I fear that some of my brothers never accepted it. All of them had difficult adult lives, and in my opinion, none of them fulfilled their potential. It was as though they were all emotionally immature. That certainly was true for me, and it was one of the reasons why I am considered to be a late bloomer by my academic colleagues. However, there is no need for me to be critical of my brothers. They are all dead now save one. They died by accident, murder, and natural causes. Kenny is my only living male sibling.

I've given a lot of thought to the demise of my brothers, and I have reached the conclusion that they died a collective death long before they were individually buried. This may seem to be a rather fanciful, or even a harsh statement, but consider this. I never felt more vital and useful than when I was doing daily battle with the soldiers of destitution, and

I think my brothers felt the same way. Together, we had a spirit of camaraderie that made us feel we could stand up to any bad situation and give it our best shot. We protected, supported, and cared for each other. Like the Three Musketeers, we were one for all and all for one. We did not always agree, and we could be intemperate competitors. But in the end, we were the Cooper brothers, and as Snotnose found out, we knew how to stand together.

When we moved away from Noble Street, my brothers and I were no longer dependent upon each other for survival. Of course, this was inevitable. We were growing up, and there had to be a parting of ways. What I didn't know was, that when we left the nest, the bonds between us would begin to unravel, and like Humpty Dumpty they could not be put right again. Why couldn't there have been a sign, some indicator, a clue about the coming change? Must there always be the element of the unexpected in this thing we call the future? Is change the mother of all our tomorrows?

When I was a child, I looked to the future, and now that I'm an adult, I look to the past. It is sad, but yet it is an awakening to realize that my best days may be behind me. I had a certain vitality in my life then that is absent now. This tells me that the past is ambiguous, and it is more difficult to understand than our memories will allow. Throughout my childhood, I lived in abject poverty, but the challenge and the daily struggle to survive kept me on my toes. It gave meaning to my hungry, cold existence. I can see it very clearly now. No endeavor can be more meaningful than when you're trying to stay alive. Because, in the end, it is the struggle to survive that gives life meaning. Why did it take me so many years to learn that simple truth? I hope you can take the lesson I learned to heart, and perhaps it will serve some useful purpose for you.

Great Lady spoke on great subject at 76th Anniversary Banquet of Friends Neighborhood Guild. Mrs. Eleanor Roosevelt is being escorted to speakers' table by John Cooper, left, and Joseph Thomas (hidden by Mrs. Roosevelt). Subject: "The American Neighborhood — A Laboratory for World Understanding."

ABOUT THE AUTHOR

John Cooper was born in Philadelphia, Pennsylvania during the height of the Great Depression. He was one of a dozen children who lived for over a decade on welfare. John overcame these social obstacles to become a professor of African-American studies at John Jay College of Criminal Justice.

www.ingramcontent.com/pod-product-compliance
Lightning Source LLC
Chambersburg PA
CBHW061342280526
45784CB00001B/102